INDUSTRIAL LOCOMOTIVES & RAILWAYS OF YORKSHIRE

Gordon Edgar

AMBERLEY

Front cover: Almost at the end of industrial steam working in Yorkshire – Hunslet Austerity SWCP No. 2 in action at Smithywood coking plant on Sunday morning, 25 July 1982. (Roy Burt)

Back cover: Former BR Class 05 Hunslet 0-6-0 diesel-mechanical No. D2607 at NCB Steetley colliery on 22 August 1982. (John Sloane)

First published 2018

Amberley Publishing
The Hill, Stroud
Gloucestershire, GL5 4EP

www.amberley-books.com

ISBN 978 1 4456 6776 8 (paperback)
ISBN 978 1 4456 6777 5 (ebook)

British Library Cataloguing in Publication Data.
A catalogue record for this book is available from the British Library.

Typeset in 10pt on 12pt Sabon LT Std.
Origination by Amberley Publishing.
Printed in the UK.

CONTENTS

INTRODUCTION & ACKNOWLEDGEMENTS

This is the seventh book to be published in this regional series, examining the industrial railways of England, Wales and Scotland. This volume covers the former Ridings of Yorkshire, from the Pennines on the Lancashire county boundary in the west, to the fringes of the Nottinghamshire coalfield in the south, through to the county boundary with Lincolnshire in the east. The Humberside region, historically a part of the East Riding, has previously been examined in the Eastern England volume, while the Teesside region, on the south bank of the River Tees and historically a part of the North Riding, will be covered in a subsequent volume looking at the North East. These arbitrary divisions, selected on the author's part, have been chosen merely to permit a more balanced industrial railway overview for each respective book and do not observe historical regional bureaucratic jurisdictions of any period.

Following on from the previous volume, which examined Lancashire and Cheshire, a region which once boasted many collieries, some served by extensive private railway systems, Yorkshire was no less fascinating in this respect, a vast county which had numerous sprawling steel mills and foundries, particularly around the Sheffield and Rotherham areas, not to mention the widespread coal mining activities which strongly influenced the county and its fortunes over the last 200 years or so.

It is only appropriate that the greater part of this book covers the industrial railway activities based on coal mining and steel production in Yorkshire, during a period in our industrial history where sadly such concerns gradually contracted, or indeed were entirely eradicated, as was the case with the coal mining industry. Arguably, the turning point in this industry was the miners' strike during the years of the Thatcher Government; the infamous 'uprising' at Orgreave, was of course well-documented by the media. The subsequent years of the nationalised mining industry saw it decimated, although a limited number of mines continued to prosper in Yorkshire under private ownership into the twenty-first century, with the last at Kellingley closing in December 2015.

As previously documented in other volumes, at Cadley Hill colliery in Derbyshire and at Bickershaw and Bold collieries in Lancashire, the county of Yorkshire also had a significant part to play in industrial steam's last stand in Britain. Remarkably, and not entirely due to any enthusiasm or whim of a colliery or plant manager, steam activity could still be witnessed well into 1982 in the county. The Hunslet 15 and 16-inch saddle tanks and the PLA Class Hudswell Clarke 0-6-0 side tank locomotives, all sporting either red or green liveries, and often turned out in immaculate and striking external condition, were synonymous with the National Coal Board's (NCB) North Yorkshire area collieries and attracted the attention of many photographers, particularly during the post-1968 'steam-less' years of the main lines in Britain.

It was, however, at a coal by-products plant, 4 miles north of Sheffield, where regular steam activity could be observed into the early 1980s; a chance visit to Smithywood coking plant on 24 July 1982 by my lifelong friend Roy Burt found one of the Hunslet Engine Company's Austerity saddle tanks, a 1960s rebuild of a 1944-built locomotive, busy shunting wagons at the coke ovens on that glorious summer's day! This locomotive, along with a sister Austerity rebuild, had been the mainstay of motive power at Smithywood between 1964 and 1980. More widely documented at that time and since were the activities by Hunslet, experimenting on an Austerity 0-6-0 saddle tank equipped with their patent mechanical underfeed stoker and gas producer system and using various grades of coal. Load trials were conducted on the NCB running lines between Wheldale and Fryston collieries during December 1981 and January 1982. Although the detailed evaluation had been concluded during this period, the poor reliability of the resident Hunslet diesel locos at Wheldale during the exceptionally cold winter period saw Hunslet's works number 3168, built in 1944, continue to work well into 1982, a BBC Television *Look North* programme documenting the last active steam loco with the NCB in Yorkshire and the end of steam at Wheldale during week commencing 20 September 1982!

The Hunslet Engine Company had supplied hundreds of products to industry in Yorkshire since the company was first founded in 1864, but it was by no means the only Leeds-based locomotive manufacturer to show influence in this region. Hudswell, Clarke & Co. Ltd, also based at Hunslet in Leeds, supplied a variety of designs of steam and diesel locomotive for use both under and above ground at the Yorkshire collieries. Notably, the company supplied the NCB with five 0-4-0 saddle tanks in the early 1960s, a time when the Swindon Works of British Railways had just turned out the last BR Standard steam locomotives, the Class 9F 2-10-0. The Yorkshire Engine Company, based at their Meadowhall works in Sheffield, also enjoyed great success in supplying both steam and diesel locos to British industry. The steel industry in Yorkshire was especially influenced by the company's successful six-coupled 'Janus' diesel-electric design, and it is fitting that one of the oldest regular working locomotives in British industry today is a 1957-built example, to be found at the Stocksbridge works of Liberty Speciality Steels Ltd, a remarkable survivor, both in terms of the surviving railway, its branch line and of course the production at the works itself in the twenty-first century.

Unsurprisingly, the scrap metal businesses thrived remarkably during the period of industrial contraction which took place from

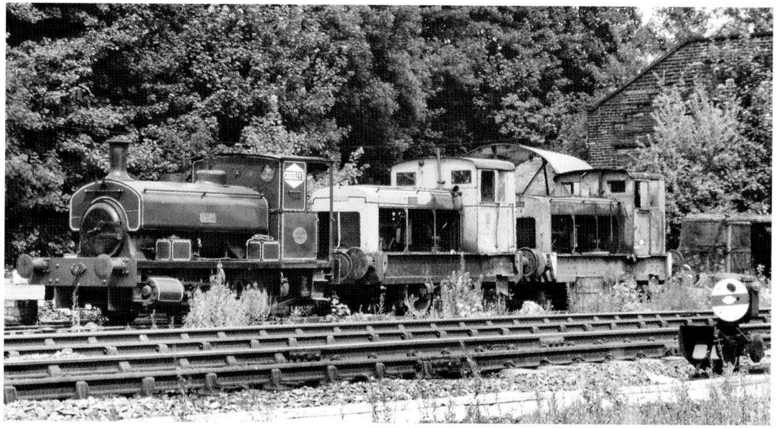

Andrew Barclay 0-4-0 saddle tank *Harry* (W/No. 1823 of 1924) stands idle in the sidings at Crossley's scrapyard at Shipley on 25 July 1982. Remarkably, the two 88DS Class Ruston & Hornsby locos *Beth* (W/No. 425483 of 1958) and 0040 (W/No. 284838 of 1050) were still dumped out of use in this same position in 2018, although surrounded by trees! (Roy Burt)

the mid-1980s, with redundant locomotives being eagerly snapped up from the ever-diminishing number of collieries and steelworks to realise their lucrative scrap value, recognised by the specialist dealers which were strategically placed around Rotherham and Sheffield. However, some relatively new examples were earmarked for refurbishment and resale to the few remaining industrial concerns still using rail freight and seeking to update existing but older motive power for shunting on their private railway infrastructure. Some of these scrap metal businesses survive to this day and still employ industrial shunting locomotives. Although by far the most prolific dealer of railway vehicles and locomotives is C. F. Booth at their Clarence Metal Works in Rotherham, the most unlikely of places where industrial steam was to survive was at the Crossley's scrapyard at Shipley. Indeed, Crossley's operation was a contender for being one of the last places where commercial industrial steam traction in Britain was called upon to work in earnest, albeit on an irregular basis up until summer 1983. The yard still has industrial diesel locomotives present, although rail traffic is irregular, if not having now finally ceased.

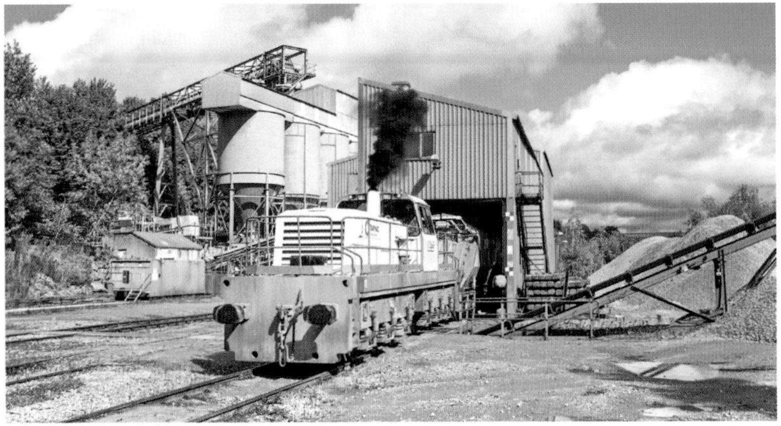

RFS-built 150-ton Co-Co diesel-hydraulic *Cracoe* (W/No.067/C4498GA/57000/01 built in 1994) roars into life with a cloud of black exhaust, before moving loaded JGA wagons off the Tarmac loading point at Rylstone in September 2016. This was the final locomotive to be built at the Doncaster Works site, just as RFS went into receivership. (Author)

In keeping with the other books in this series, this is primarily a historic photographic album, with the period covered chiefly being over the last six decades. To present as much historic photographic material as possible, I have refrained from including chapter introductions, preferring the photographs to tell their story with the use of relevant extended image captions.

In compiling this book, I have consulted numerous works of reference published by the Industrial Railway Society, which always prove invaluable in tracing the sometimes complicated trails of some locomotives, and the history of the locations in which they served. I would like to record my gratitude to Roy Burt, John Sloane, Kevin Lane, Adrian Nicholls, Duncan McEvoy, John Brooks and the Industrial Railway Society for making available historic material from their collections and archives. Without such support a work of this scope would have been impossible to produce. I would also like to thank Richard Stevens for not only providing some of his splendid action photographs and associated historical information and captions, but also for reviewing the draft copy, although I accept full responsibility should any errors have crept in. Finally, and by no means least, I would particularly like to pay tribute to my wife Valerie for her support and patience while I have been engaged in producing not just this book, but the entire series.

Gordon Edgar
Ripon, North Yorkshire
June 2018

1

CONSTRUCTION

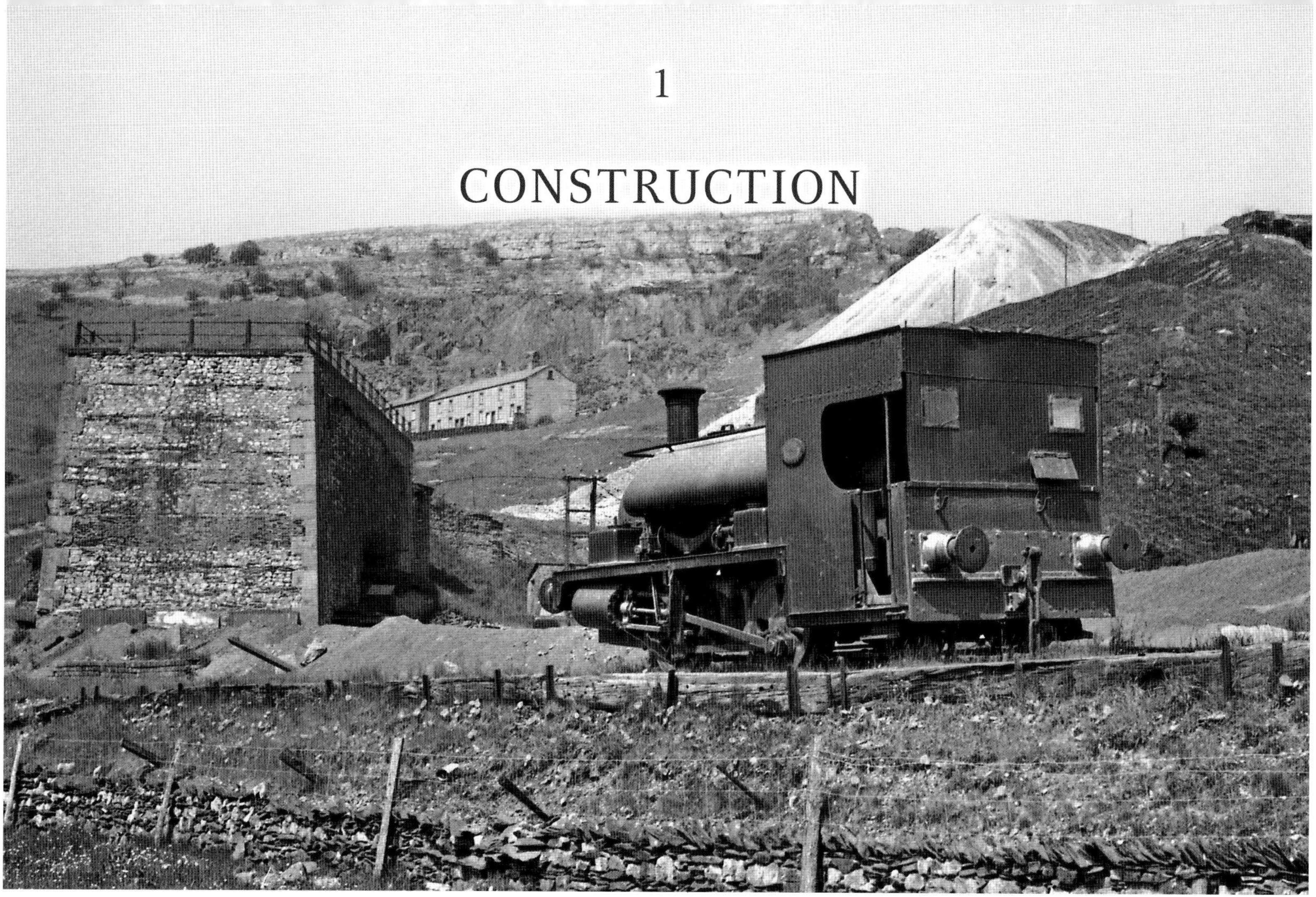

Hudswell Clarke 0-4-0 saddle tank *Ribblesdale* (W/No. 1546 of 1924) at Settle Limes Ltd, Austwick Lime Quarry, Helwith Bridge, near Settle on 13 June 1967. (Peter Eckersley – author' s collection)

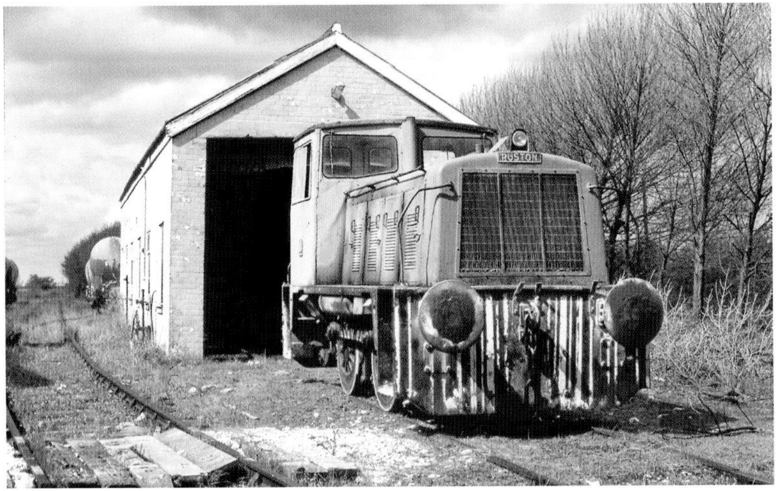

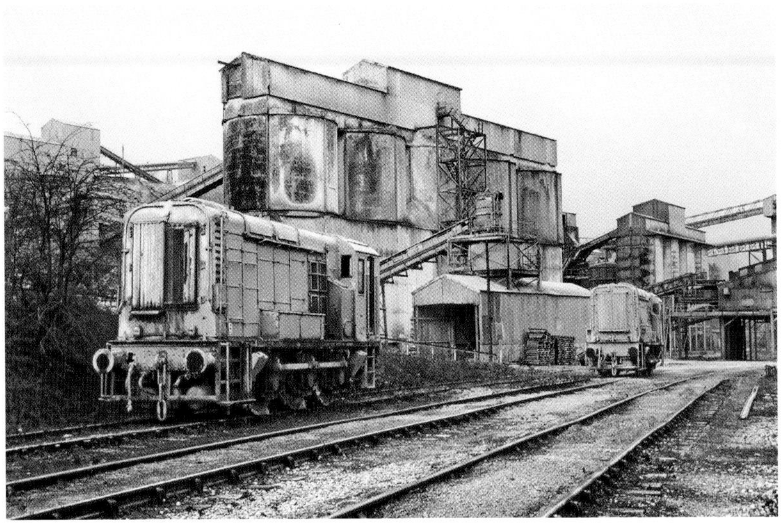

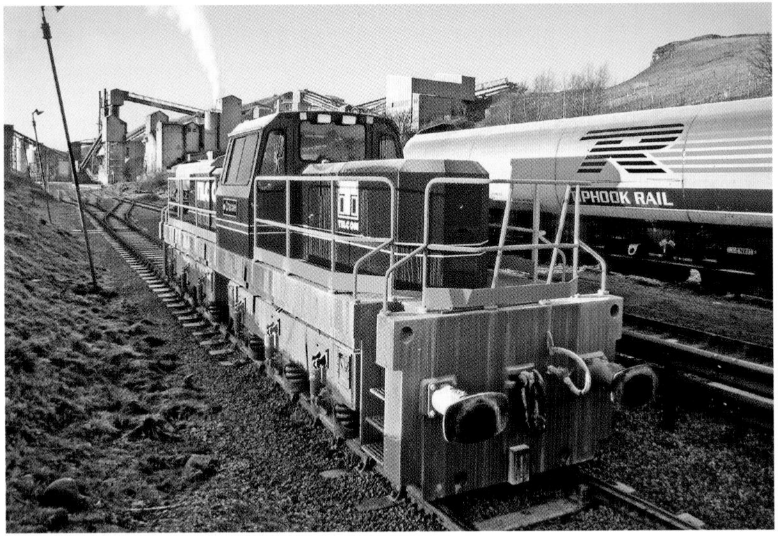

Above left: Ruston & Hornsby Class LPSH 192 hp 0-4-0 diesel-hydraulic (W/No. 513139 of 1967), formerly named *Herbert Turner*, at the Melton Works of Croxton & Garry Ltd near Hull on 13 April 1992. (Author)

Left: Wearing a striking red livery that it was not to display for long due to a company change (see page 6), RFS Ltd's massive 150-ton Co-Co diesel-hydraulic shunting locomotive *Cracoe* (W/No. 067/C4498GA/57000/01 of 1994) at Tilcon's Rylstone Quarry sidings on the frosty morning of 23 December 1994. The final locomotive built at Doncaster Works for domestic use, the design was loosely based on the popular Thomas Hill Ltd's Steelman range of industrial locomotives. It is quite fitting that the last standard gauge locomotive built in Yorkshire for industry should remain in the county and, furthermore, emerge from the world-renowned Doncaster Works. (Author)

Opposite page top right: Former LMS and BR 350 hp Class 11 shunter No. 12083 retained as standby at Swinden limeworks on 8 February 1993. Behind it is the working loco, former BR Class 08 No. 08054 (originally D3067). No. 12083 arrived at Swinden following withdrawal from BR service at Carlisle Kingmoor, which took place in October 1971. No. 12083 is now to be found on the Battlefield Line in Leicestershire. No. 08054 had been withdrawn from BR in February 1980 and worked at the quarry exchange sidings until 1998. It was donated to the nearby Yorkshire Dales Railway by Tarmac in 2008. The lime kilns towering above the locos continued to burn lime until 1996. (Author)

Right: The Plasmor building block works at Heck in North Yorkshire is home to the last John Fowler locomotive in industrial service in Britain. This Leeds-built 1966 vintage 203 hp 0-4-0 diesel-hydraulic (W/No. 4220038) is used to position the PNA wagons about the Plasmor works for loading, prior to being despatched to either Biggleswade, Bow or Dowlow by the main line freight operator. In November 2016 it was stabled between duties in its usual location during the lunch-break, by this splendid section of trackwork. Plasmor established the works in 1959, using power station waste ash mixed with concrete to manufacture lightweight light grey blocks for the building construction industry. The Plasmor four-wheel concrete block-carrying PNA wagons have raised ends, fitted to allow product double-stacking. Fowler built their final loco, also of this 422 Class, in January 1968, which was supplied to Cargo Fleet steelworks in Middlesbrough. The John Fowler & Co. (Leeds) Ltd business and goodwill were subsequently acquired by Andrew Barclay Sons & Co. Ltd. (Author)

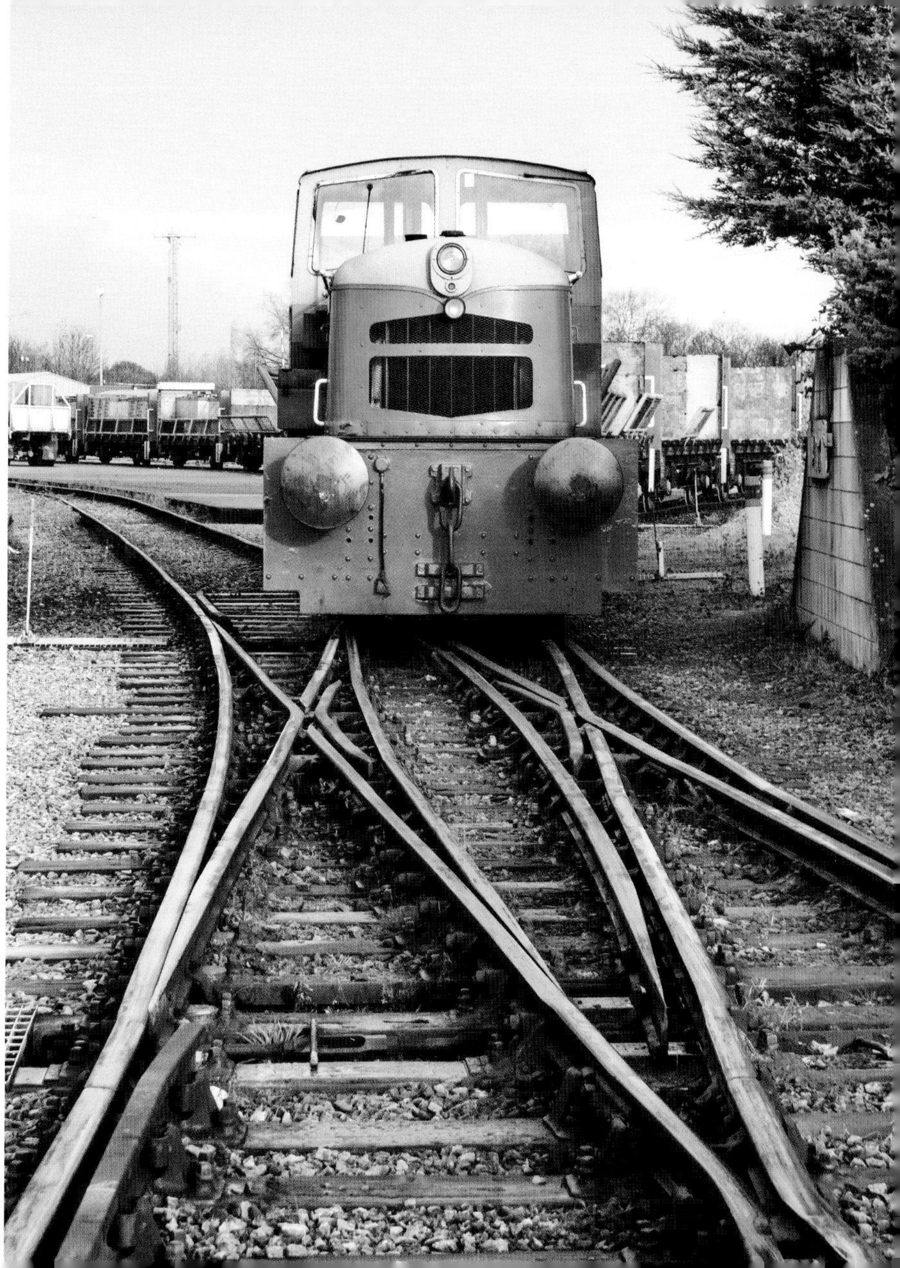

2

COAL

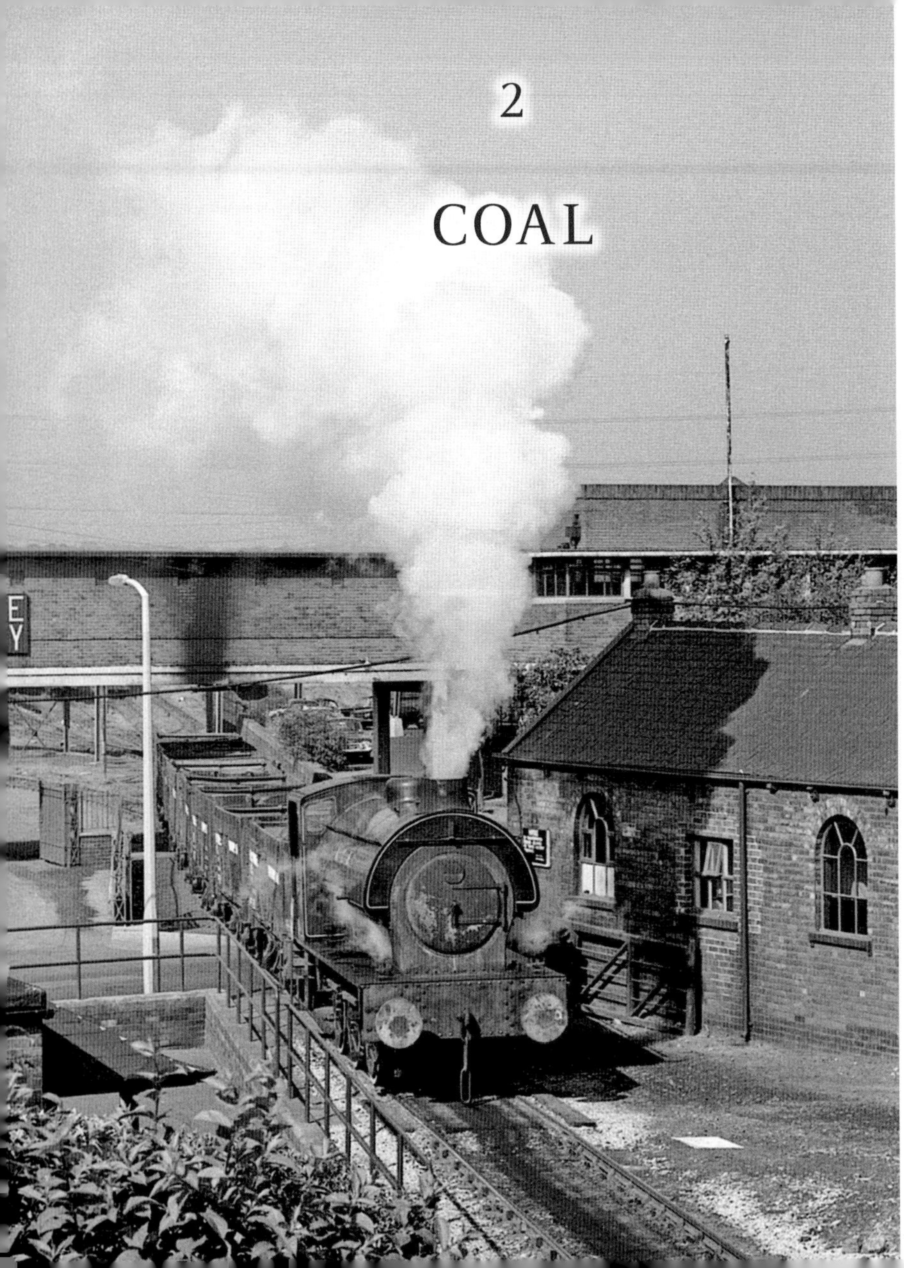

Left: Arguably, within railway circles, the most well-known of all the Yorkshire collieries was Wheldale. Located alongside the Aire Navigation, east of Castleford, Wheldale first commenced production in 1870. An amalgamation of the Wheldale and Fryston Coal Companies with the Allerton Bywater colliery took place in 1899, forming Airedale Collieries Ltd. Wheldale had no coal washing plant, so an internal railway of just over 1 mile was installed in the 1930s between Wheldale and Fryston collieries, where Wheldale coal was subsequently washed. The complex also had no coal preparation plant, so coal smaller than 1 inch was despatched to Glasshoughton Coking Plant (see page 65) or by 'Tom Puddings' compartment boats from a rail-connected basin to Ferrybridge power station, located close by. The NCB lines ran east under the BR line to extensive tips on the south bank of the River Aire, between the colliery and Ferrybridge power station. In the early 1980s, Wheldale colliery was producing in the region of 400,000 to half a million tons of coal per annum, employing a workforce of 650. Fryston colliery closed in 1985, followed shortly after by Wheldale in October 1987. By August 1988, the complete site had been cleared and levelled off. The highlight of Wheldale was the steeply graded line that led from the staithes and the Fryston branch to the sidings adjacent to the BR Castleford–York line, crossing en route a moderately busy public road that bisected the colliery, before bending slightly right and uphill. An anonymous Hunslet Austerity 0-6-0 saddle tank (W/No. 2879 of 1943) crosses Wheldon road and takes a run at the bank with a string of internal user wagons on 7 September 1971. (Richard Stevens)

Opposite page: During the very last week of steam activity in Yorkshire, Wheldale colliery's Hunslet Austerity 0-6-0 saddle tank No. 7 (W/No. 3168 of 1944) rests in the sidings outside Fryston Colliery on 21 September 1982. Following the series of Hunslet Engine Company Ltd tests with the mechanical underfeed stoker fitment and various grades of coal conducted during the preceding December and January, the Austerity had been maintained in reserve at Wheldale, due to ongoing reliability issues with the resident diesel locos, also supplied by Hunslet. The steam workings during this week were to be the very last hurrah for industrial steam in Yorkshire. A close contender in Yorkshire was at Smithywood coking plant, where the last recorded steam working was in July 1982 (see page 67). As documented in the book in this series covering the North West of England, regular commercial industrial steam traction in Britain finally bowed out at Bickershaw colliery, in Lancashire, one year later, in October 1983. (John Brooks)

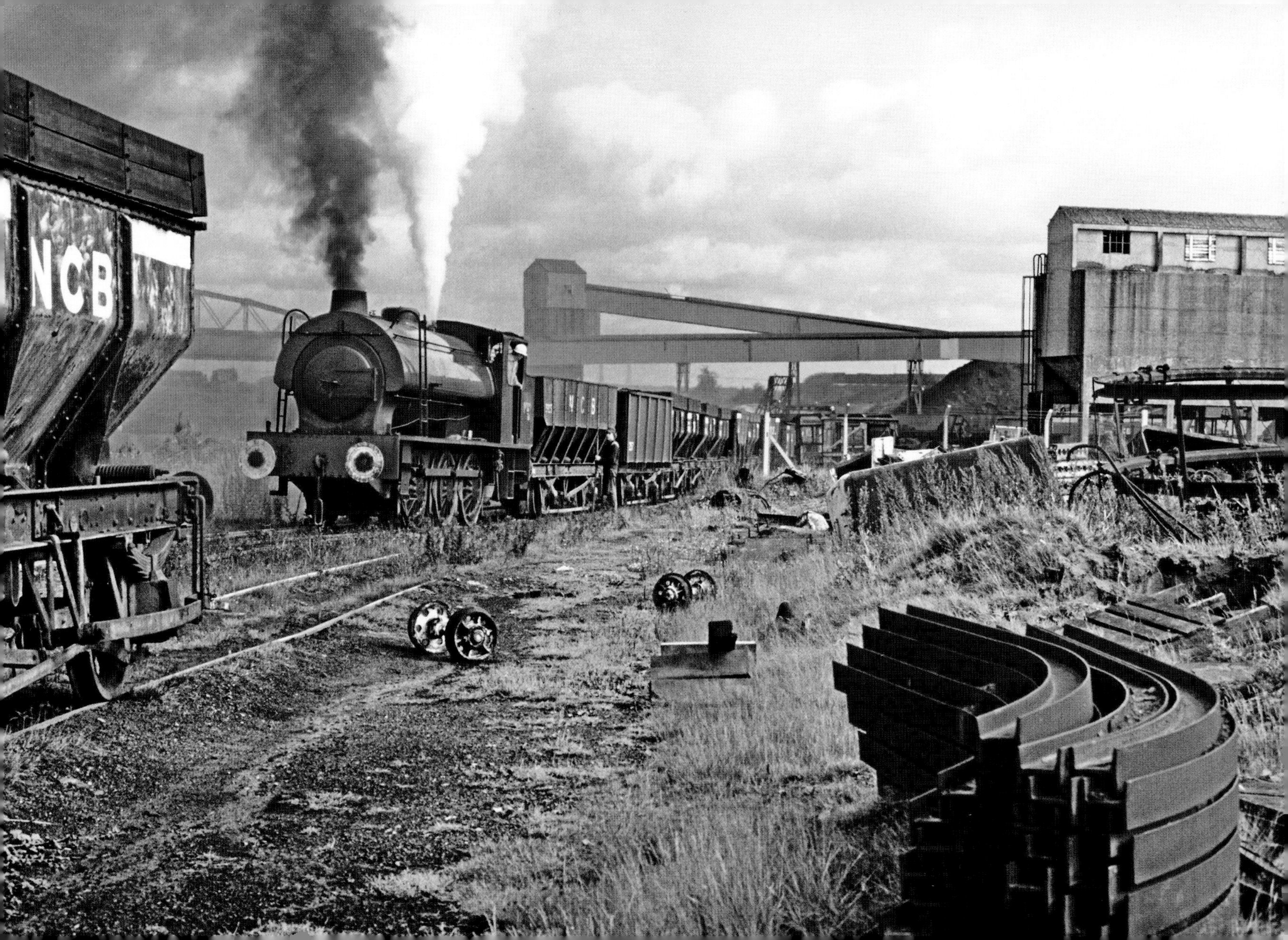
NCB

Right: J. G. Russell-owned bulk 30-foot ISO containers mounted on FPA container flat wagons await collection at Manton colliery, with Hudswell Clarke No. 20 *Manton* (W/No. D1121 of 1958) standing by as duty loco on 14 June 1987. (Author)

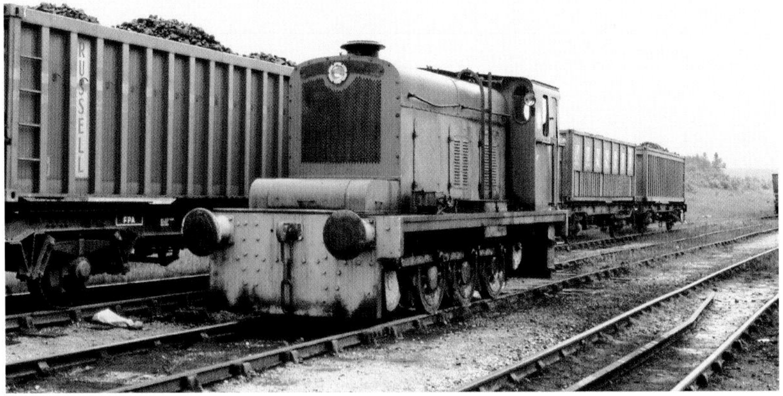

Below: Two Leeds-built six-coupled veterans dumped out of use at Bullcroft colliery, Carcroft, on 8 November 1969, (*left*) Hunslet No. 2 *Tom* (W/No. 1826 of 1939) and (*right*) Hudswell Clarke No. 50 (W/No. 1532 of 1924). Both locos were scrapped on site during November 1969. The colliery, located on the Adwick Junction to Stainforth & Hatfield line, was merged with Brodsworth colliery in September 1970. Rail traffic subsequently ceased at Bullcroft in 1971, but Brodsworth survived until September 1990. (John Sloane)

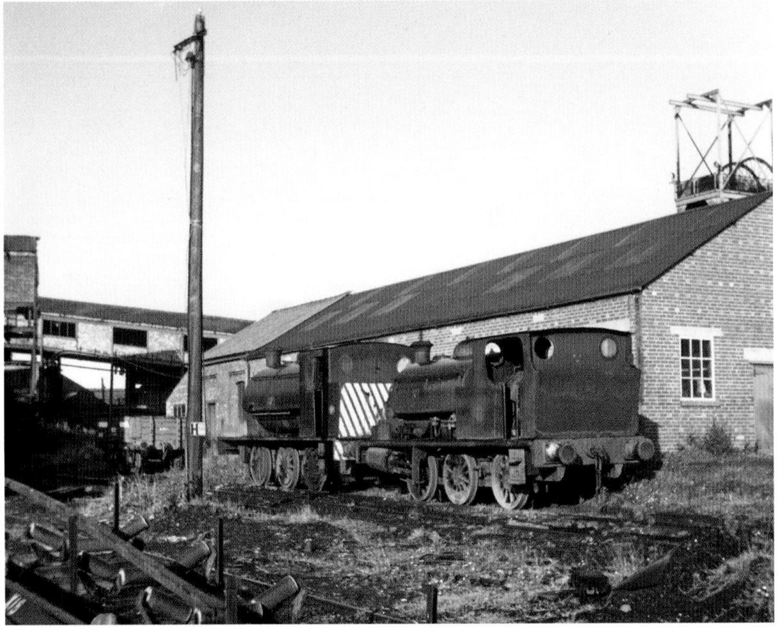

Opposite page: Former BR Drewry Class 04 No. D2322 alongside the No. 1 Winding House at Kiveton Park colliery on 16 March 1983. Delivered new to BR Heaton depot in March 1961, it was withdrawn from Gateshead depot in August 1968 and sold to the South Yorkshire area of the NCB in February 1969. As No. 24 in their fleet, it served at various South Yorkshire area collieries, moving to Kiveton Park in April 1980. It was one of three former BR Class 04 Drewry locos to be found at the colliery in the early 1980s (see page 77), which resultantly attracted much interest from railfans at the time. It was broken up at Kiveton Park by November 1985. Use of NCB shunting locos at the colliery ceased by June 1985, although the colliery continued in production for almost a further decade, until its final closure in September 1994. (Roy Burt)

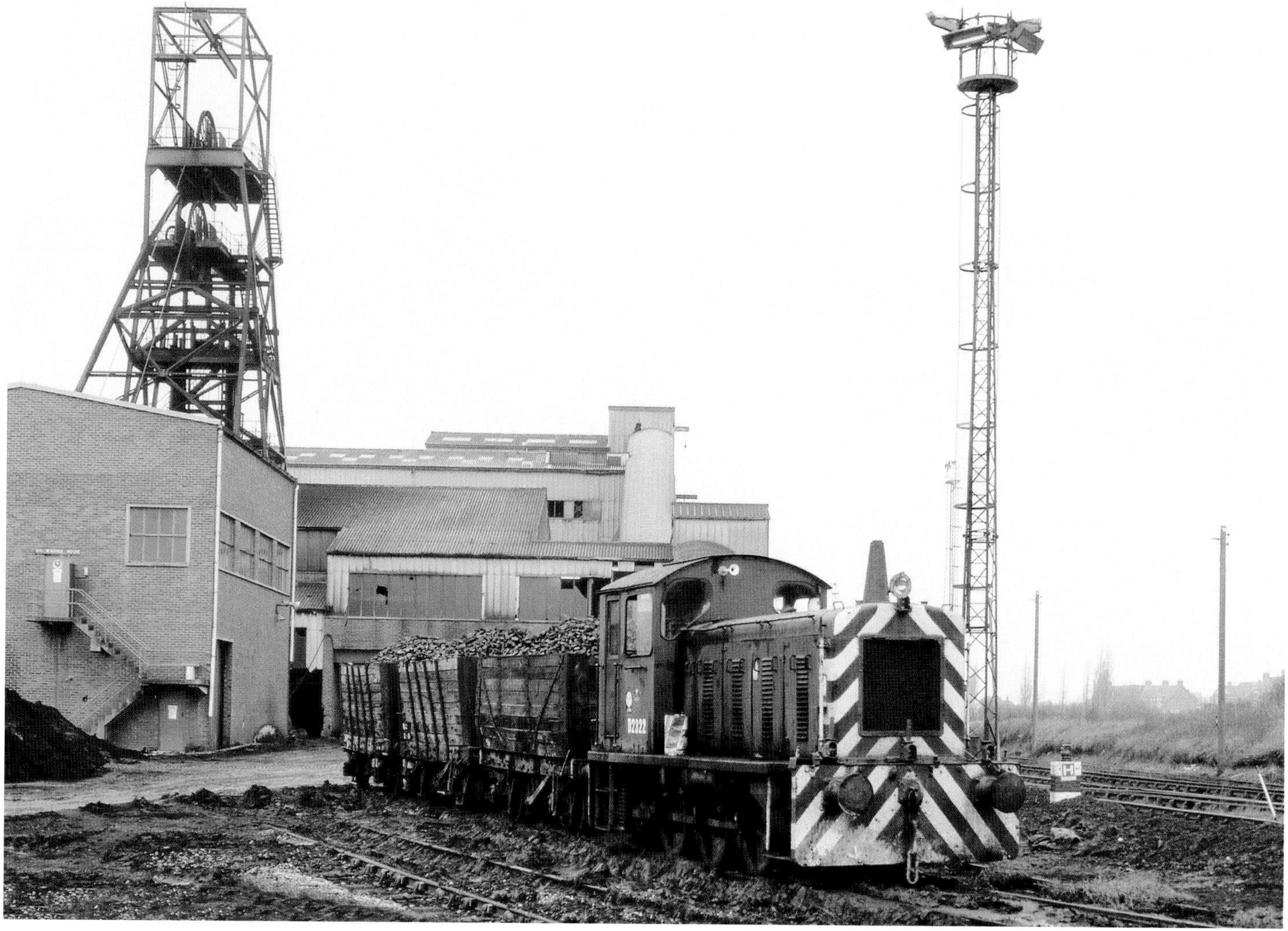
D2322

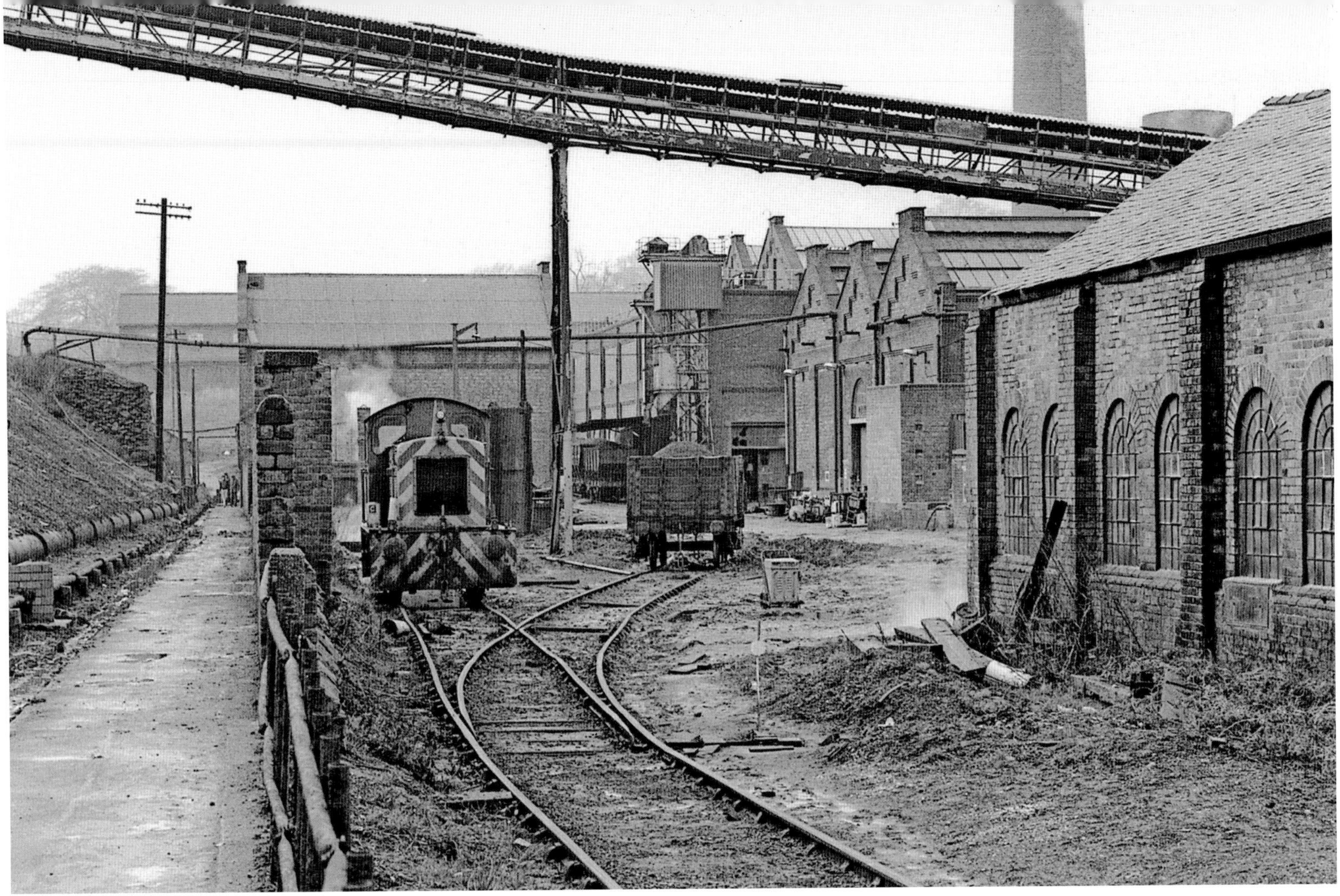

Railway shunting activity at Orgreave colliery and the coke and chemical plant in South Yorkshire could be observed from an adjacent open access footpath; Orgreave colliery's ex-BR Class 04 No. D2322 was busy shunting on 21 March 1977. The colliery closed in October 1981 and the Drewry loco was passed on to Kiveton Park Colliery (as featured on the previous page) for further use. (Kevin Lane)

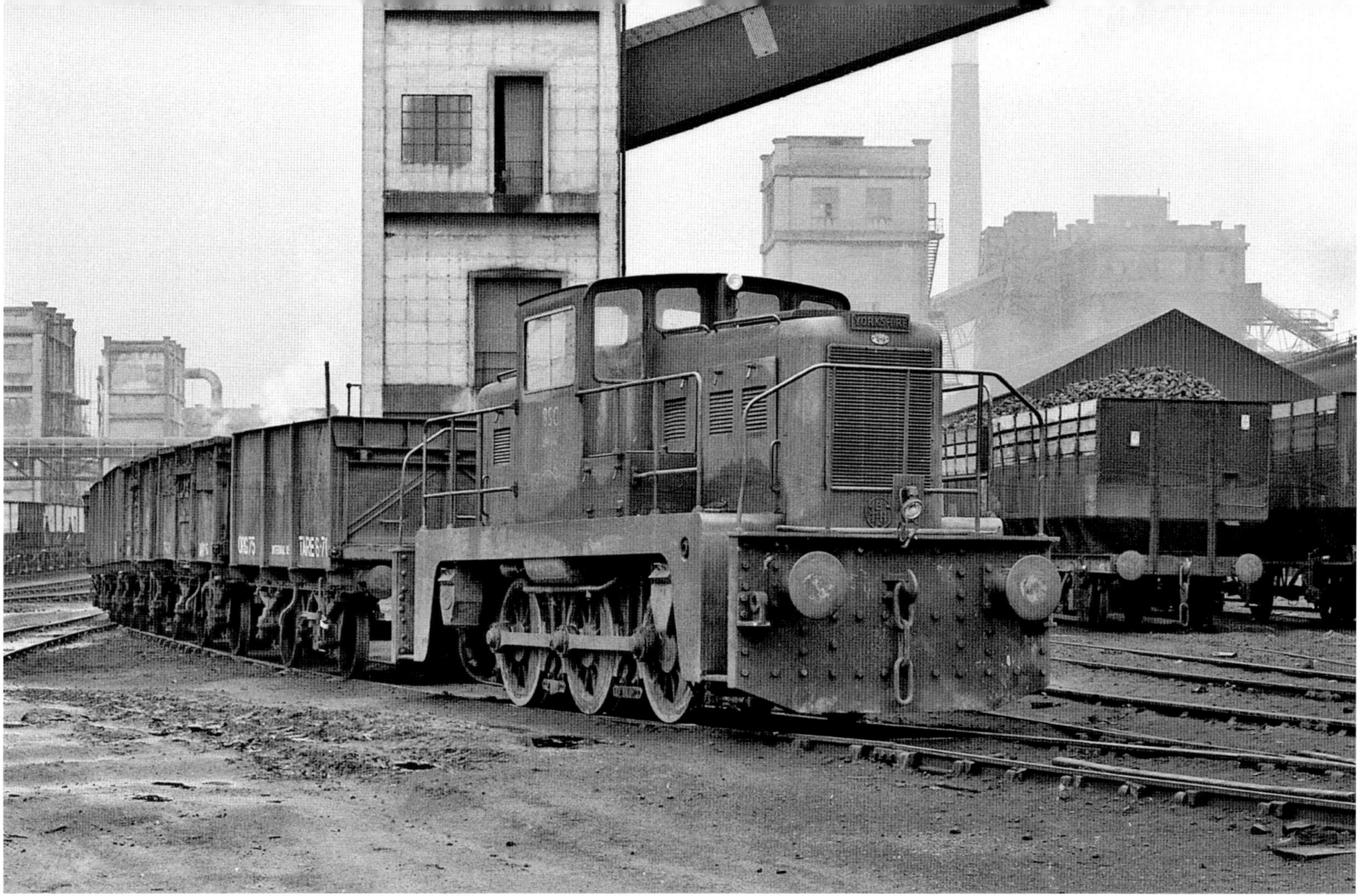

On Sunday 20 March 1977, Yorkshire Engine Company Janus Class 0-6-0 diesel-electric No. 2444/20 (W/No. 2670 of 1958) was shunting the British Steel Corporation's Orgreave coke and chemical works yard, which was adjacent to the colliery and washery. A nearby field was the scene of the controversial, brutal events of 18 June 1984, during the prolonged miners' strike. This works was closed in 1990. (Kevin Lane)

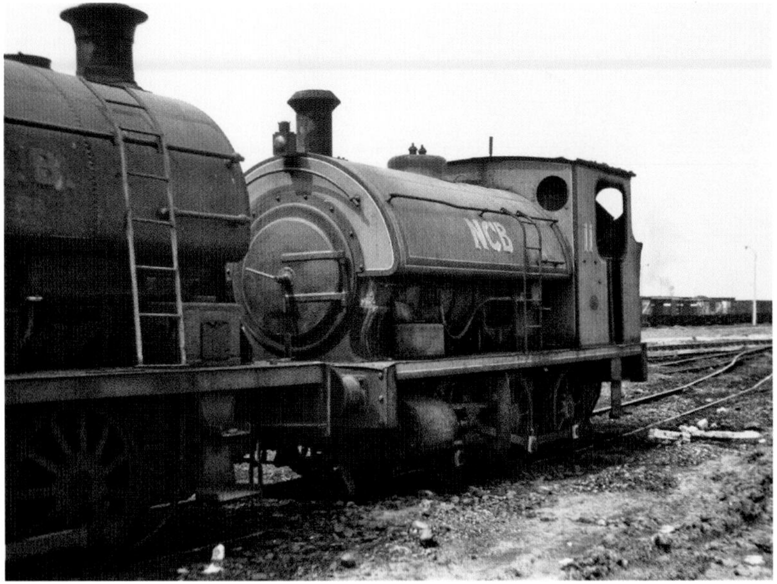

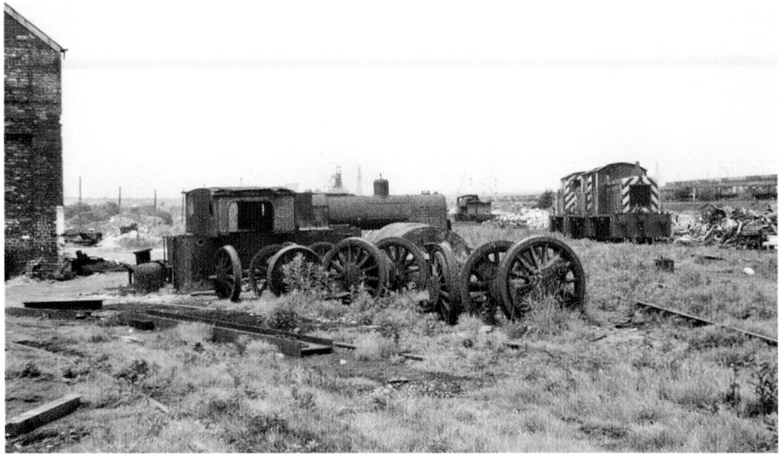

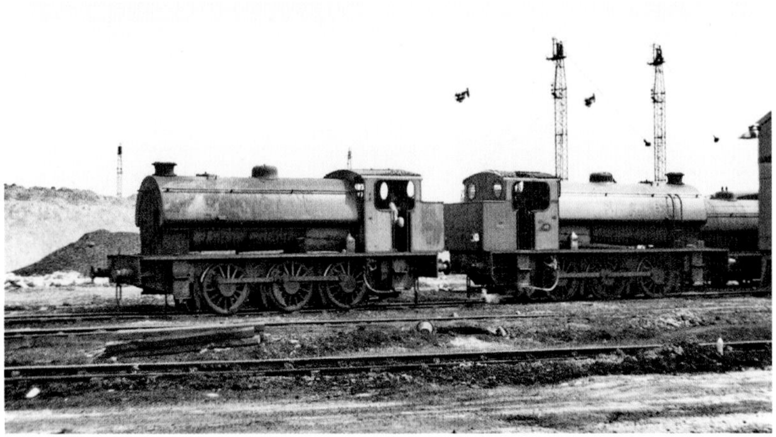

Above left: Manvers Main shed on 14 June 1969, with Yorkshire Engine Company 0-6-0 saddle tank No. 11 (W/No. 1823 of 1922) and (*below left*) Hunslet Austerity 0-6-0 saddle tanks No. 57 *Raymond* (W/No. 3839 of 1955) and No. 49 *Ted* (W/No.3701 of 1950). Manvers Main was one of the largest colliery complexes in the country, with numerous yards and sidings, coking, benzole and coal preparation plants, a branch connecting Barnburgh Main colliery and a large loco shed and workshops, all surrounded by a complicated network of main line railways; in fact, one could say it was a railway enthusiast's dream location, particularly with the nearby BR motive power depot at Wath and supporting marshalling yard with BR Class 76 electric locos for added interest! A colliery was first sunk on the site as early as 1868, but a century later, when these photos were taken, the UK coal mining industry was about to contract. Mining and by-products would last just two further decades at this Wath-upon-Dearne complex and Manvers colliery closed in March 1988, followed by its coal preparation plant and the Barnburgh Main colliery during 1989. (Both John Sloane)

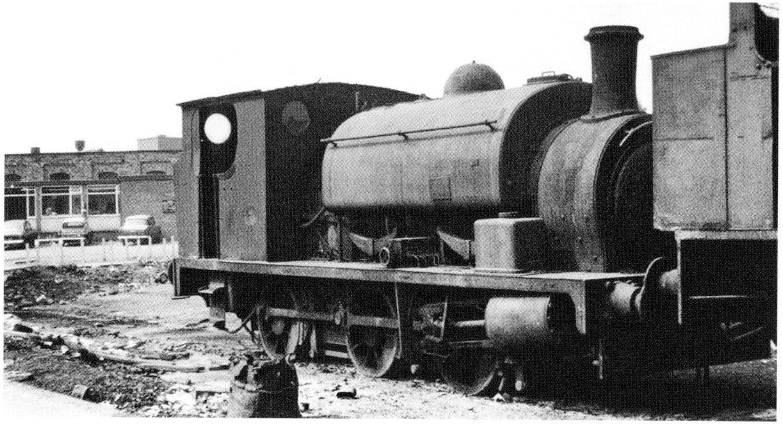

Above: Hudswell Clarke 0-6-0 saddle tank No. 18 *Eddie* (W/No.1178 of 1916) at NCB Yorkshire Main colliery, Edlington. The chunky 15 x 22-in. (OC) loco had been acquired from the Appleby Frodingham Steel Company Ltd at Scunthorpe in June 1950, but by the time of this photograph, on 14 June 1969, it had fallen into disuse and was eventually scrapped in early 1972. (John Sloane)

Opposite page top right: Manvers Main Works on 14 June 1969 with active locos, ex-BR Drewry Class 04s Nos D2334, D2335 and D2337 stabled, and parts of redundant steam locos scattered outside the workshops, marking the end of large-scale steam working there. Between September 1968 and June 1970 no fewer than fourteen Class 04 Drewry locos were acquired from BR. Some were transferred to other South Yorkshire collieries and some dismantled for spares, but Manvers relied on around six and a couple of other diesel locos which replaced the steam fleet, except for one solitary Hunslet Austerity; this was maintained on a standby basis only and saw very little work after 1971 (see page 125). (John Sloane)

Right: Hudswell Clarke 16 x 24-inch Class (OC) 0-6-0 tank No. 34 (W/No. 1523 of 1925) dumped at Elsecar Main colliery on 14 June 1969, a few months before meeting its fate. The colliery survived until October 1983. (John Sloane)

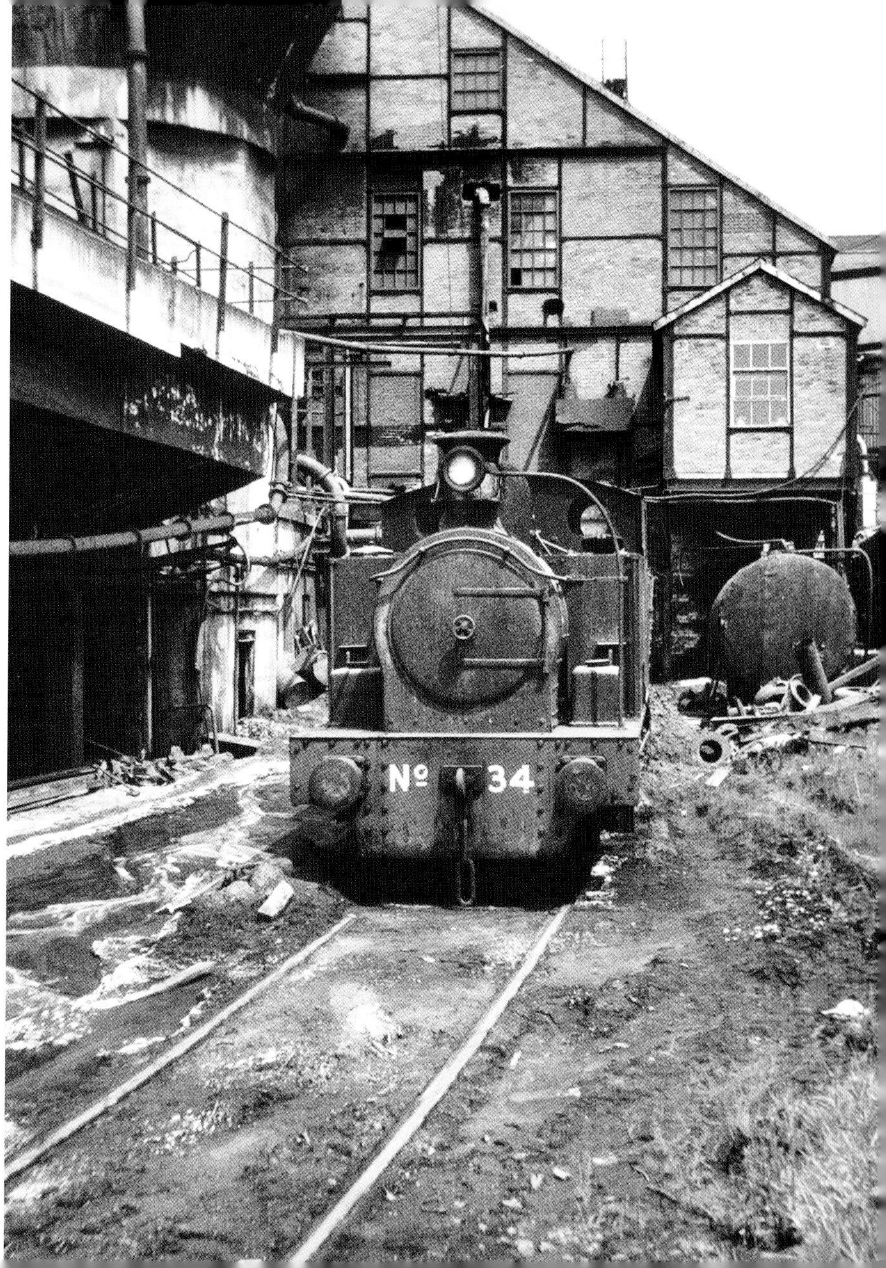

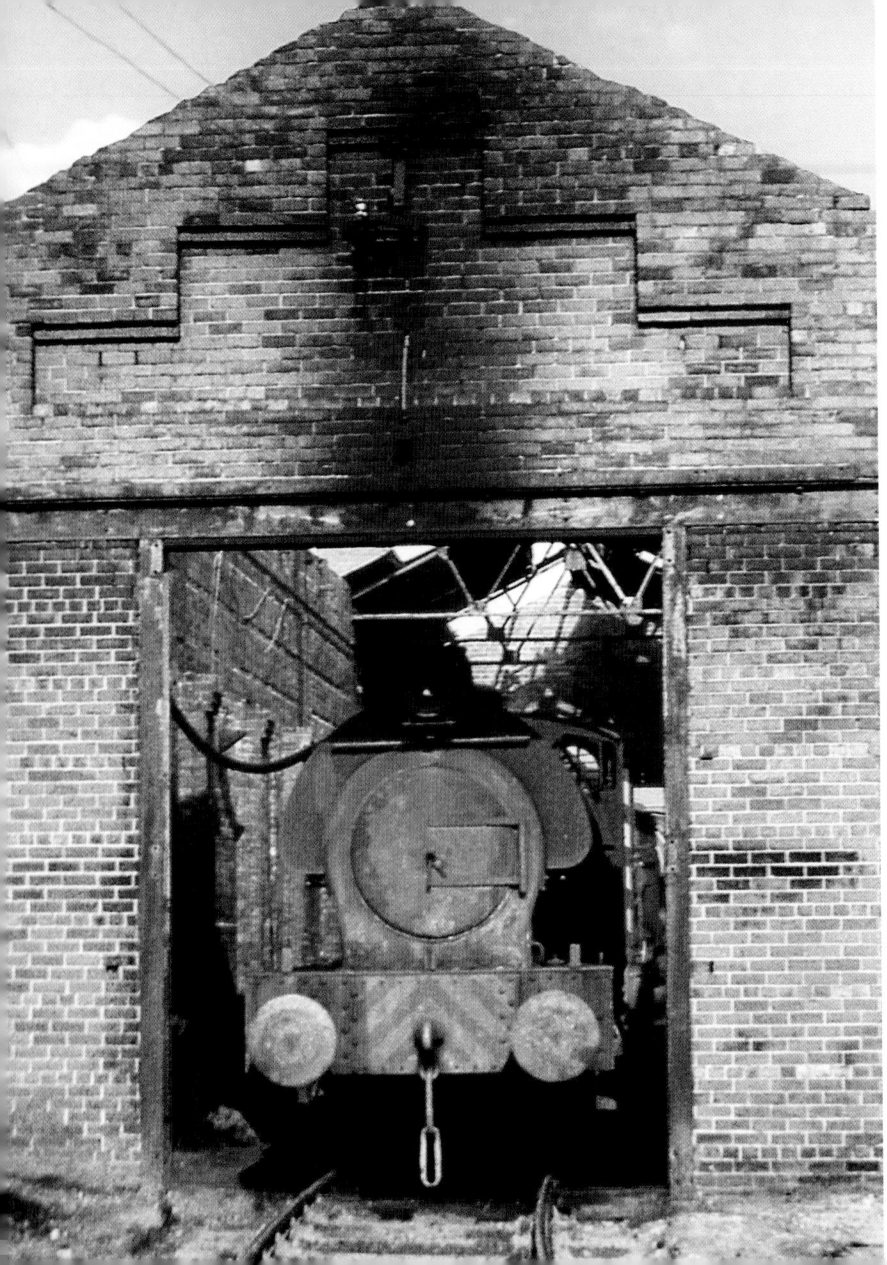

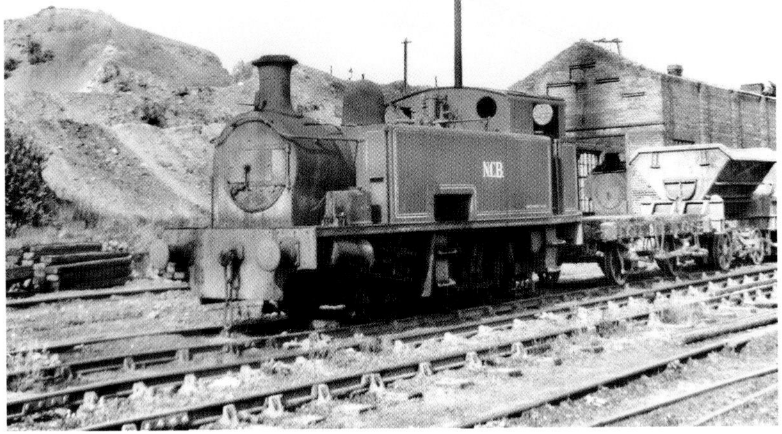

Left: Hunslet Austerity 0-6-0 saddle tank *Monckton No. 1* (W/No. 3788 of 1953) at North Gawber colliery, Mapplewell, on 30 July 1971. It was to continue to work there for a few more years, being acquired for preservation by the Yorkshire Dales Railway in February 1980. North Gawber was one of the longer-lived Barnsley-area collieries, producing around half a million tons of coal per annum, when its workings were merged with Woolley colliery in January 1986 and the surface pit closed. (Roy Burt)

Above: Hudswell Clarke PLA Class 0-6-0 tank N2 (W/No. 1857 of 1952) at North Gawber colliery on 30 July 1971. It was to pass into preservation at the Shackerstone Railway (now the Market Bosworth Light Railway) some four years later. (Roy Burt)

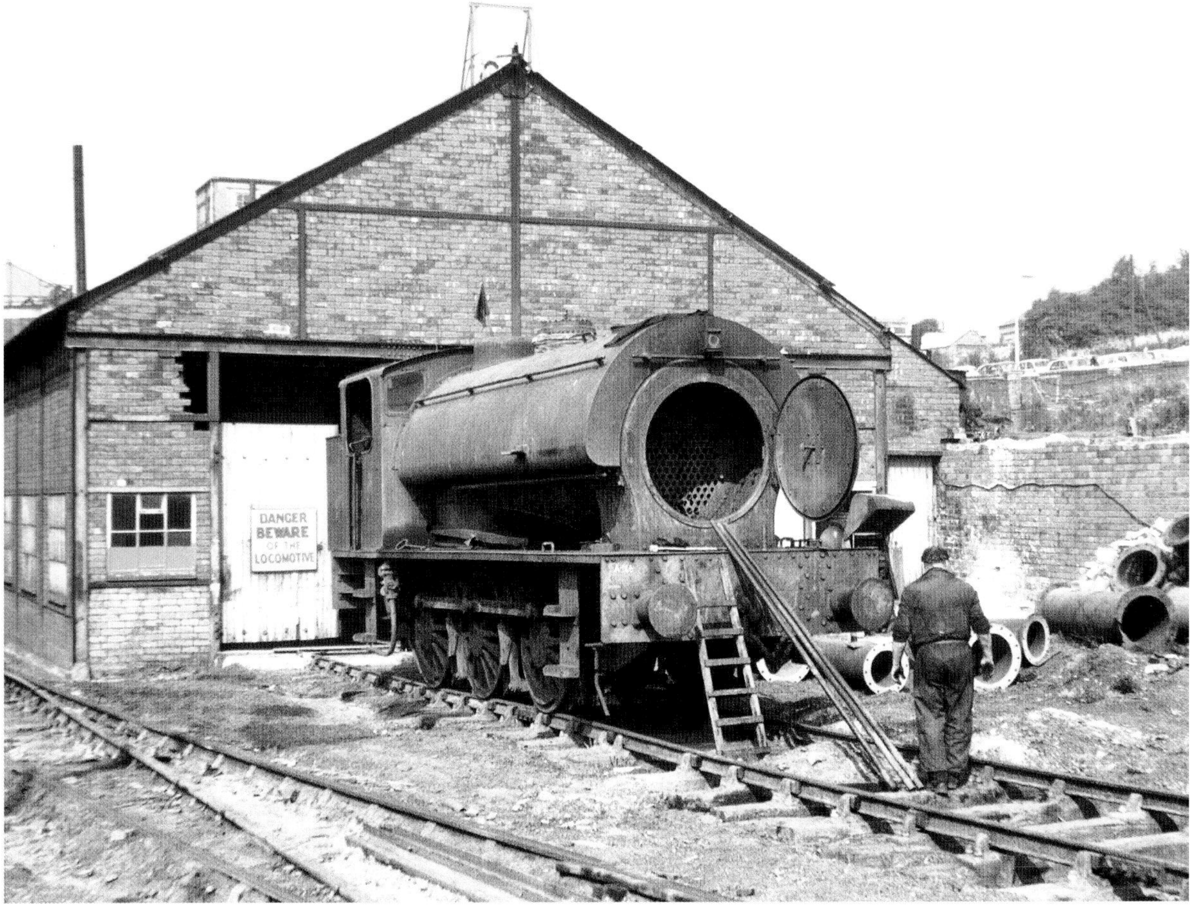

William Bagnall Austerity 0-6-0 saddle tank A146 (W/No. 2753 of 1944) receiving front end attention at Woolley colliery on 8 September 1969. A former War Department Shoeburyness loco, *WD No. 146*, it was purchased by the NCB from Hunslet in 1966, but its immaculate Army green and red livery was soon to be smothered in a liberal coating of colliery grime. It was scrapped on site by Wakefield Metal Traders in March 1973. (John Sloane)

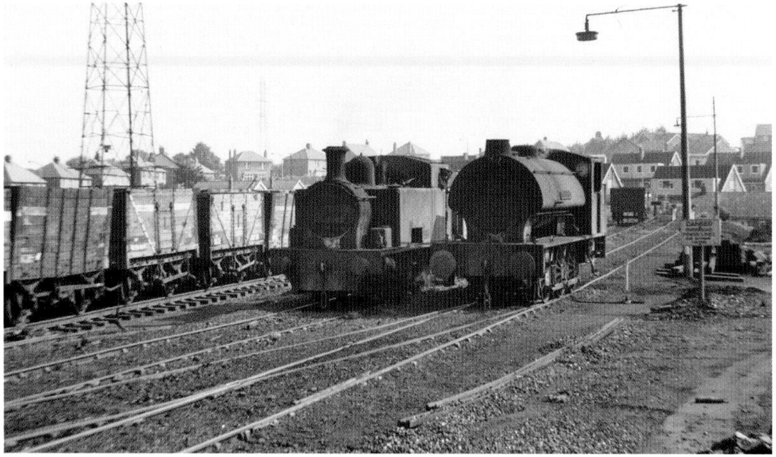

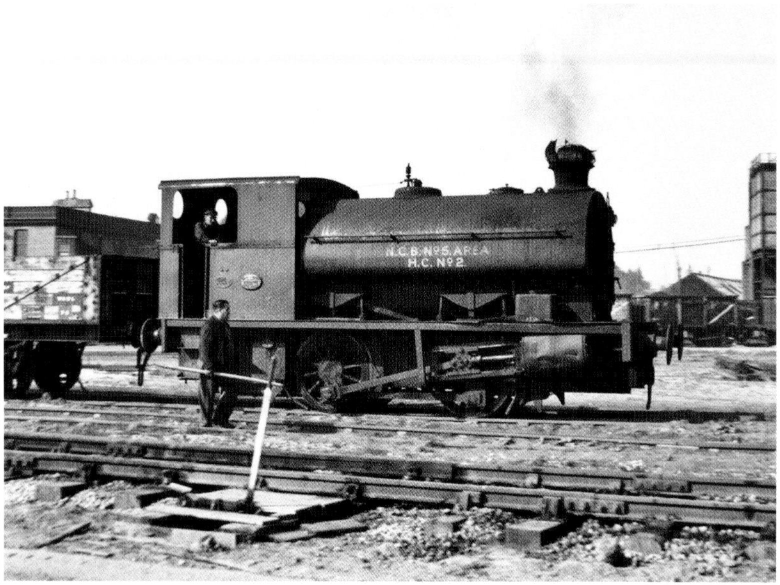

Above left: Both previously featured locos at North Gawber colliery were in action at the east end of the site on 8 September 1969, namely Hudswell Clarke 0-6-0 tank N2 and Hunslet Austerity *Monckton No. 1*. (John Sloane)

Above right: Hudswell Clarke 0-4-0 saddle tank *HC No. 2* (W/No. 1890 of 1960) at Dodworth colliery on 8 September 1969. Having seen barely nine years of action at the time of this visit, it was to see no more than six years of further service, being scrapped on site during March 1975. (John Sloane)

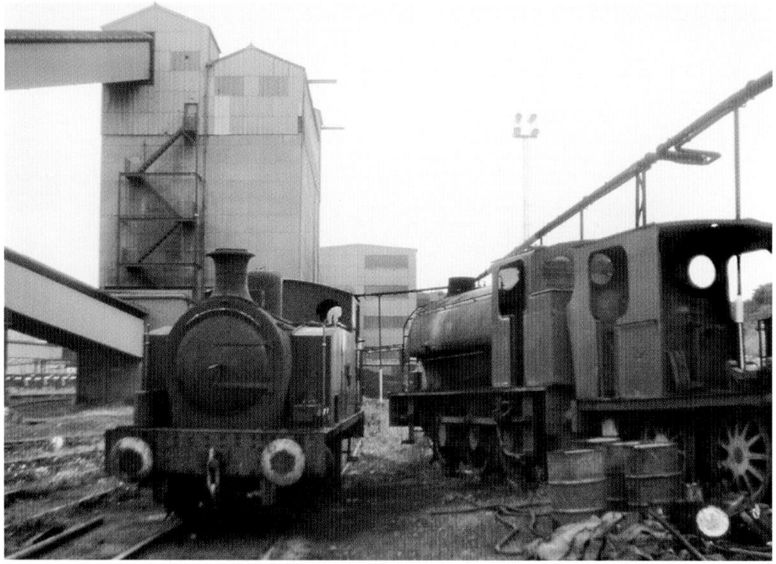

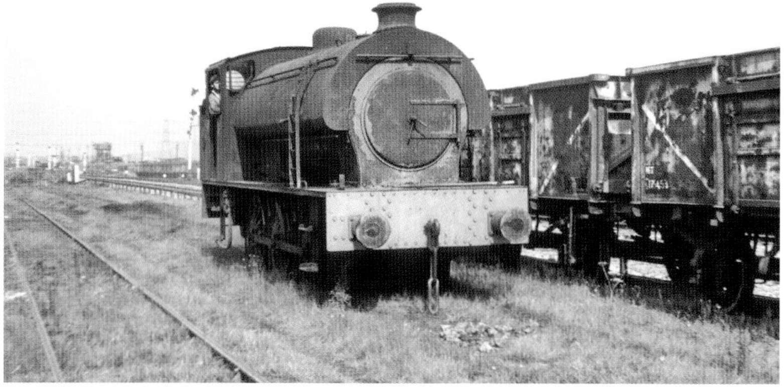

Above: Hunslet Austerity 0-6-0 saddle tank (W/No.3208 of 1945) was another former MoD Army Department locomotive (*WD No. 158*) acquired by the NCB, as late as February 1965 from their Chilwell depot in Nottinghamshire. By this 8 September 1969 photograph it had already acquired the signature 'NCB grime and rust' appearance as it was captured running through the yard at Wharncliffe Woodmoor colliery, Carlton, near Royston. (John Sloane)

Opposite page below left: Cadeby colliery at Conisbrough was located north of the BR Mexborough–Doncaster line and the colliery enjoyed a connection to nearby Denaby colliery via the BR bridge over the River Don. Coal from Cadeby was, until 1964, transported to a staith at Denaby. There was interworking between the two collieries, although railway operations were concentrated at Cadeby. Diesel traction had virtually taken over by the time of this visit on 28 July 1971 when out of use were (*left*) Hudswell Clarke 0-6-0 tank No. 20 (W/No. 1731 of 1942) and (*centre right*) Hunslet Austerity 0-6-0 saddle tank No. 66 (W/No. 3890 of 1964). This was the last entirely new Austerity to be constructed (see page 125). Displaced by ex-BR Class 04 and 05 diesel shunters at the colliery in 1970, the loco had a commercial working life of less than six years. (Roy Burt)

Below: A Hunslet Austerity 0-6-0 saddle tank (W/No. 2857 of 1943) hard at work on BR metals in the rain at Dodworth colliery on 3 August 1971. The NCB had running rights on to BR and across the level crossing with the main A628 Barnsley to Penistone road due to the restricted length of the colliery's headshunt, much to the disapproval of motorists delayed at the crossing gates! The Hunslet was transferred to Cadley Hill colliery in January 1976 and was to hold the distinction of being one of the last working Austerity locos active in British industry. (Roy Burt)

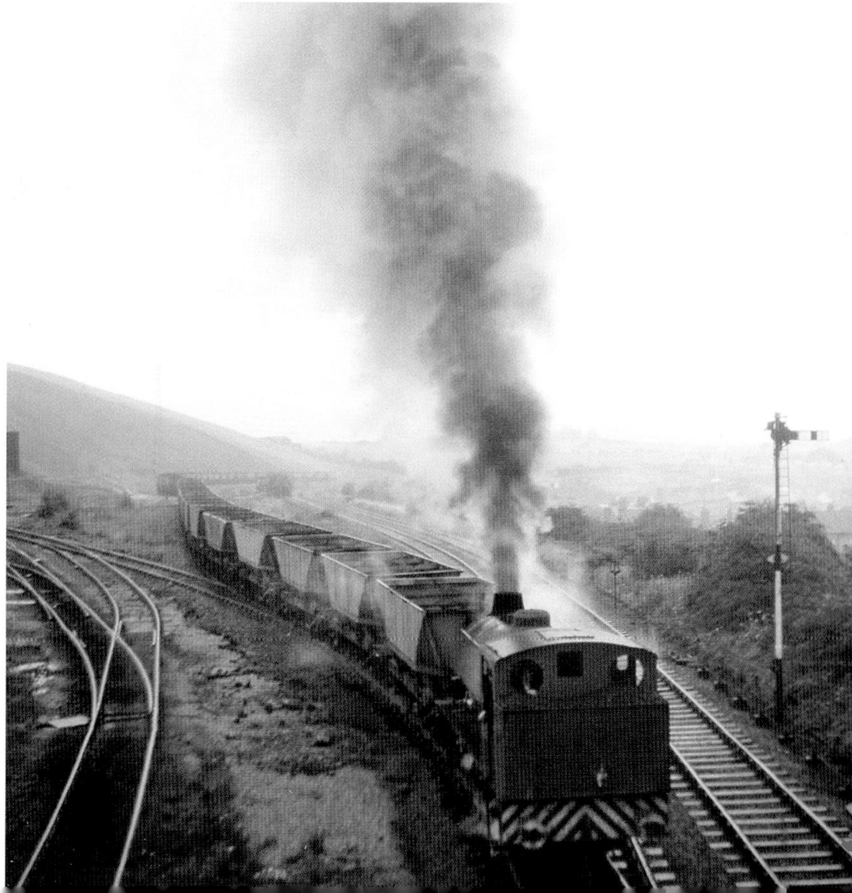

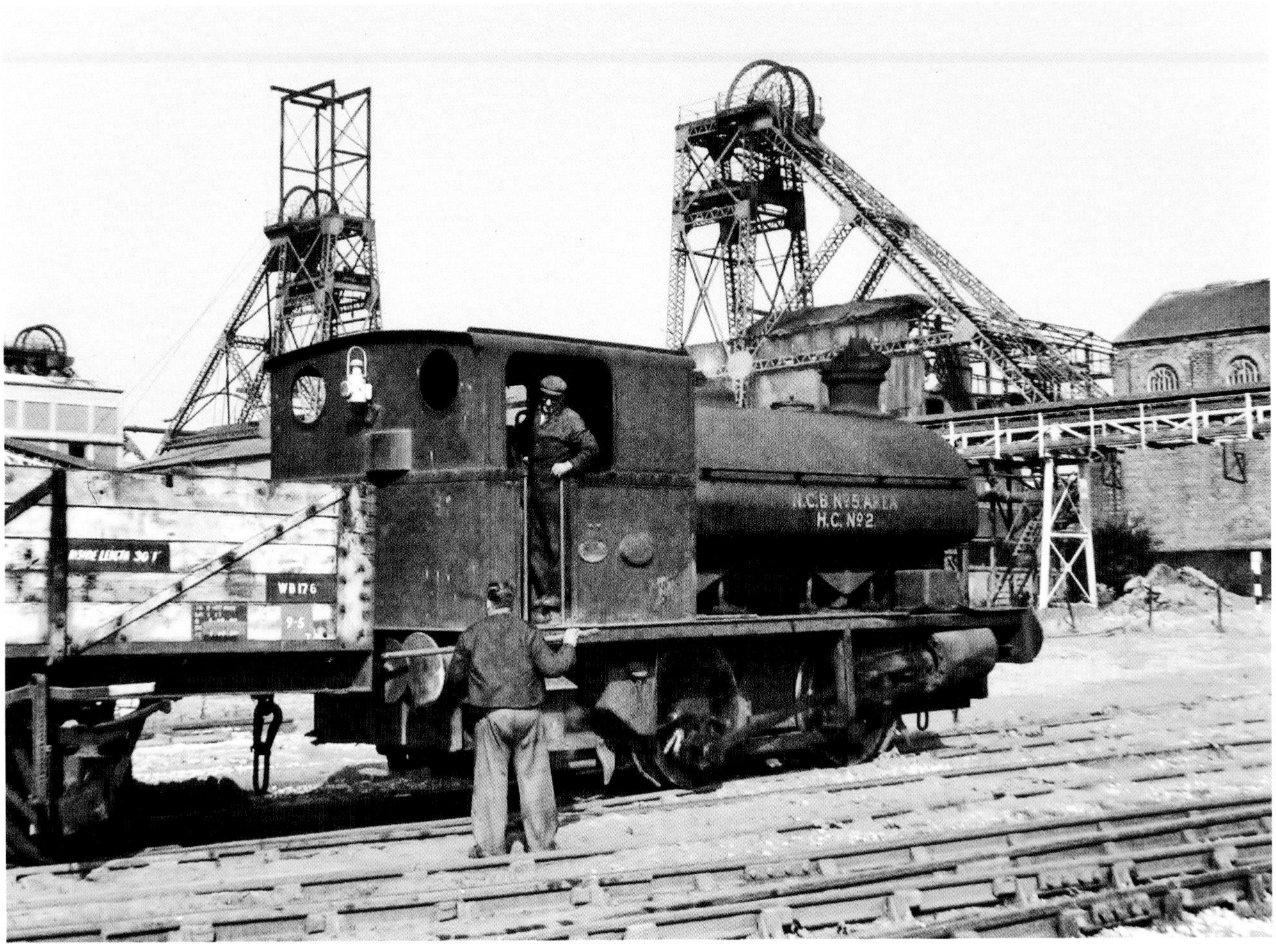

On 8 September 1969, one of five Hudswell Clarke 0-4-0 saddle tanks supplied new to the NCB Barnsley area in the early 1960s, *HC No. 2* (W/No. 1890 of 1960), fitted with a rudimentary spark arrestor, is in action shunting wagons at the Dodworth colliery pit head. (Further coverage, the last steam locos constructed by Hudswell Clarke, can be found on pages 127 and 128). (John Sloane)

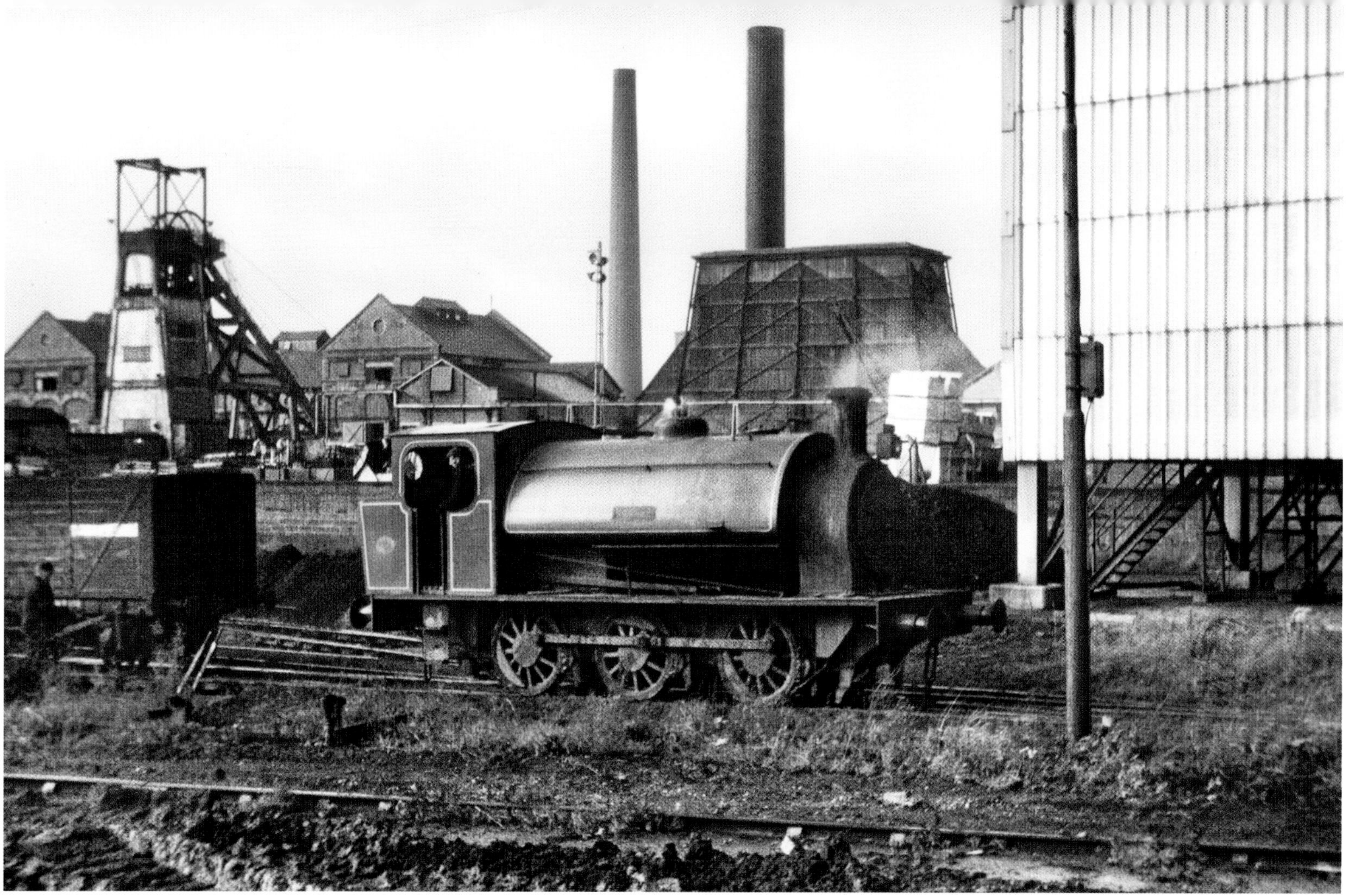

Markham Main colliery, Armthorpe, on 8 November 1969 with Hunslet 16 x 22-in. inside-cylinder (IC) Class *Arthur* (W/No. 3782 of 1952) shunting. The colliery, first sunk in 1914, was the last in the Doncaster area to use steam traction, until around 1976, when *Arthur* failed its boiler inspection. It is now preserved at the Buckinghamshire Railway Centre. (John Sloane)

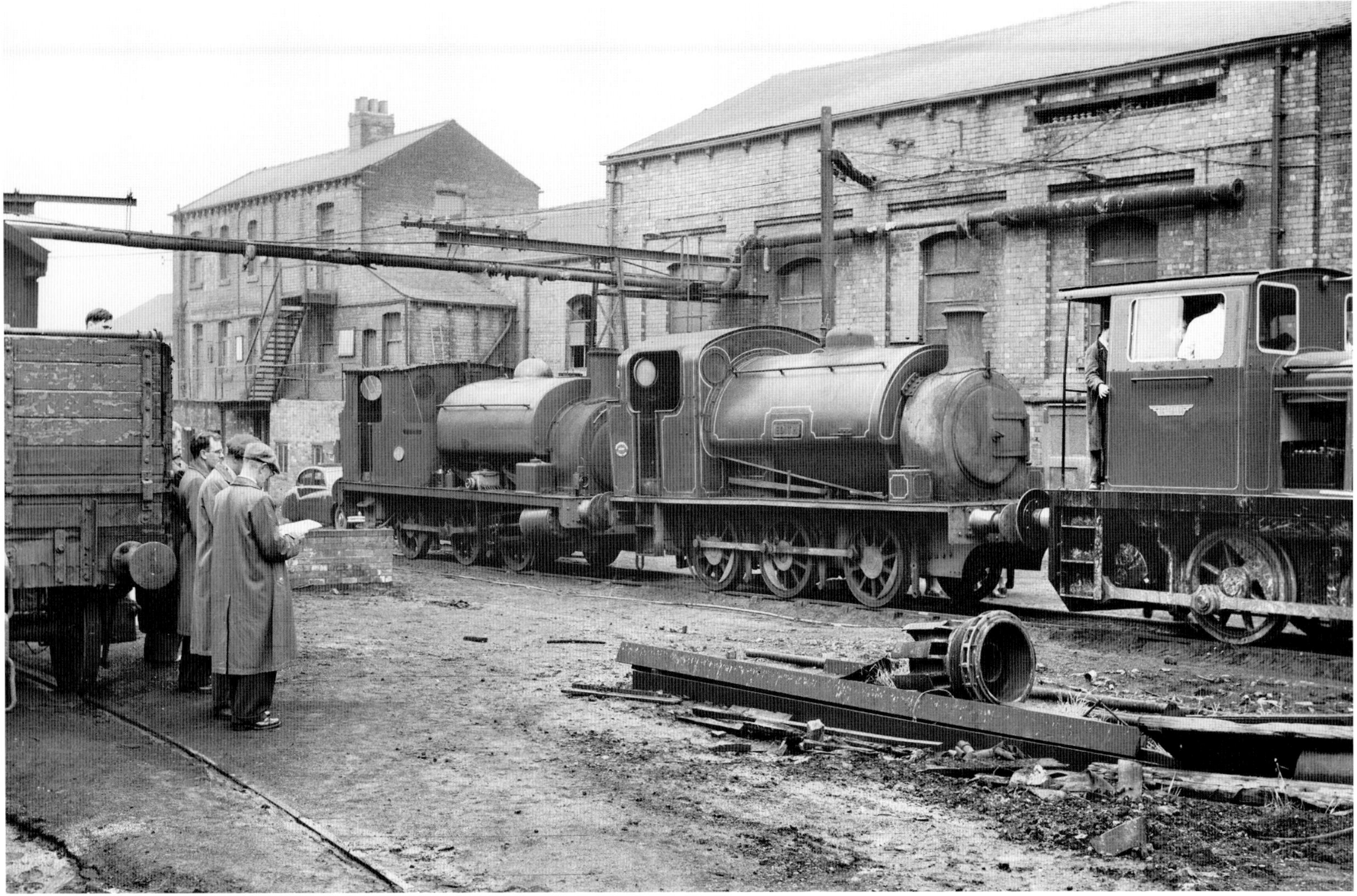

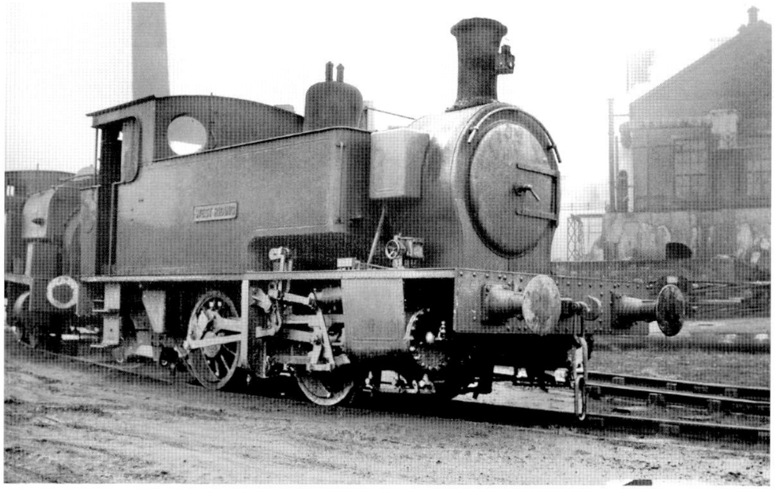

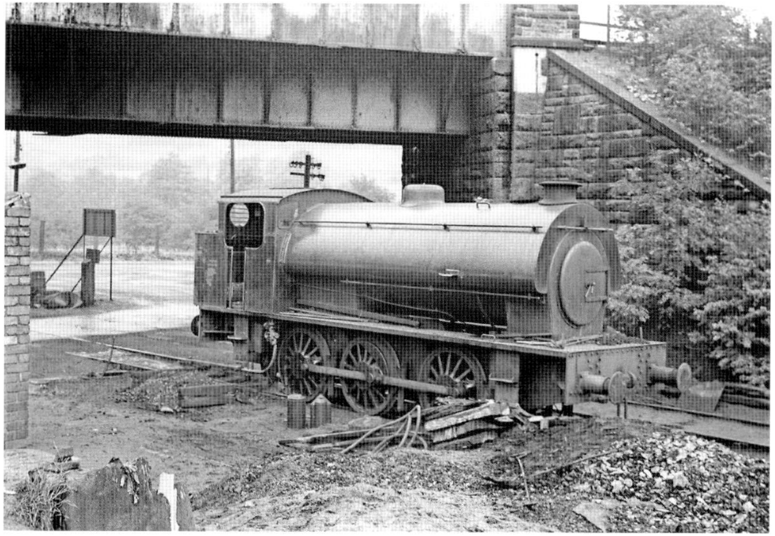

Opposite page: A colliery scene that typifies the popularity of visits undertaken over many decades by railway societies specialising in the industrial railway scene. This is Middleton Broom colliery near Leeds on 7 June 1958, with visitors observing a shunting operation for two out-of-service locos using a newly constructed 185 hp John Fowler 0-4-0 diesel-hydraulic (W/No. 4230001 of 1957). The Fowler would have been under evaluation on loading tests, which was a regular arrangement between the builder and the NCB at this time. The steam locos are (*left*) former Appleby Frodingham Steel Company Hudswell Clarke 15 x 22-in. (OC) 0-6-0 saddle tank No. 69 (W/No. 1175 of 1916) and Hunslet 14 x 20-in. (IC) Class 0-6-0 saddle tank *Edith* (W/No. 1482 of 1925). The Hudswell Clarke was purchased by the NCB in 1950 and, following work at Middleton, moved to Lofthouse colliery, where it survived until it was scrapped in August 1968. Following repairs at Hunslet, *Edith* moved on to Old Roundwood colliery at Ossett, where it met its fate at the beginning of 1966. Coal traffic on the Middleton Railway ceased in July 1967 and the colliery was to close during the following May. Following the clearance of the colliery site, the Middleton Railway Society was able to extend its running line from Middleton to Park Halt. (See pages 122 and 123 for further information on the Middleton Railway). (Author's collection)

Above right: Hunslet 16 x 24-in. (OC) 0-4-0 tank *West Riding* (W/No. 1488 of 1925) at West Riding Colliery, Altofts, in the mid-1960s. Behind it is veteran 15 x 20-in. (OC) Hunslet 0-4-0 saddle tank *Altofts* (W/No. 940 of 1907). *West Riding* was scrapped at Allerton Bywater Central Workshops in 1965 and *Altofts* at the colliery site in 1968, following the colliery's closure during the previous year. (Author's collection)

Below right: William Bagnall Austerity 0-6-0 saddle tank *Pepper* (W/No. 2761 of 1944) at the British Oak Disposal Point (DP) at Calder Grove on 9 August 1958. The DP was opened by the Ministry of Fuel & Power during the Second World War and was connected by a branch from the Wakefield main line north of Crigglestone West station. A further branch from the DP ran to staithes on the Calder & Hebble Navigation (see also page 72). (Author's collection)

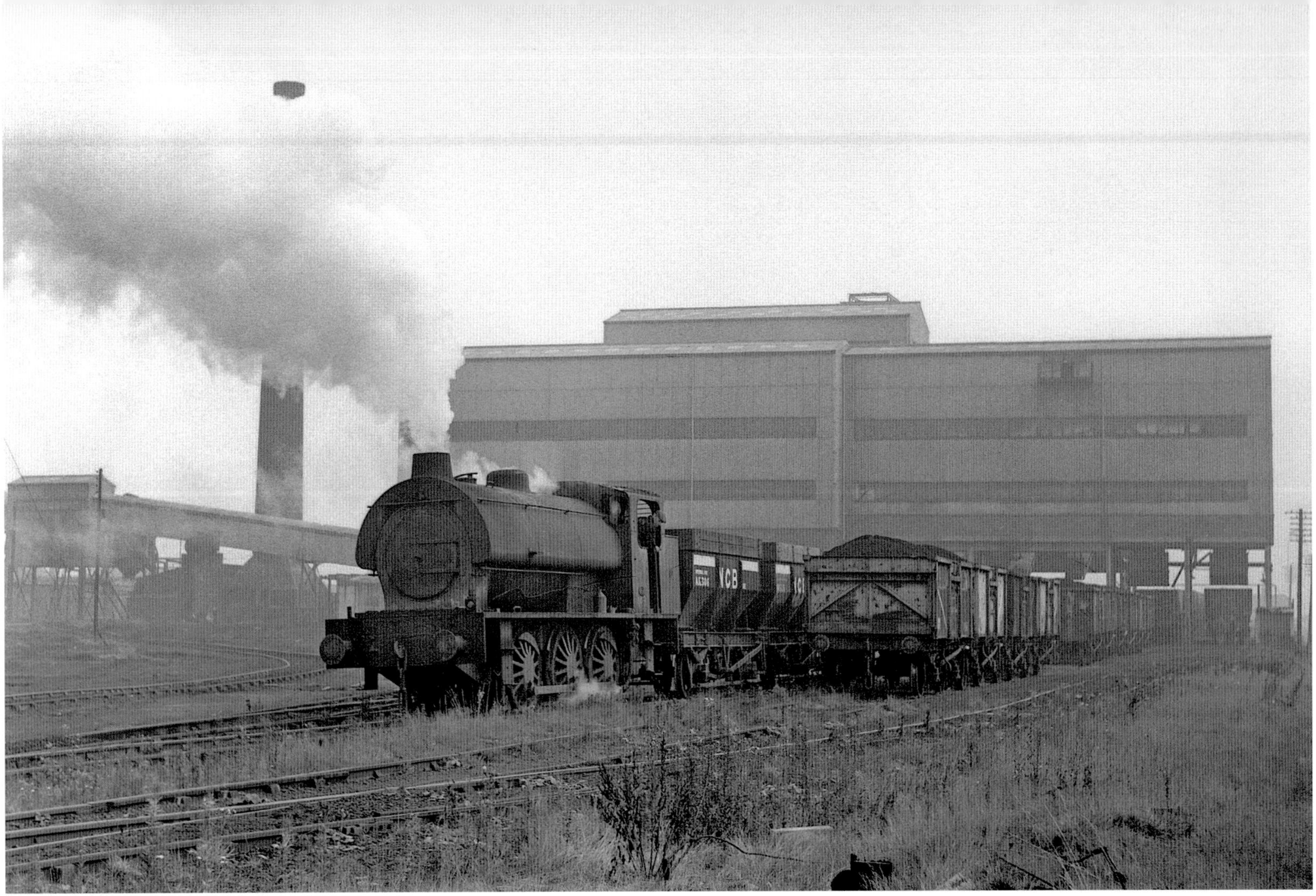

Ackton Hall was a large colliery alongside BR's Wakefield–Pontefract (Monkhill) line, close to Featherstone station. On 7 September 1971 William Bagnall Austerity 0-6-0 saddle tank No. 143 (W/No. 2740 of 1944) shunts the coal screens. (Richard Stevens)

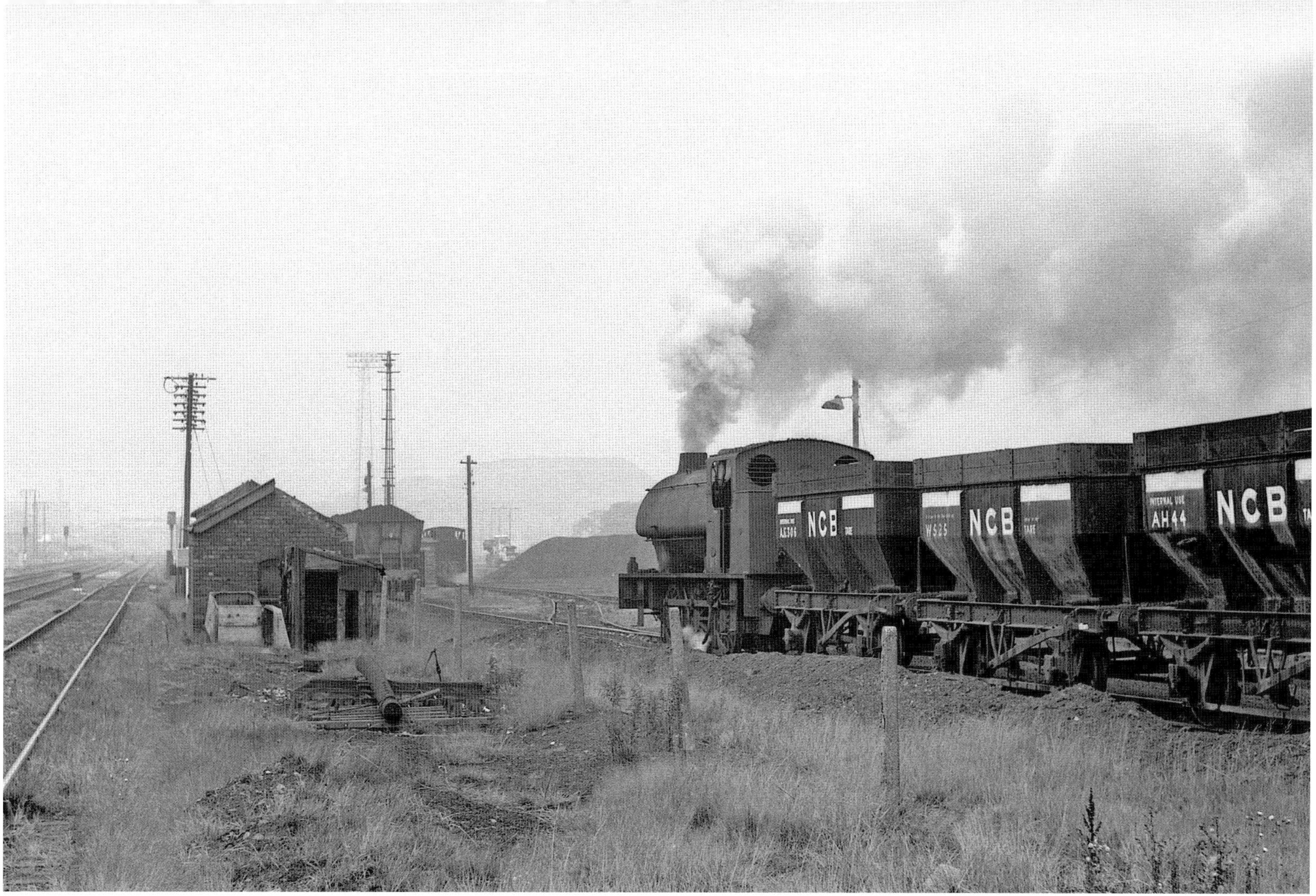

Also on 7 September 1971, Austerity No. 143 positions internal hopper wagons, setting back towards the screens, with the BR Wakefield–Pontefract line located on the left. The volume of work at Ackton Hall was such as to require two locos in use every day. (Richard Stevens)

Right: Peckett X2 Class 16 x 22-in. (IC) 0-6-0 saddle tank *Ackton Hall No. 3* (W/No. 1567 of 1920) out of use at Ackton Hall colliery on 24 June 1972. The Bristol-built loco wore a non-standard green livery and was of the unusual inside-cylinder type from this manufacturer. It was moved to the Keighley & Worth Valley Railway for preservation in April 1973. (Author)

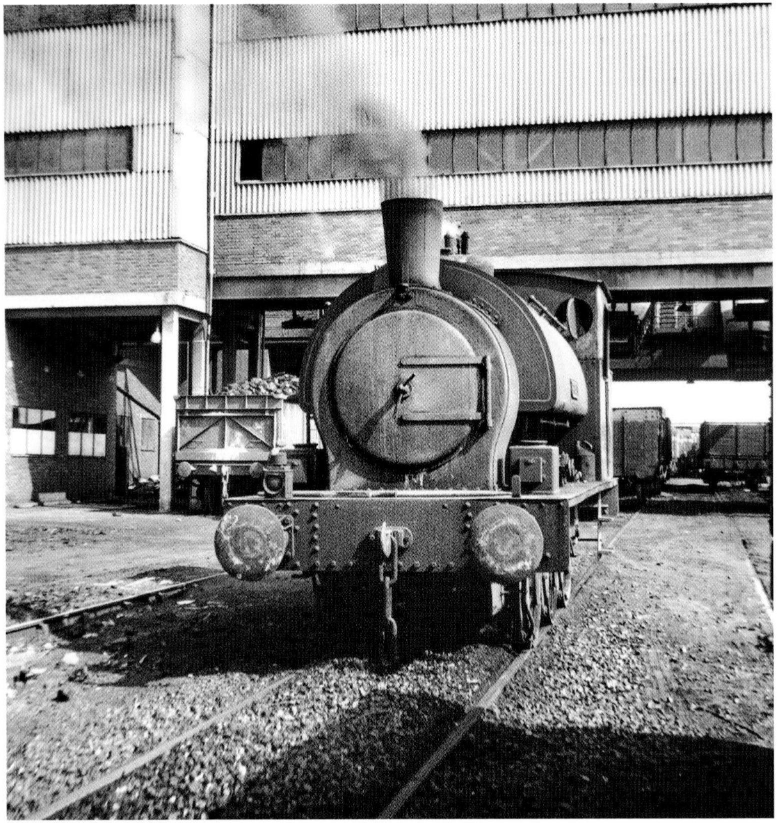

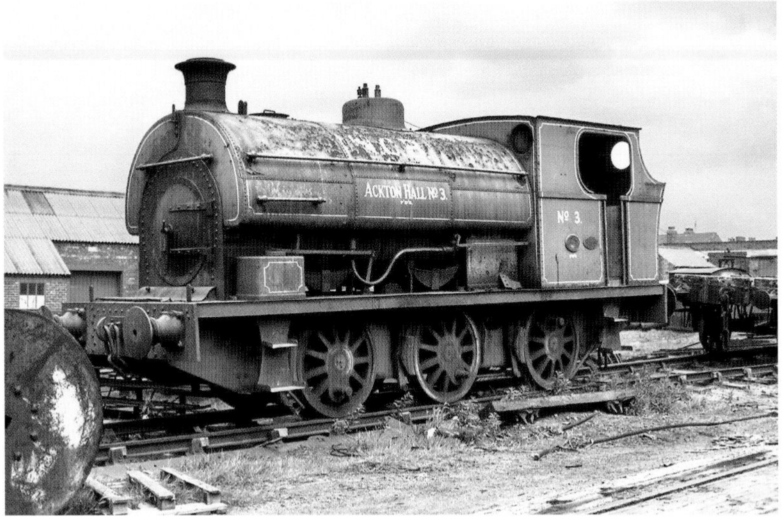

Left: Hunslet 15 x 20-in. (IC) 0-6-0 saddle tank S106 *Airedale* (W/No. 1440 of 1923) at Ackton Hall colliery on 8 September 1969. This was another loco from the colliery that did not escape the attention of preservationists, moving to the Yorkshire Dales Railway (YDR) in December 1975. (John Sloane)

Opposite page: Ackton Hall colliery on 24 June 1972, with (*left*) Peckett *Ackton Hall No. 3* and (*right*) Hunslet S106 *Airedale*, William Bagnall Austerity 0-6-0 saddle tank No. 143 and a Hunslet 400 hp 0-6-0 diesel-hydraulic (W/No. 7062 of 1971). Dismantled Hunslet 16 x 22-in. (IC) 0-6-0 saddle tank S119 *Beatrice* (W/No. 2705 of 1945) is in the foreground. She also survived the torch and was acquired by the YDR. The new Hunslet diesel in the running shed was soon to follow the fate of many steam locos before it, being scrapped by C. F. Booth of Rotherham in March 1986, following the colliery's closure during the previous July after the miners' strike. The three prominent sets of headgear are Haigh Moor, Warrenhouse and Silkstone. (Author)

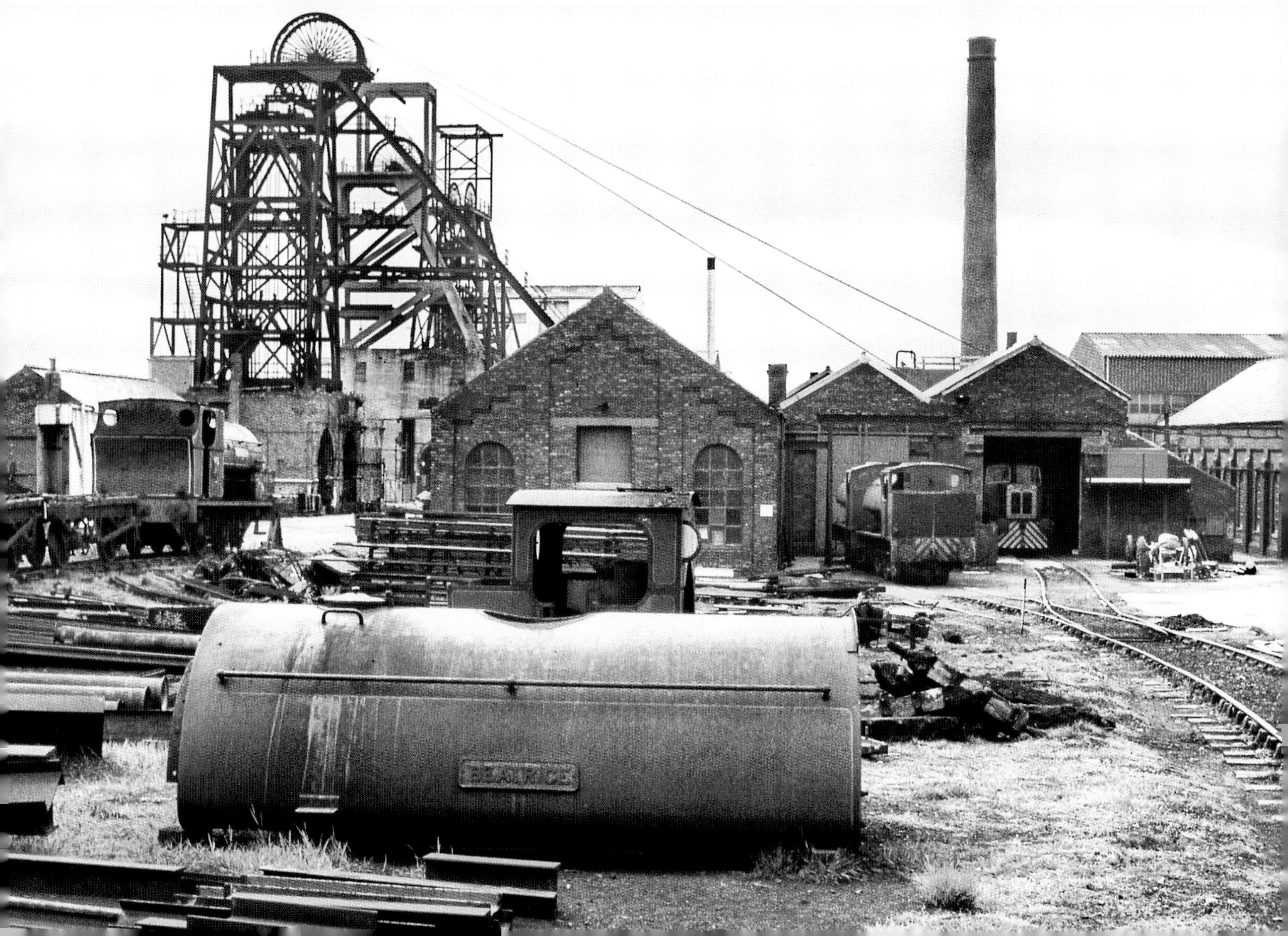
BEATRICE

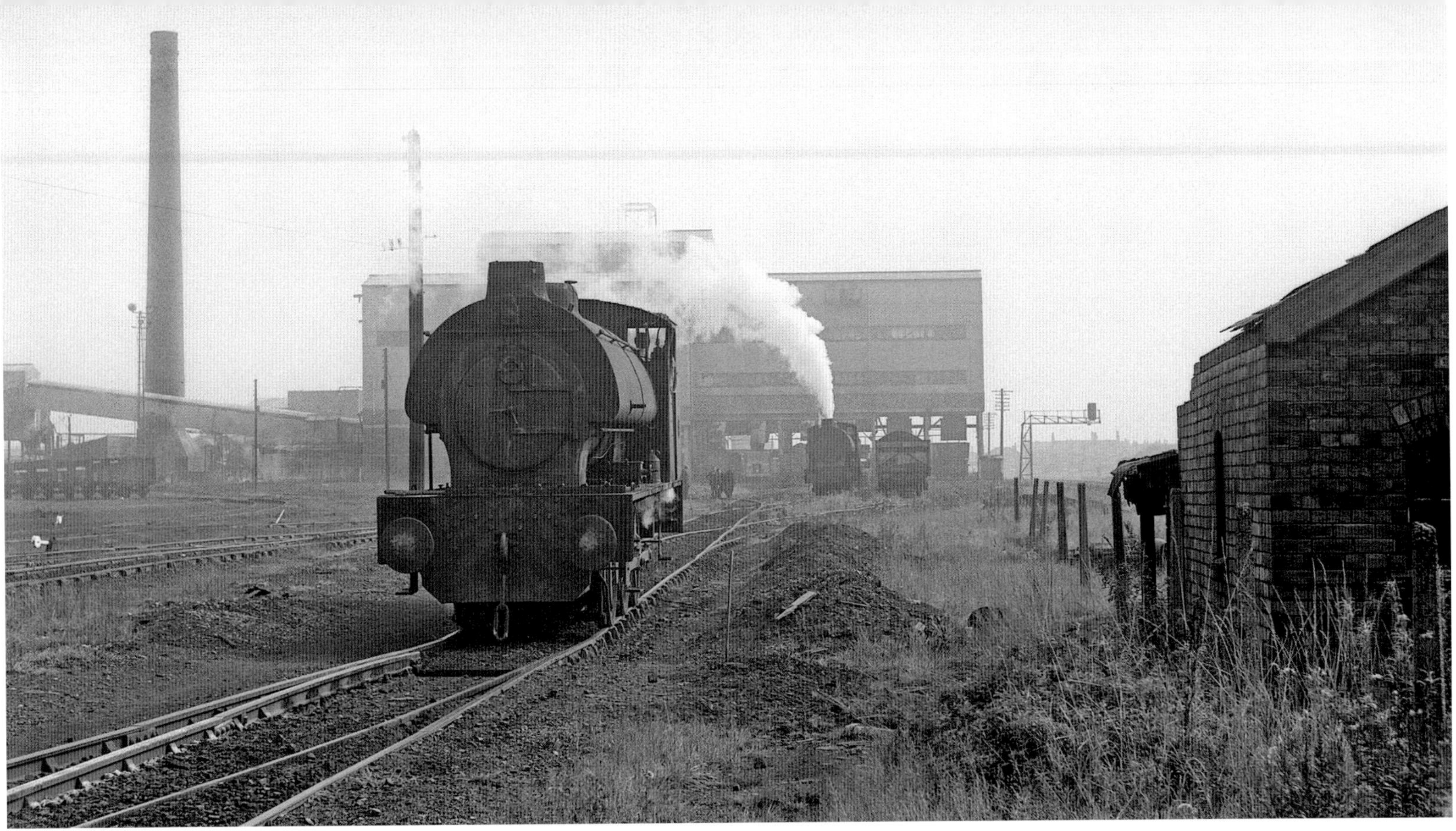

Above: Hunslet 18 x 26-in. (IC) 0-6-0 saddle tank S112 (W/No. 2414 of 1941) was one of only eight members of Hunslet's 50550 Class, the precursors of the Austerity 0-6-0 saddle tank, and the only example to enter NCB service. It had been supplied new to the Port of London Authority (PLA) and was No. 79 in their fleet, the chamfering on the buffer beam originating from PLA ownership. Hunslet undertook repairs and fitted a mechanical stoker in January 1963, which undoubtedly assured its longevity at Ackton Hall, it being acquired by the YDR in June 1976. It is seen backing towards Ackton Hall colliery's screens on 7 September 1971. Beyond is Austerity No. 143, waiting to move loaded wagons.

Opposite page: Hunslet S112, easily identified by its sloping coal bunker, crosses Station Lane, Featherstone, where some other vintage transport is also on display, including a horse-drawn rag and bone cart. The scene today is almost unrecognisable, with only the bridge abutments surviving. The dip in the road has been levelled out and all the houses have been flattened and replaced by more modern ones set back from the road. (Both Richard Stevens)

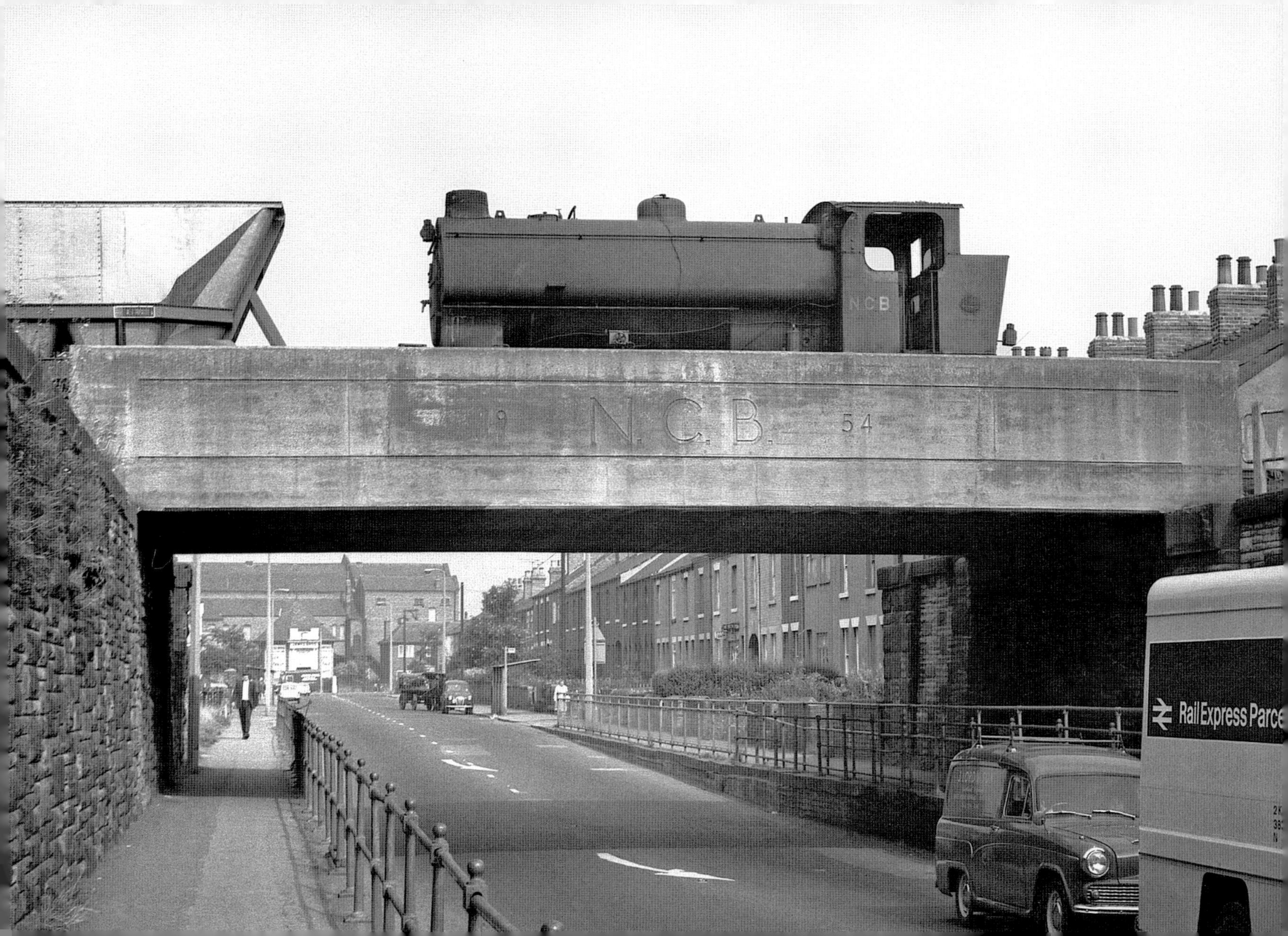
N C B
N.C.B.
54
Rail Express Parce

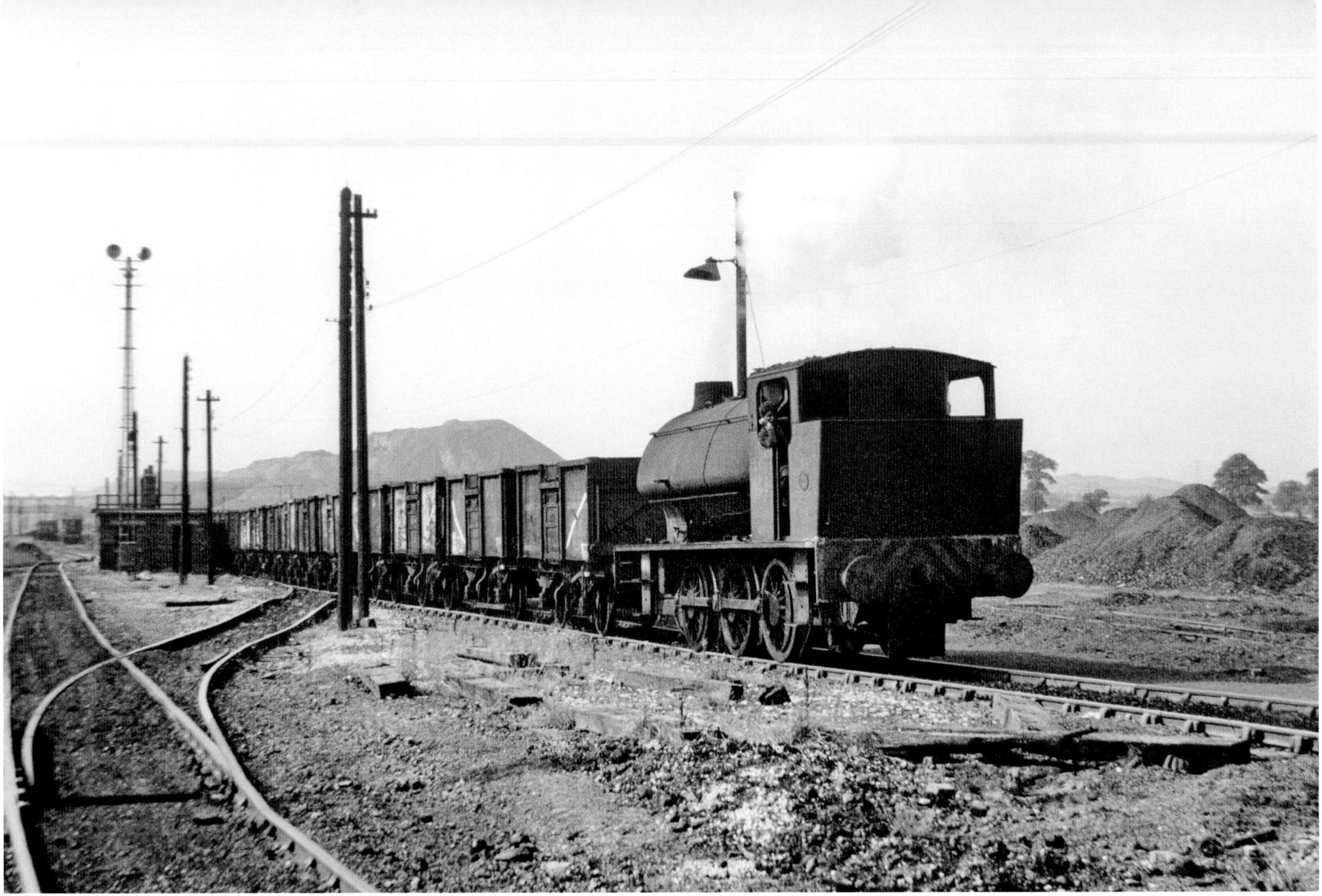

Another view of the 50550 Class 0-6-0 saddle tank at Ackton Hall, positioning loaded BR 16-ton wagons over the exchange sidings weighbridge on 8 September 1969. (John Sloane)

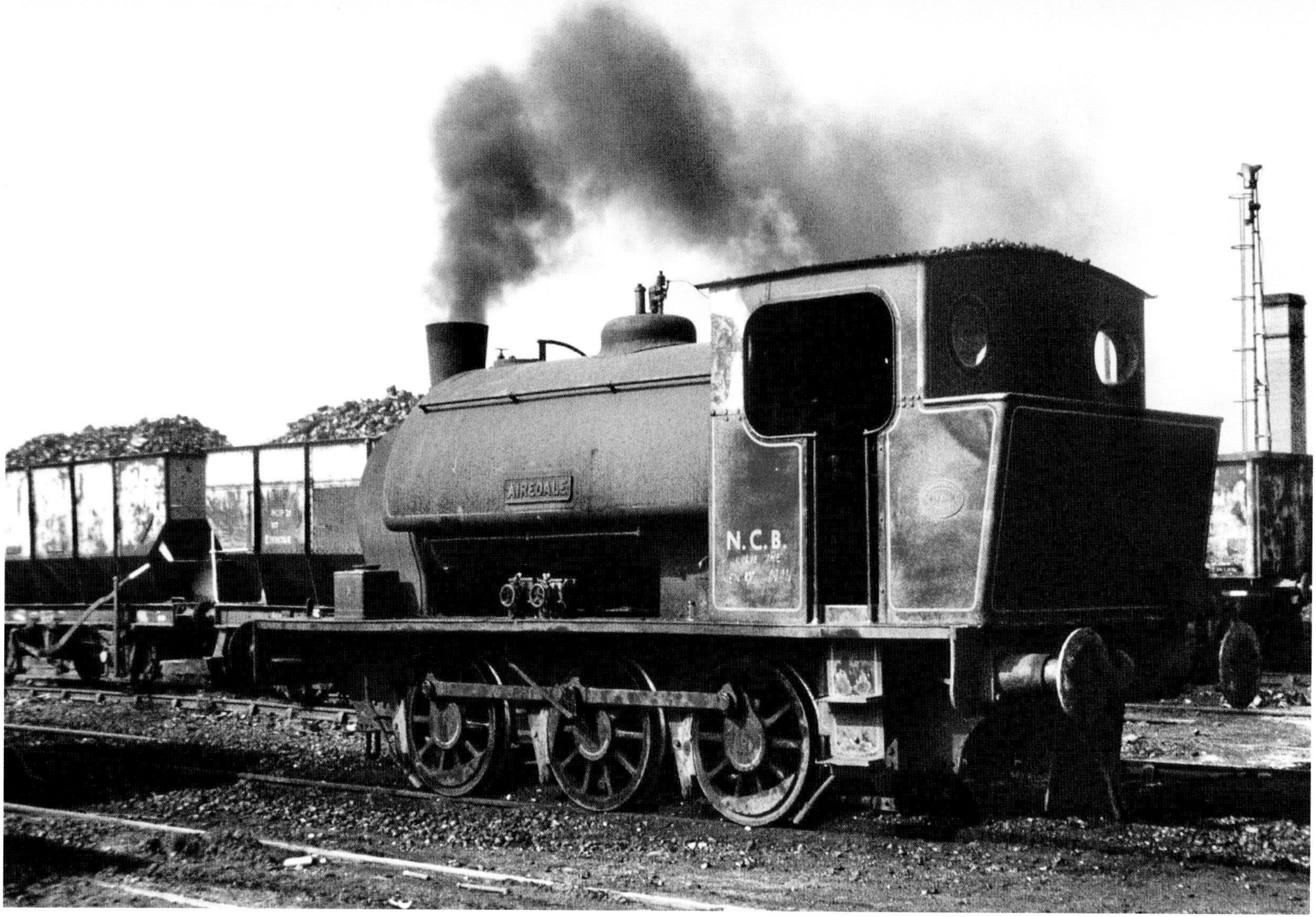

Workworn Hunslet 0-6-0 saddle tank *Airedale* 'brewing up' between duties at Ackton Hall on 8 September 1969. (John Sloane)

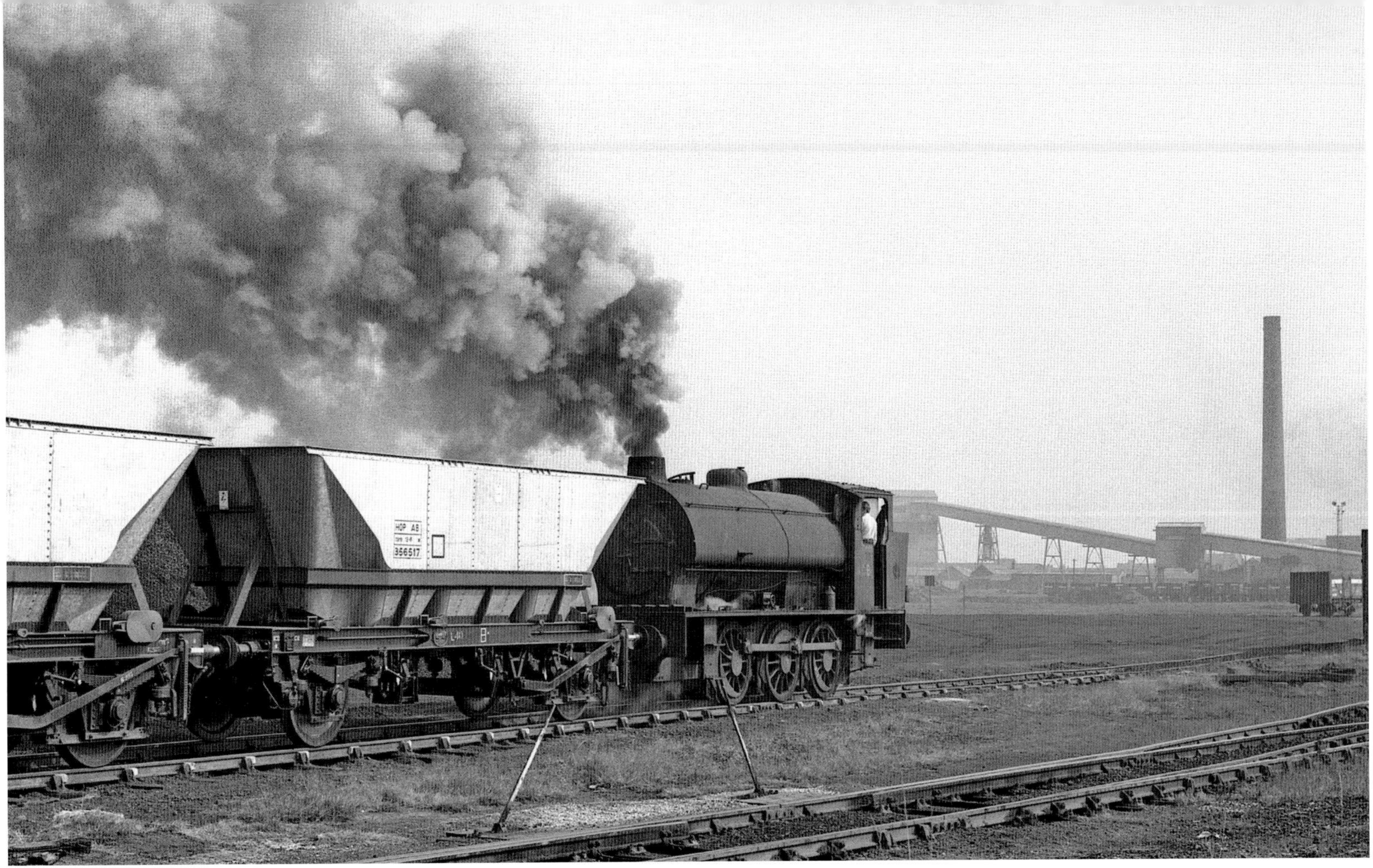

Ackton Hall's Hunslet S112 heads from the exchange sidings towards the colliery with a rake of empty merry-go-round (MGR) wagons on 7 September 1971. The vastness of the colliery site can be appreciated in this view. *Opposite page*: Looking towards the BR exchange sidings and taken just before the above photo, S112 makes an impressive storming departure with its long rake of MGR wagons. The last steam working at the colliery was on 26 June 1975 with Hunslet *Beatrice*. A Bagnall Austerity was transferred from Prince of Wales colliery in January 1977 (see page 50), ostensibly to deputise for one of the Hunslet diesels, but it was never used; it remained there until 1983, becoming one of the last two NCB steam locos remaining in the area. (Both Richard Stevens)

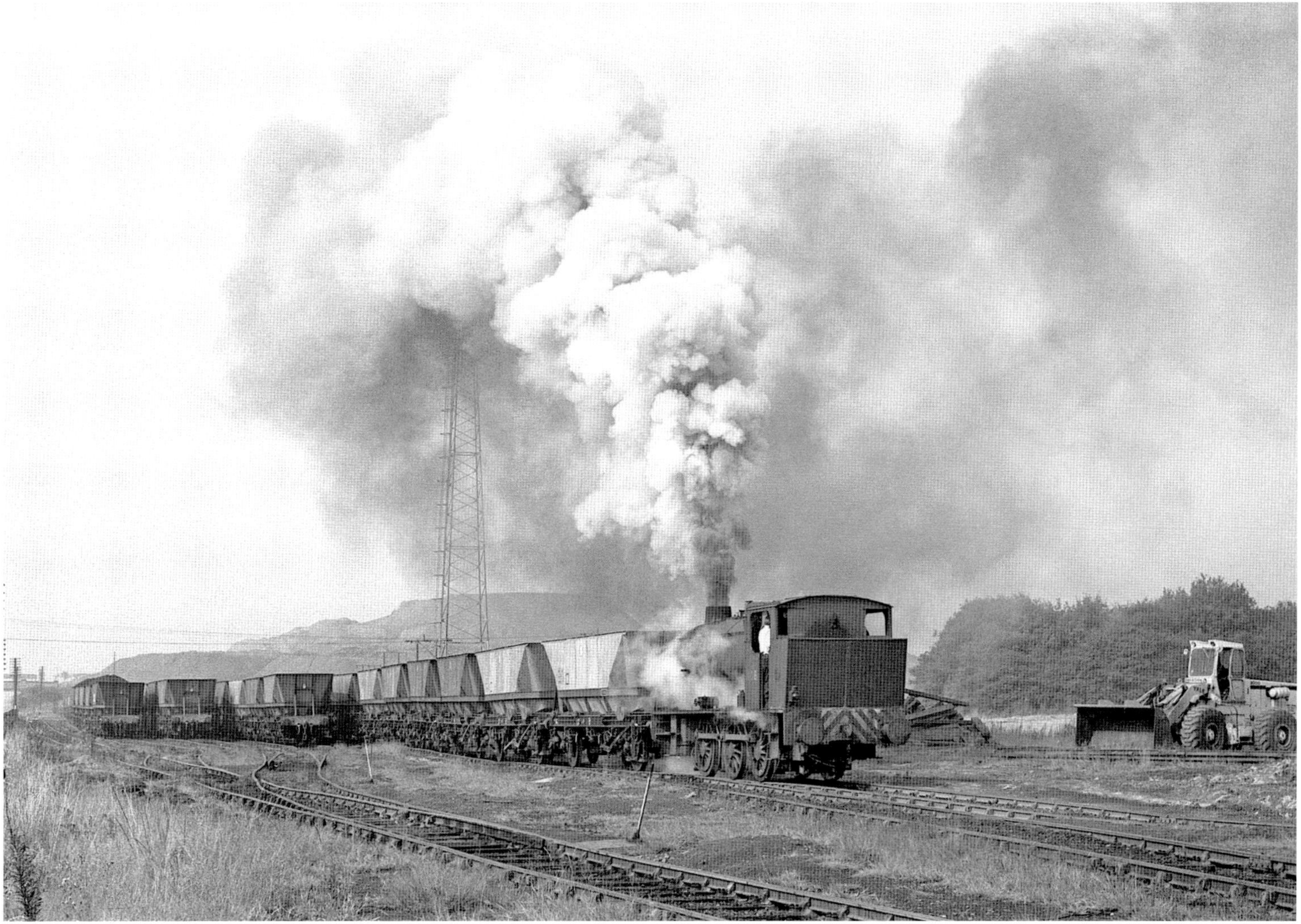

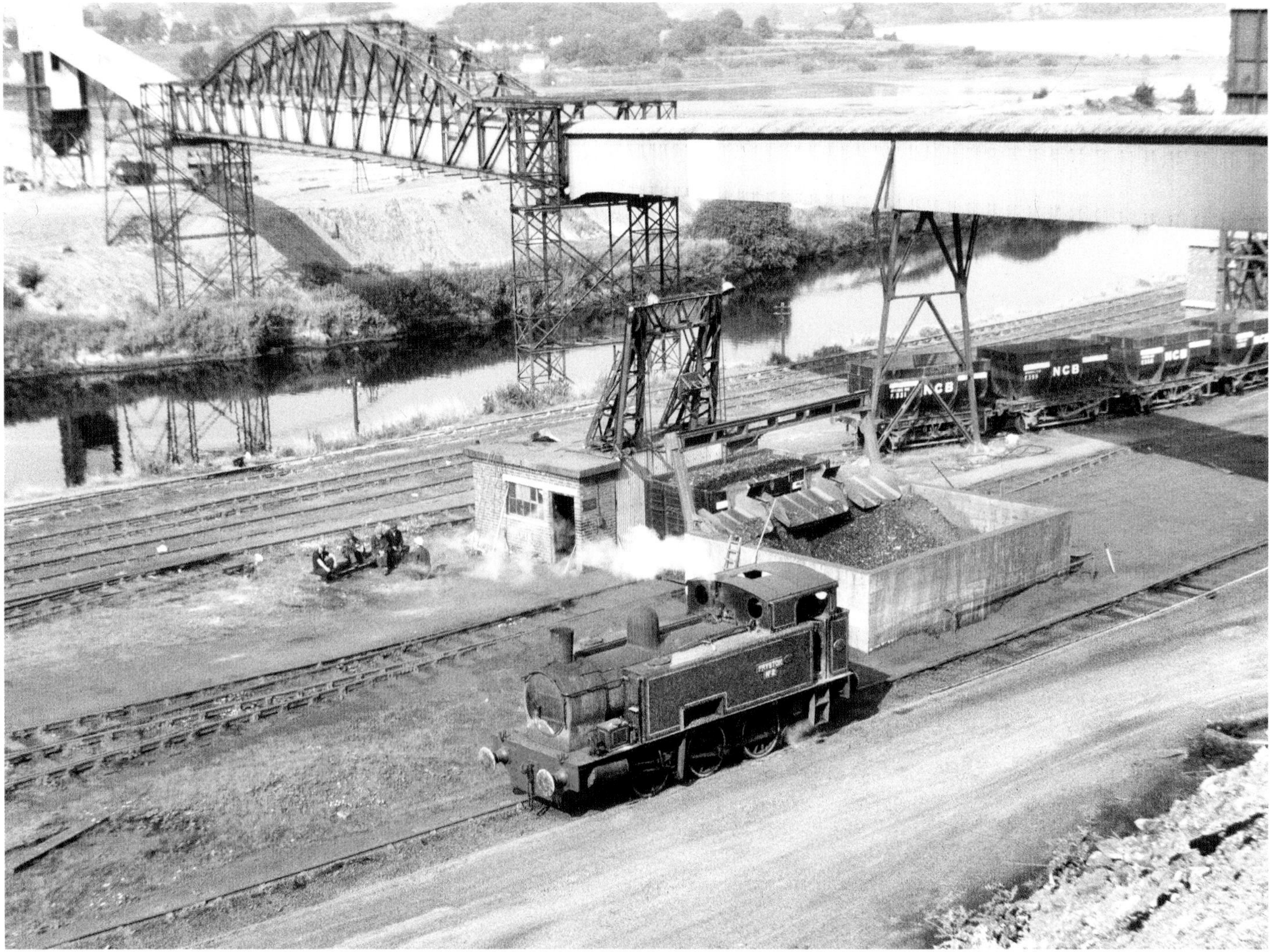
NCB
NCB
NCB

Opposite page: On 8 September 1969, Fryston colliery's Hudswell Clarke PLA Class 0-6-0 tank *Fryston No. 2* (W/No. 1883 of 1955) rests between shunting duties alongside the Aire Navigation, below the conveyor taking Fryston colliery's spoil to the Ings tipping area, now part of the Fairburn Ings Nature Reserve. The 16 x 24-in. (OC) loco was fitted with a mechanical stoker at the Hunslet works in 1964 and, despite this and its presentable external condition, it was scrapped on site by Wakefield Metal Traders Ltd, exactly three years later. (John Sloane)

Right: With the Fryston colliery headstocks dominating the scene, Robert Stephenson & Hawthorns 0-6-0 saddle tank No. 26 *Parkhill* (W/No. 7291 of 1945) shunts the colliery yard on 8 September 1969. The immaculate Austerity had been transferred to Fryston from Park Hill colliery in the June of that year but was another from the fleet there to suffer a fate at the hands of Wakefield Metal Traders Ltd, in October 1973, shortly after the arrival of new Hunslet diesel-hydraulic locos. The colliery was served by BR sidings east of Castleford station and was connected to Wheldale colliery and tips by an NCB line of just over a mile. Wheldale coal was also brought to Fryston for washing. (John Sloane)

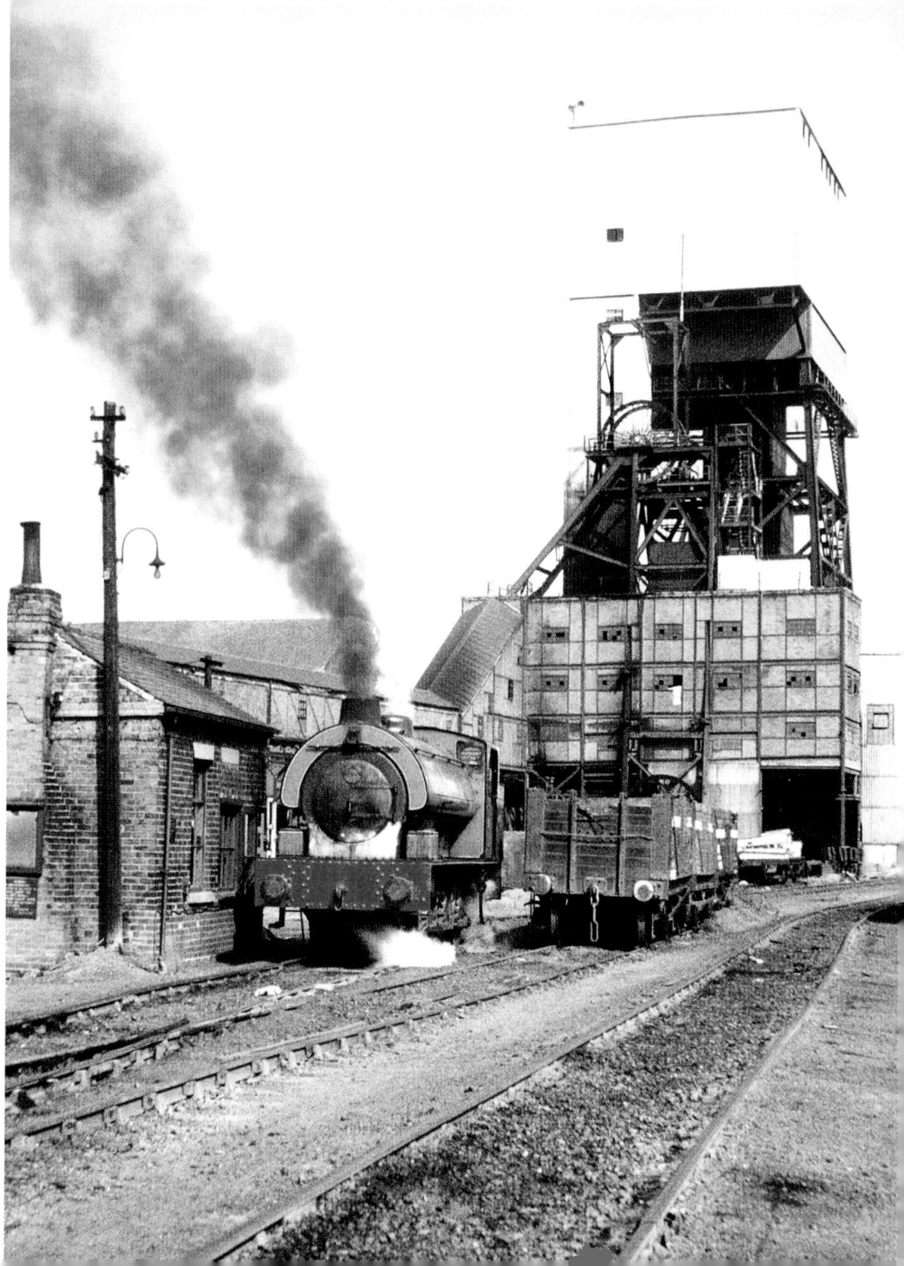

Right: Well-kept 16 x 24-in. (OC) cylinder Hudswell Clarke 0-6-0 tank *Cathryn* (W/No. 1884 of 1955), the penultimate member of the PLA Class built, was used at St John's colliery and coal preparation plant at Normanton, close to Goose Hill Junction. She is seen resting between her very intermittent duties near Locke's sidings on 23 March 1972, used just once per week at this time while the diesel loco was serviced. The colliery was connected to Park Hill colliery via a branch line. When St John's colliery closed during the following June *Cathryn* was transferred to Park Hill. The coal preparation plant, which received coal from Park Hill, closed in March 1980, shortly after the closure of that Wakefield colliery. *Cathryn* was acquired for preservation in March 1977. (Richard Stevens)

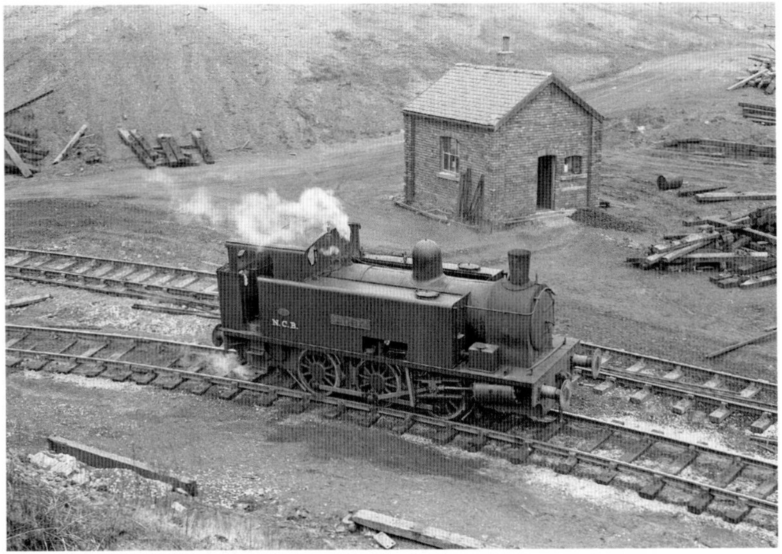

Below: Another view of the green-liveried Hudswell Clarke 16 x 24-in. (OC) 0-6-0 tank, *Fryston No. 2*, in steam and basking in the sunshine between duties at Wheldale Colliery on 20 September 1971, one year before meeting its fate. (Derek J. Lowe – author's collection)

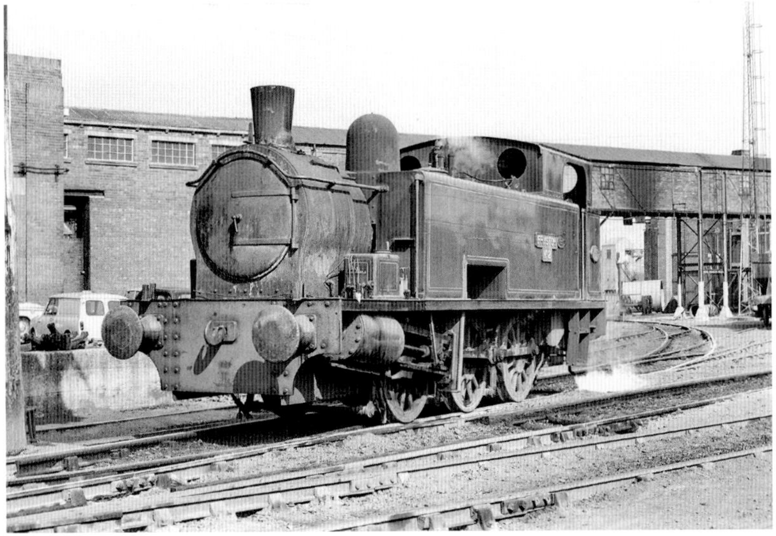

Opposite page: *Fryston No. 2* was busy at work on 20 April 1970, shunting a short rake of BR 16-ton wagons at Fryston colliery. The colliery was about a mile east of Wheldale, to which it was connected by the internal NCB line, which allowed Wheldale coal to be brought there for washing. Like Wheldale, it had staithes on the Aire Navigation, and was alongside the BR Castleford–York line. A field on the southern side of this line provided a convenient platform for viewing movements in the colliery yard! Fryston appeared to refuse to toe the NCB North Yorkshire area line in terms of loco liveries, using differing green liveries on its locos in preference to the standard maroon. *Fryston No. 2* was dark green with yellow and red lining. (Richard Stevens)

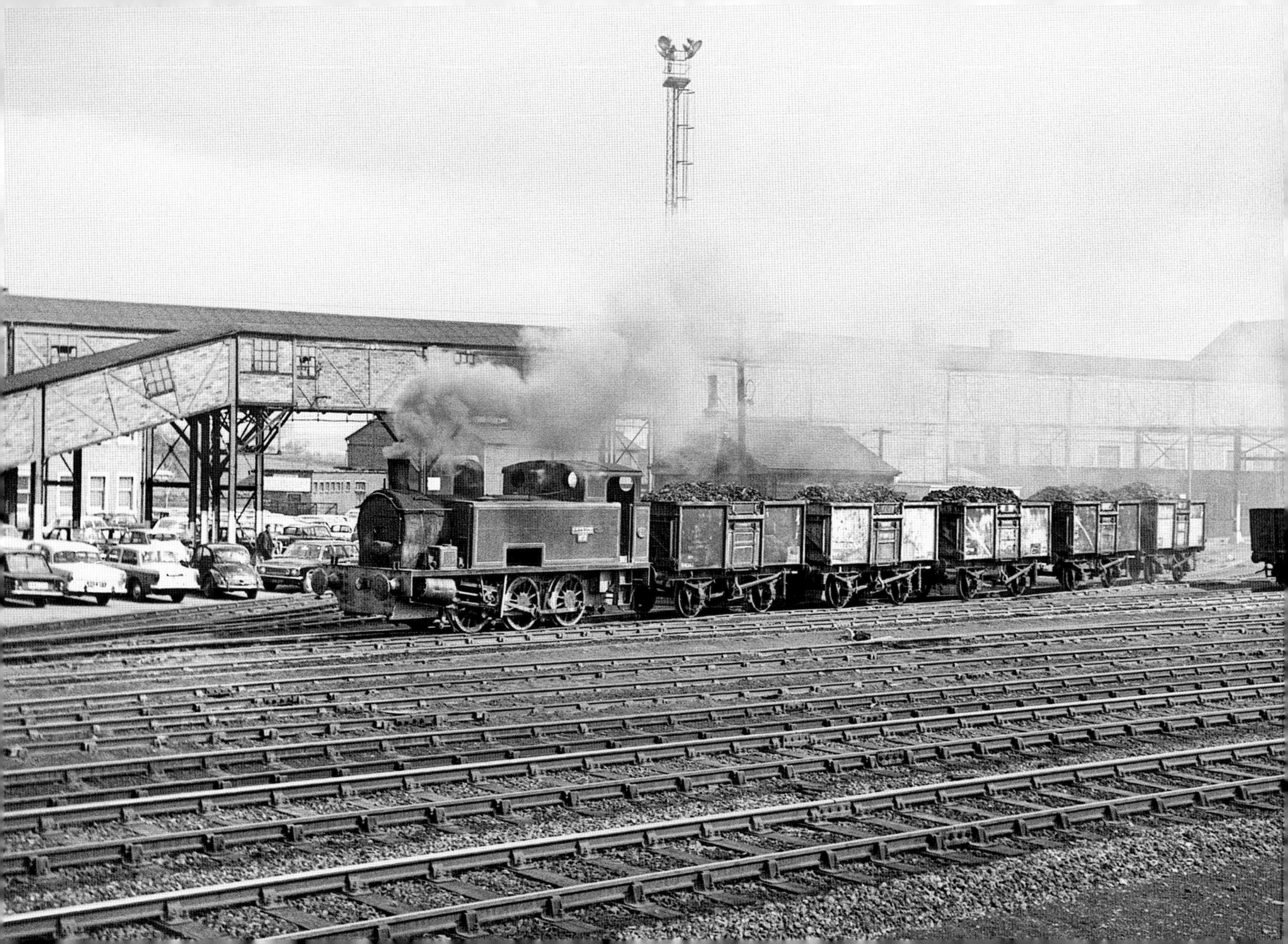

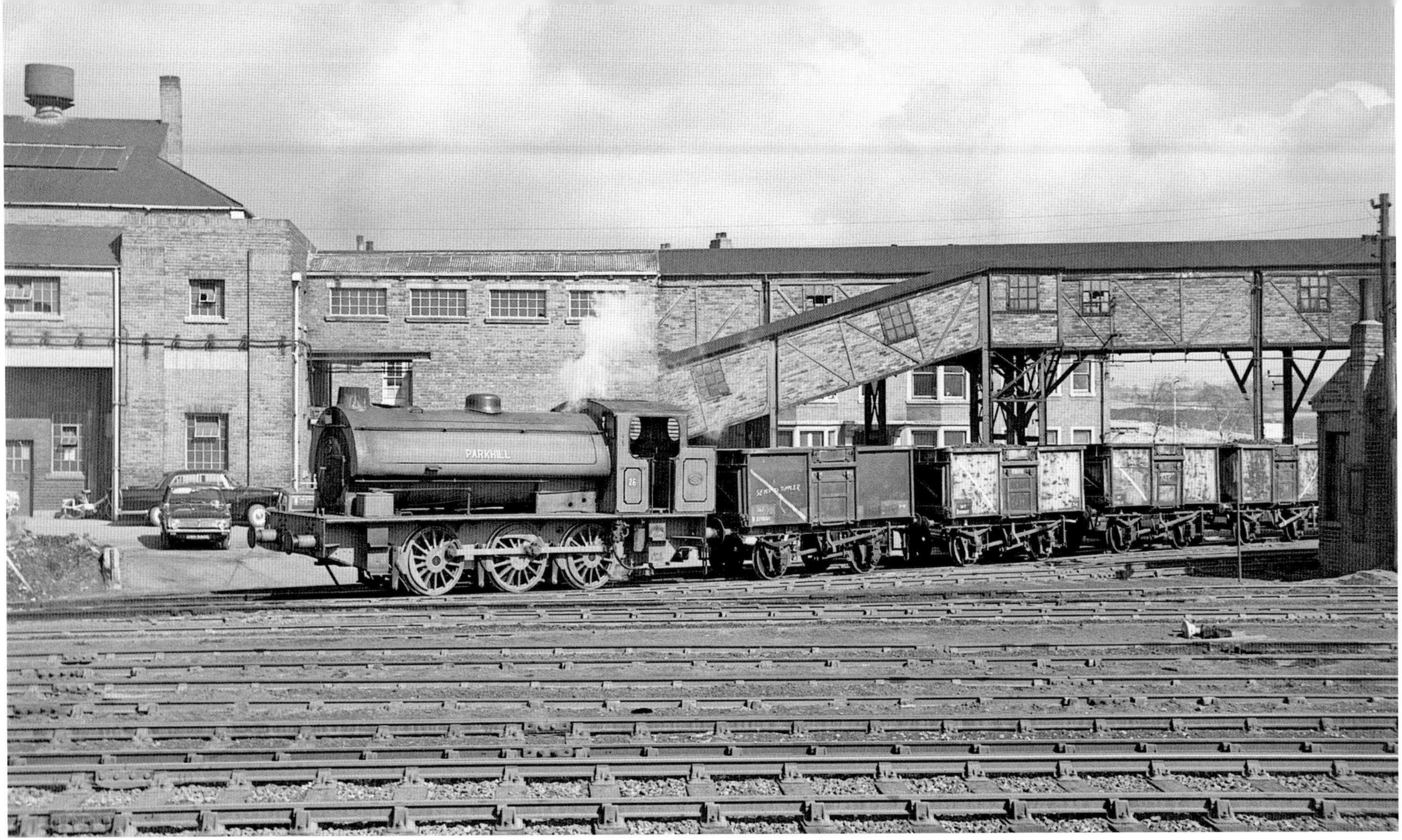

Austerity No. 26 *Parkhill*, another green-liveried loco at Fryston, eases empty 16-ton wagons down the grade into the colliery on 20 April 1970. Wheldale and Fryston collieries were witness to a return to steam for a short period from late 1981, and well into 1982, when Hunslet Austerity No. 7 (W/No. 3168 of 1944), fitted with the Hunslet patent underfeed stoker and gas producer system, underwent a period of load tests using various grades of coal (covered in *British Austerity Saddle Tanks* by this author). The use of the extensive system at Fryston, with its rail-served tips along the south bank of the River Aire between the colliery and Ferrybridge power station and provision of staithes on the Aire Navigation from which 'Tom Pudding' compartment boats were loaded, all came to an end in December 1985. The Wheldale branch was used for a short period in 1986 for the tipping of waste, but by August 1988 the site had been totally cleared and levelled over. (Richard Stevens)

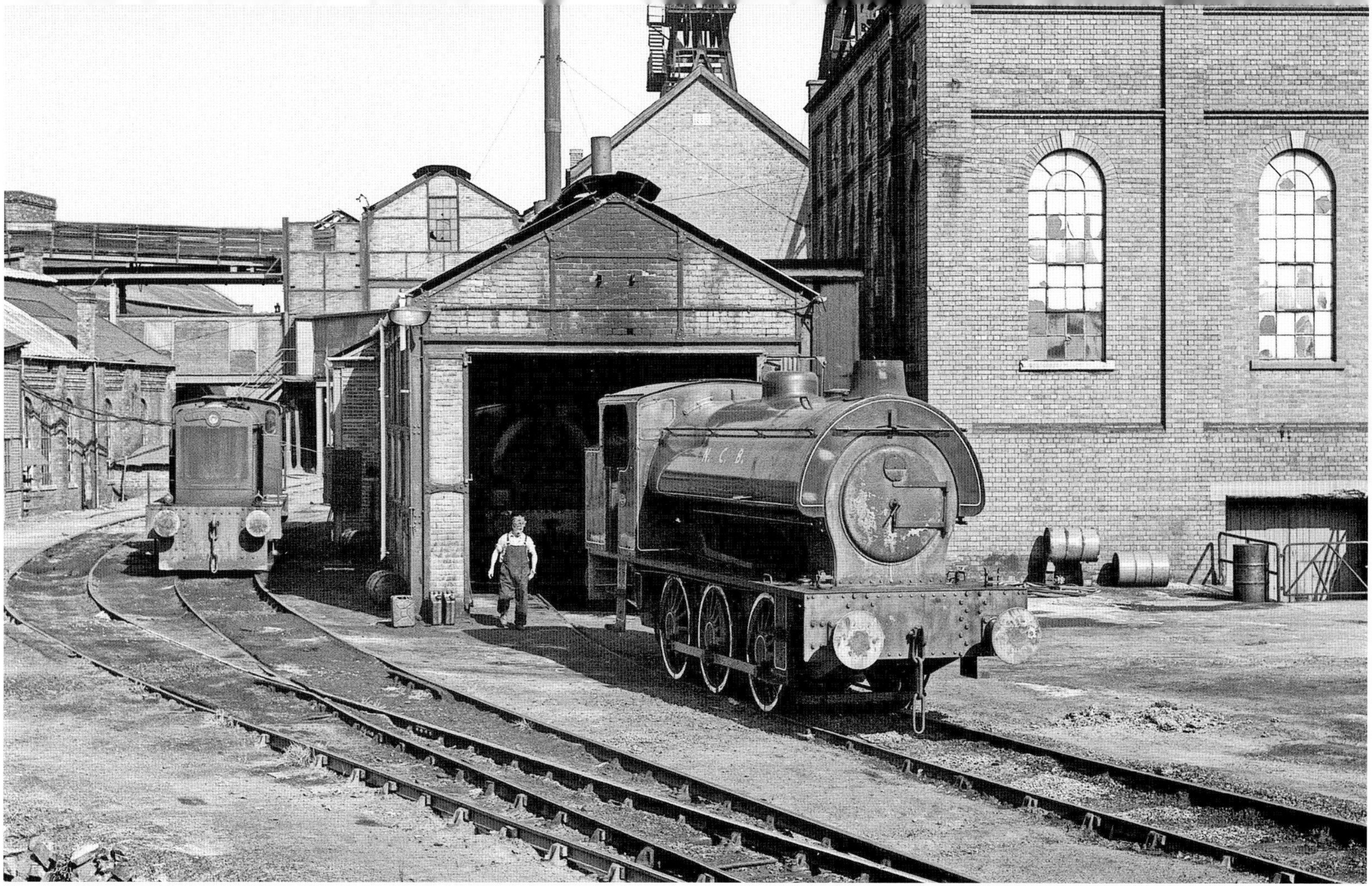

Wheldale colliery was quite small and did not have its own washery but, like Fryston, also had staithes on the Aire Navigation for the transport of coal in 40-ton 'Tom Pudding' barges to power stations. By July 1969 most of its coal was being barged, with domestic coal being tripped by rail to Fryston for washing or landsale. On 7 September 1971 a Hunslet Austerity (W/No. 2879 of 1943) stands outside the loco shed. A Hudswell Clarke six-coupled diesel-mechanical (W/No. D976 of 1957) stands alongside the shed. (Richard Stevens)

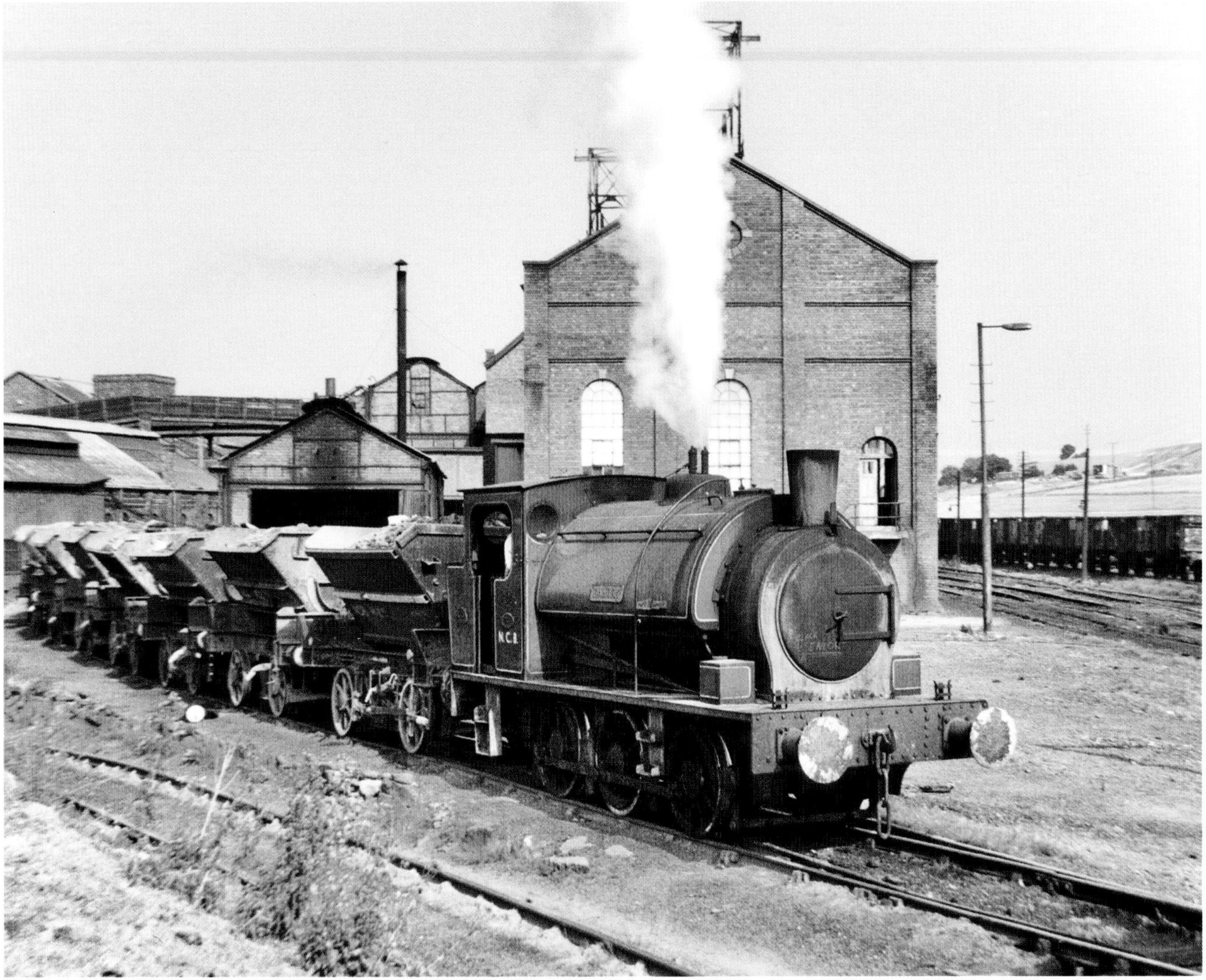
NCB

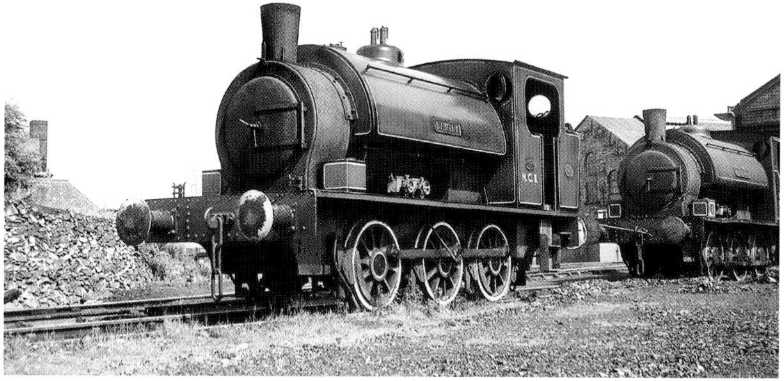

Opposite page: Wheldale colliery on 8 September 1969 with Hunslet 15 x 20-in. (IC) 0-6-0 saddle tank *Bawtry* (W/No. 1698 of 1932) at the pit head with internal side-tipping spoil wagons. It was scrapped on site by W. H. Arnott, Young & Co. Ltd of Bradford during December 1972. (John Sloane)

Above: Another view of *Bawtry*, resplendent in the striking green, black and red livery with straw lining, along with grubby sister 15 x 20-in. (IC) Hunslet 0-6-0 saddle tank *Wheler* (W/No. 1449 of 1928), at Wheldale colliery. *Wheler* was transferred to Prince of Wales colliery in February 1958, so this un-dated photo is quite likely to predate that event. (Author's collection)

Right: On 7 September 1971, an anonymous Austerity 0-6-0 saddle tank (W/No. 2879 of 1943), named *Diana* prior to an overhaul at Allerton Bywater workshops, stands in steam inside the shed at Wheldale. Although the smokebox shows evidence of hard work, the lined maroon livery of the NCB North Yorkshire area is still in very good condition. (Richard Stevens)

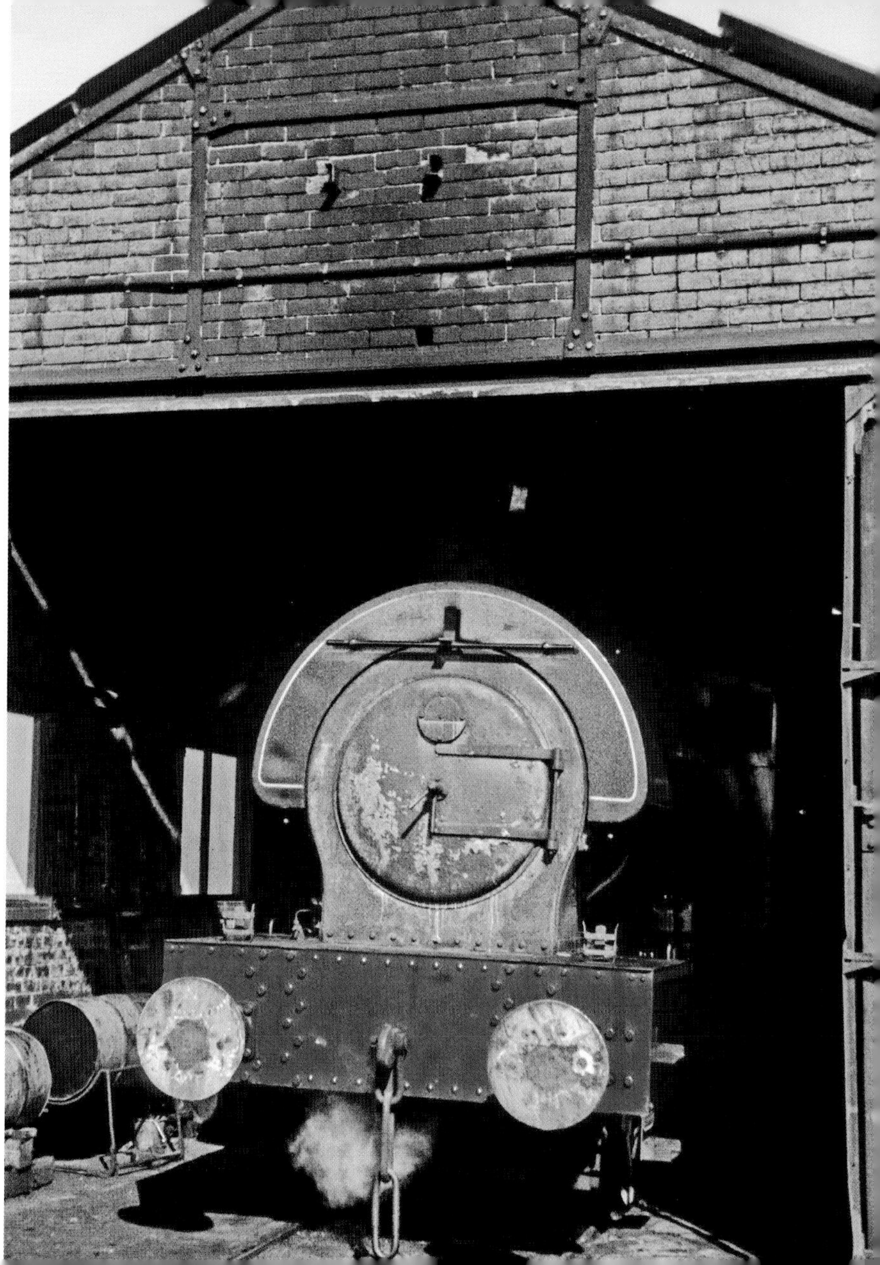

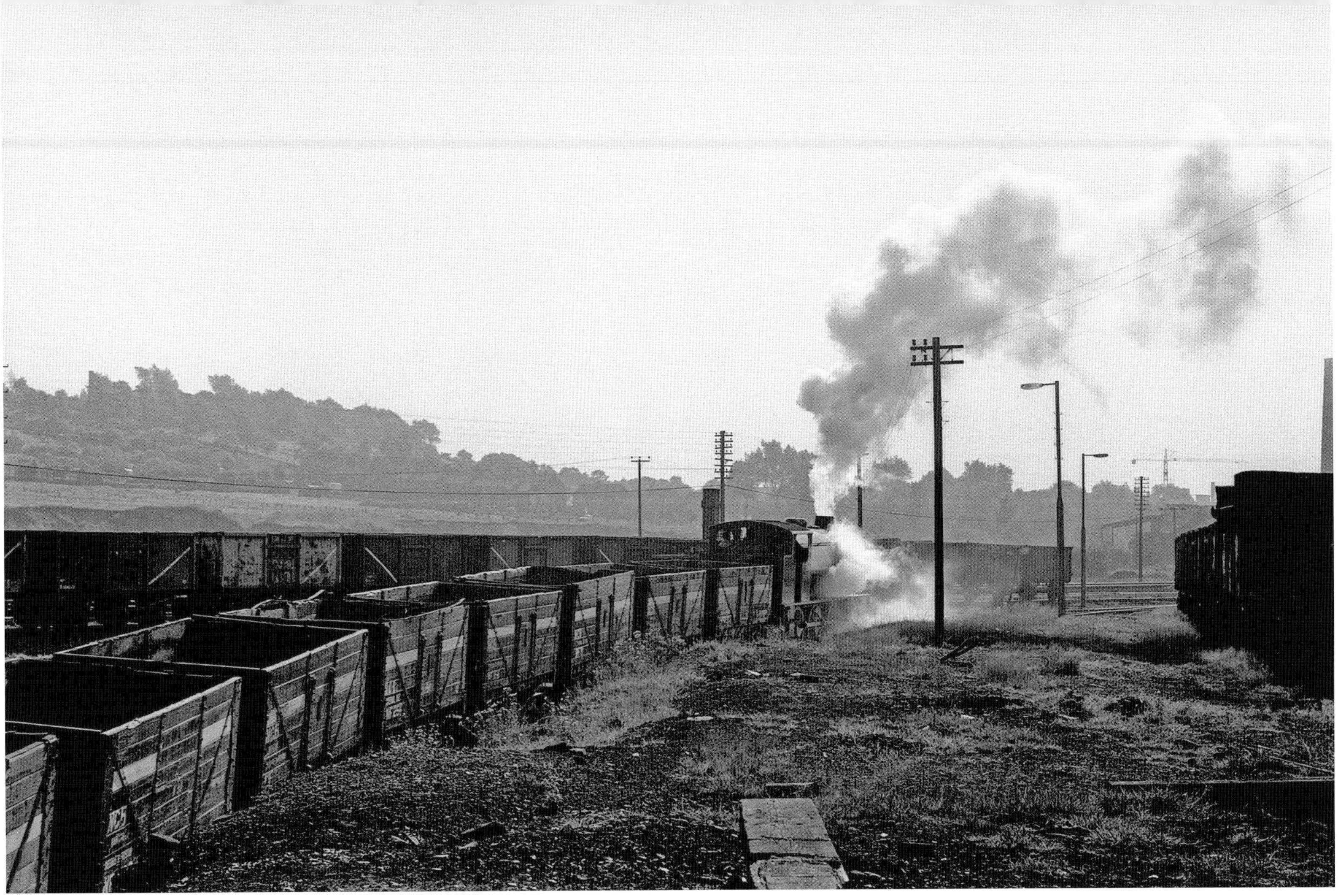

The highlight of steam workings at Wheldale was the steeply graded line that led from the staithes and the Fryston branch to the sidings adjacent to the BR Castleford–York line. The severity of the curve and gradient can be appreciated in this view of Hunslet No. 2879 climbing up to the BR exchange sidings on 7 September 1971. (Richard Stevens)

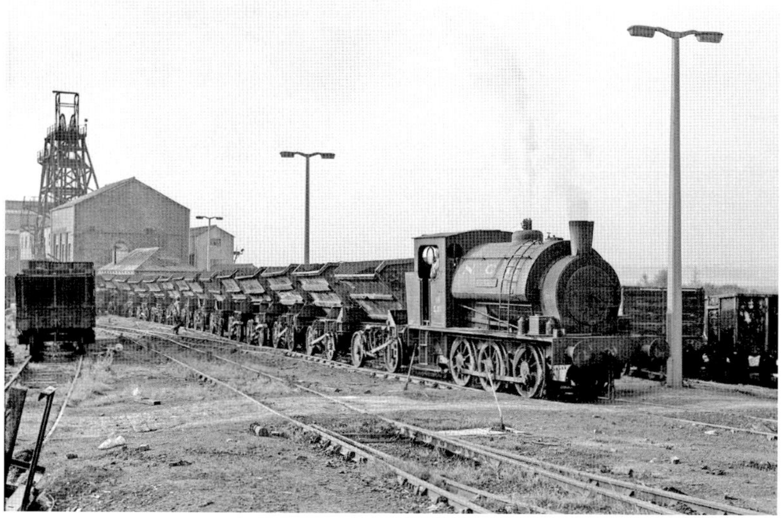

Savile was another colliery that despatched much of its output by water, via the adjacent Aire & Calder Navigation. By the time of its closure in 1986 its entire output was conveyed by canal to power stations, mainly Ferrybridge, in Hargreaves' barges fed directly from the screens in a basin that was only a stone's throw from Primrose Hill's Astley staithes, on the opposite bank of the canal. A smaller, older basin was served by the internal railway system, and this, together with spoil trains, provided much of the work for the colliery's steam locos. *Above*: On 7 September 1971, three months before the end of regular steam working, Hunslet 15 x 20-in. (IC) 0-6-0 saddle tank S111 *Airedale No. 2* (W/No. 1956 of 1939) shunts tipper wagons in the colliery yard, and (*right*) pauses between duties near the screens. These wagons were officially known as Jubilee wagons but were more commonly referred to locally as dirt cans or muck cans! (Richard Stevens)

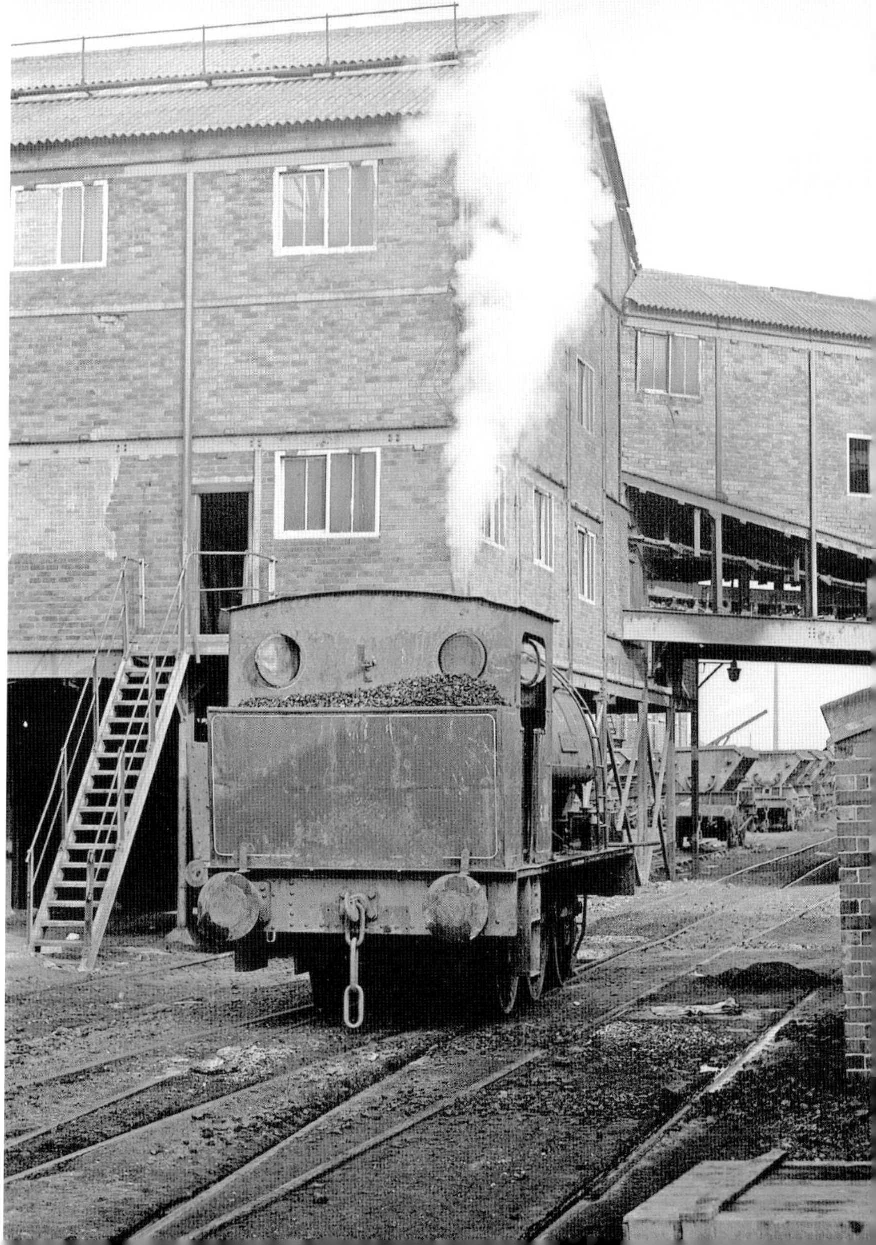

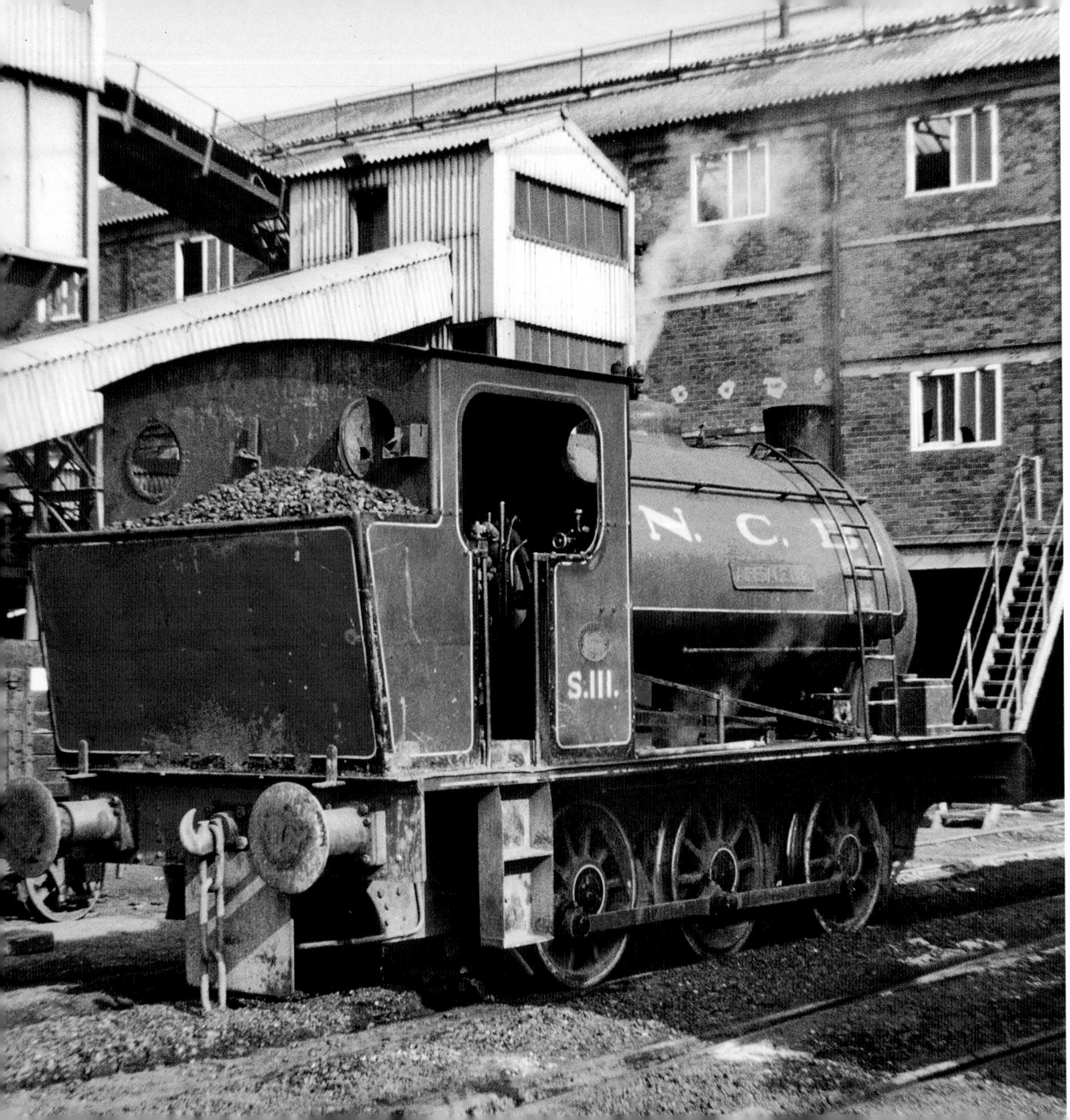

Left: Hunslet S111 *Airedale No. 2* in the striking NCB North Yorkshire area red livery pauses between duties at the Savile colliery screens on 8 September 1969. (John Sloane)

Opposite page: S111 *Airedale No. 2* shunts tipper wagons on the Savile colliery tip on 7 September 1971. The British Legion Nissen hut survives today in modified form, though is now branded as Methley Ex-Services Club, and probably serves something more palatable than Younger's beers these days. Not everything from the 1970s is remembered with affection! The fate of the Savile colliery site was highly unusual; in 1988, three years after the colliery closed, opencast workings on the other side of the River Aire led to a breach in the river bank, causing the opencast workings to flood. The remedial works included the combining and re-channelling of the river and canal into a new course south of the original – and part of the new course included the west end of the Savile colliery site, including part of the screens. Perhaps an appropriate end for a colliery that shipped so much of its coal out by water. (Richard Stevens)

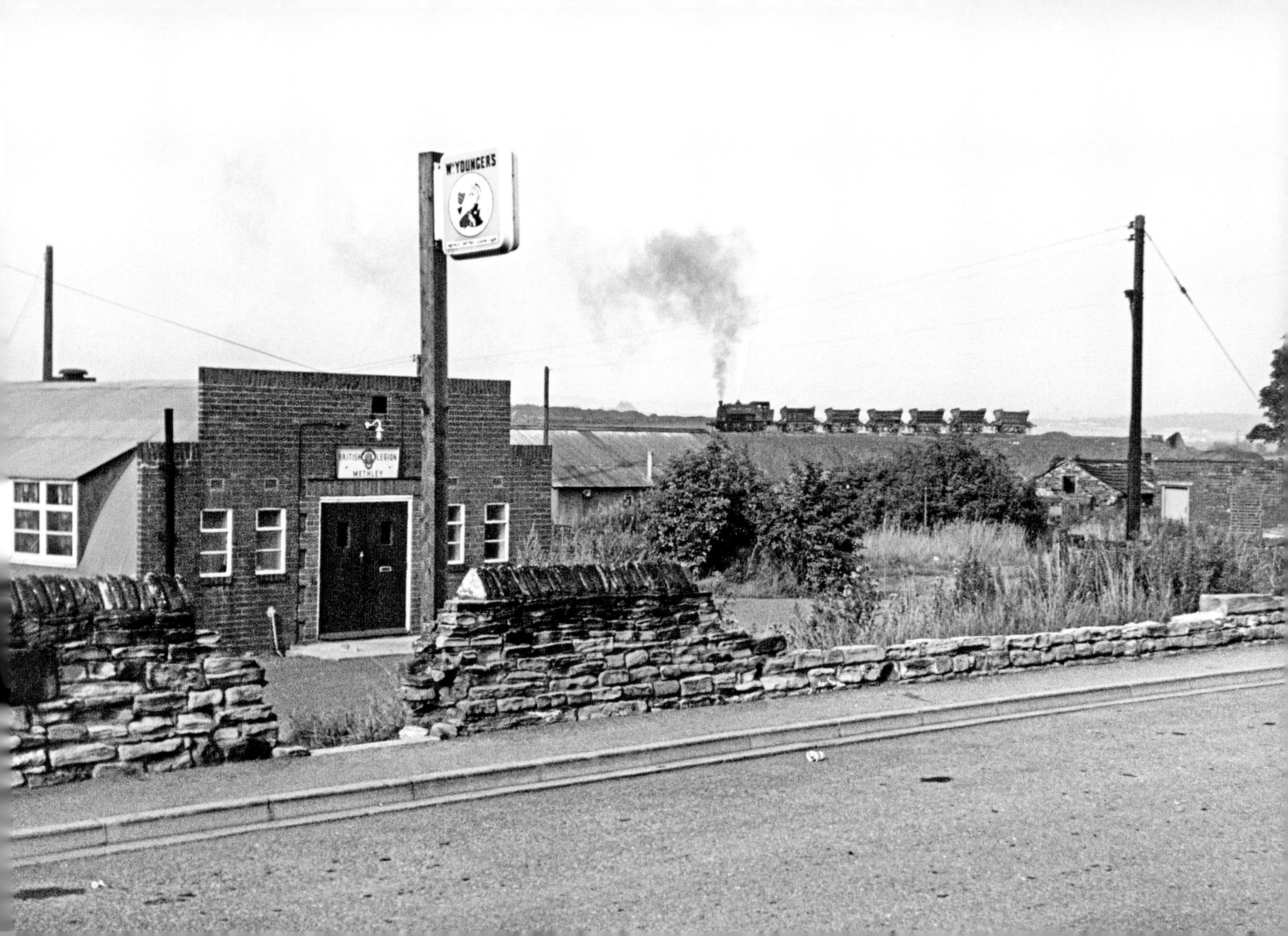
Wm YOUNGER'S
BRITISH LEGION
METHLEY

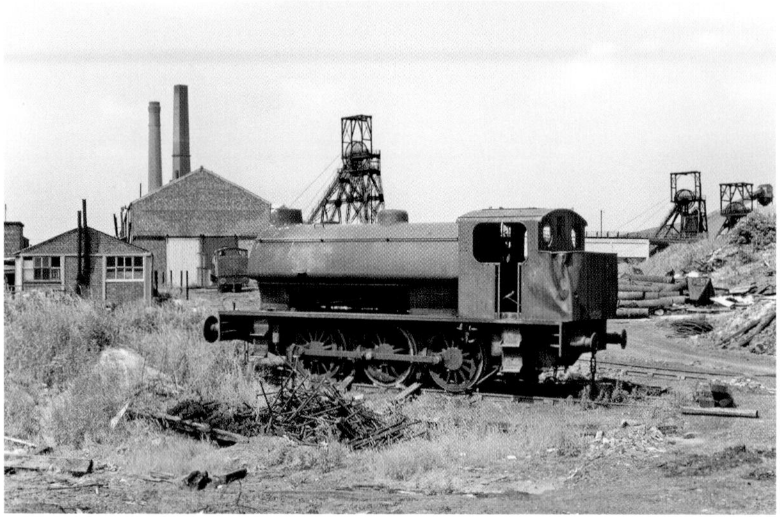

Above: Prince of Wales was a large colliery, north of Pontefract, connected to BR's Pontefract (Monkhill)–Castleford line. Converted in 1980 from a deep mine to a drift mine, which probably extended its life as it did not close until 2002, steam traction also enjoyed an extended life here compared with most other pits in the area. Steam was frequently used, albeit in a standby capacity to a Hudswell Clarke and a Hunslet diesel. On 15 July 1972, a battered Vulcan Foundry Austerity (W/No. 5276 of 1945), ex-Army Shoeburyness in July 1965 and still showing some evidence of its previous owner's livery, languishes out of use at the colliery. A William Bagnall Austerity (W/No. 2746 of 1944) stands beyond. Despite the fitting of a Hunslet underfeed stoker system at the Allerton Bywater workshops in 1967, the former *Army No. 185* may well have been a suspect acquisition, for it was scrapped on site by Wakefield Metal Traders Ltd during November 1972. (John Sloane)

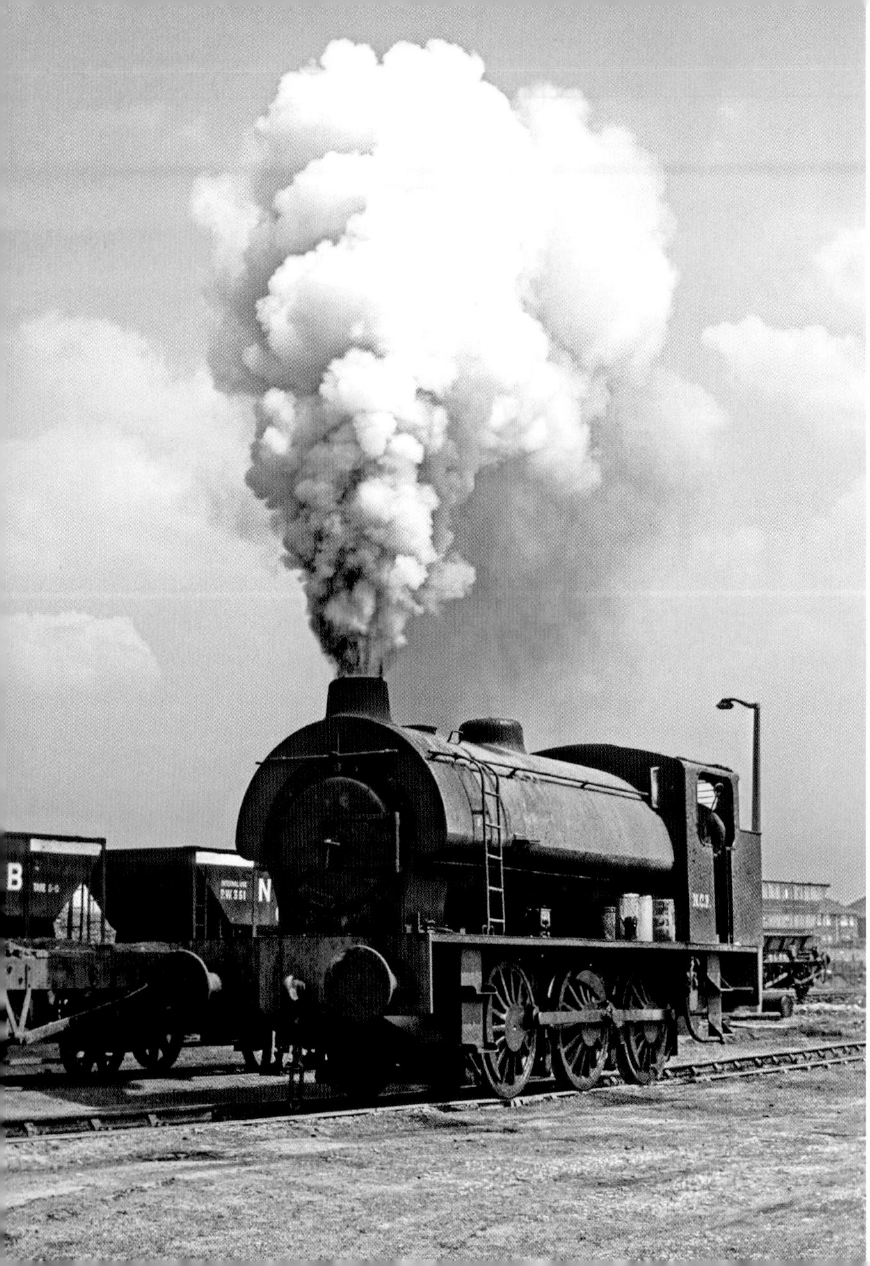

Left: On 7 June 1976 a William Bagnall Austerity (W/No.2746 of 1944) was being tested following repair and was to be transferred to Ackton Hall in January 1977. (Richard Stevens)

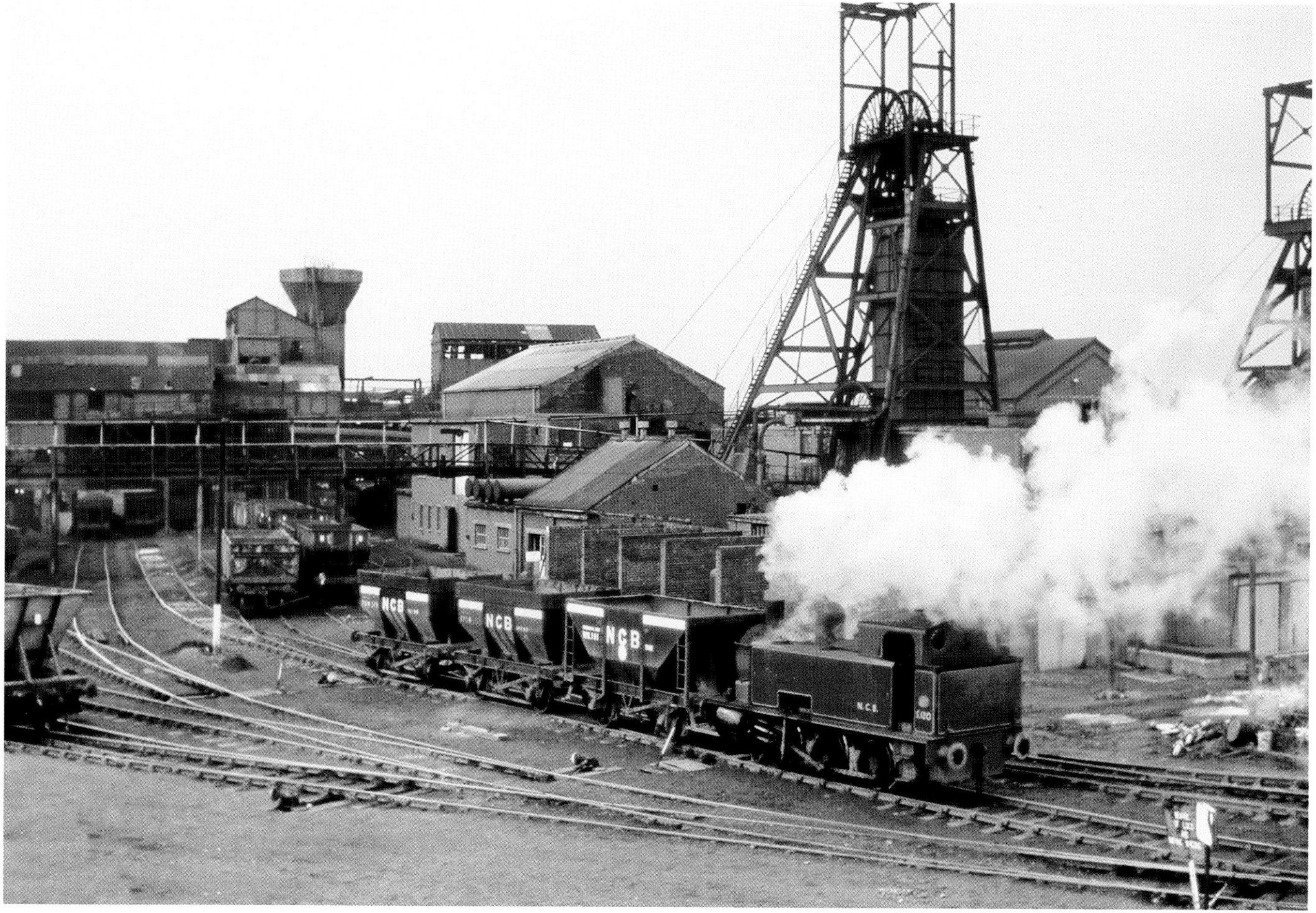

Prince of Wales colliery, located opposite the Pontefract racecourse, commenced full production in 1870. Hudswell Clarke 0-6-0 side tank S120 (W/No. 1886/1955) is shunting internal hopper wagons at the pit head on 1 March 1971. The 16 x 24-in. (OC) PLA Class side tank was cut up on site by W. H. Arnott, Young & Co. Ltd of Bradford in December 1972. (Author's collection)

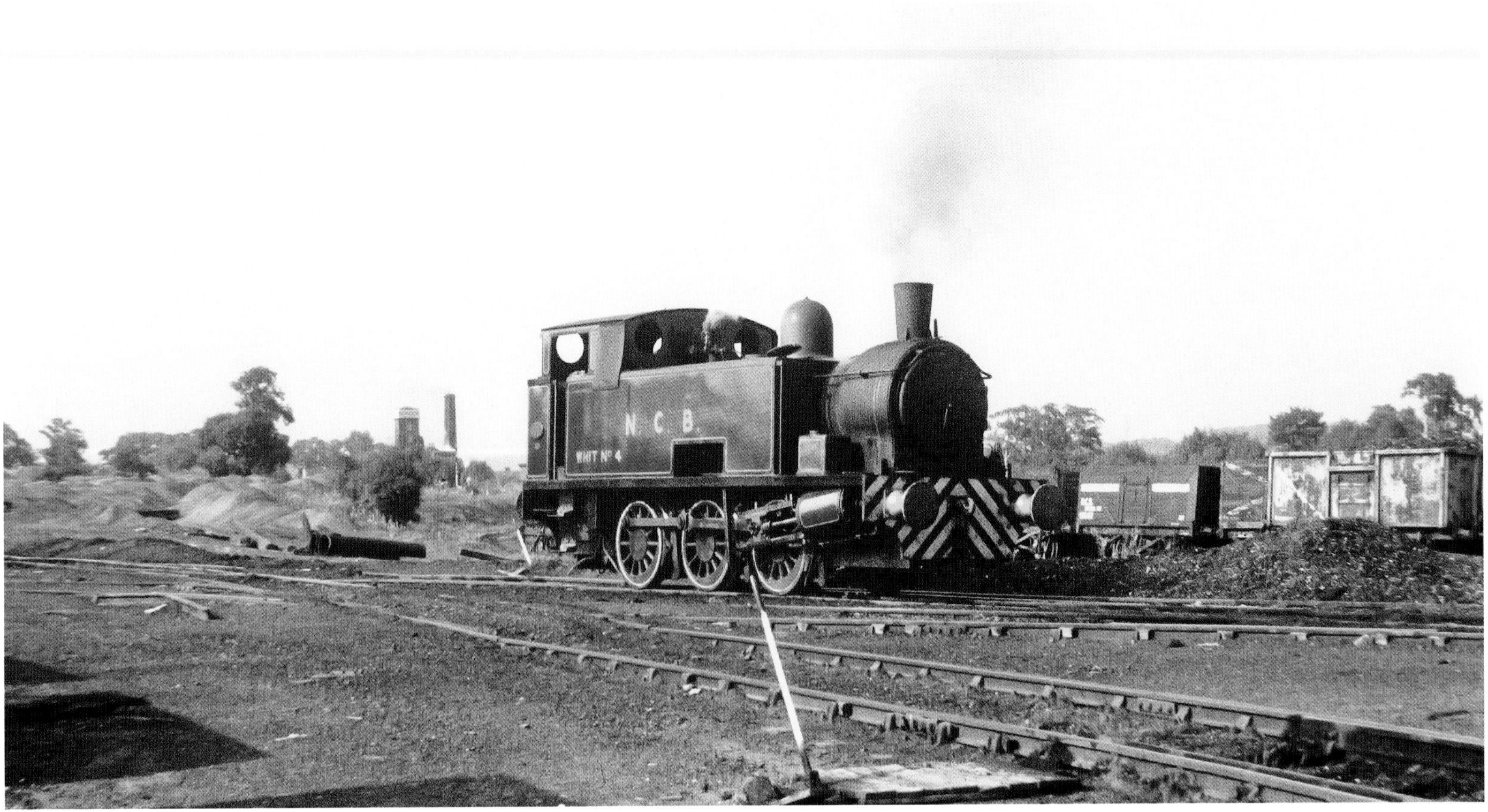

Water Haigh colliery at Woodlesford shipped much of its coal out by water. The colliery was on the south side of the former Midland Railway line into Leeds, but its railway system included a line which passed under the main line to reach staithes on the Aire & Calder Navigation and a tipping area, although most pit waste for disposal was conveyed by aerial ropeway, passing over the BR line to tips between the canal and the River Aire. Water Haigh had a reputation for immaculately turned-out locos and Hudswell Clarke 16 x 24-in. (OC) 0-6-0 tank *Whit No. 4* (W/No. 1844 of 1951) was upholding this tradition on 8 September 1969. The colliery closed in April 1970 and the coal preparation plant during April 1971, after which *Whit No. 4* was transferred to Prince of Wales colliery. It was acquired by the Nene Valley Railway for spares in February 1976. (John Sloane)

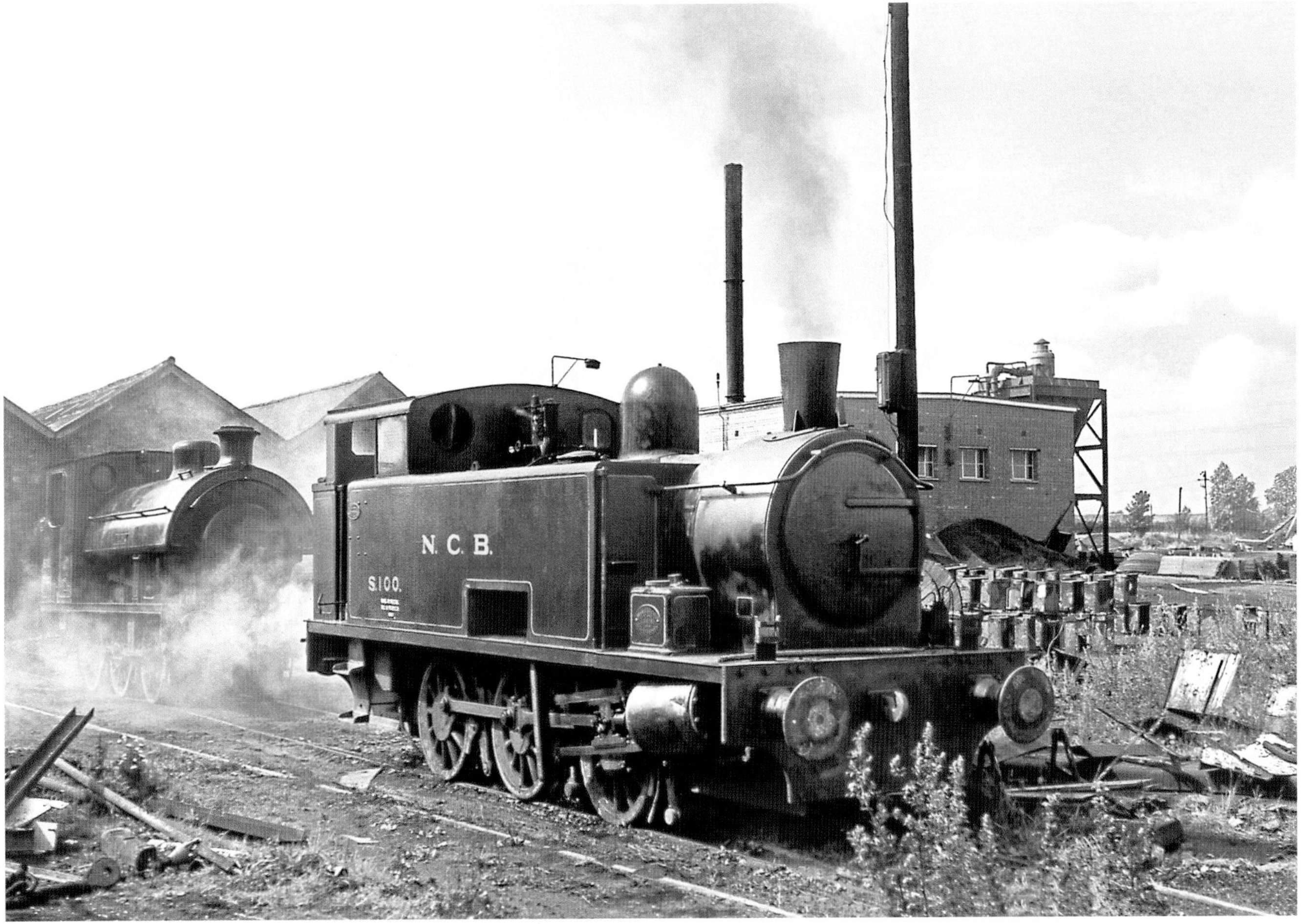

A summer 1968 scene at Peckfield colliery loco shed with Hudswell Clarke 16 x 24-in. (OC) PLA Class 0-6-0 tank S100 (W/No. 1822 of 1949) and Hawthorn Leslie 15 x 22-in. (OC) 0-6-0 saddle tank S115 *Frank* (W/No. 3534 of 1922), both in steam and resplendent in the striking NCB North Yorkshire Area maroon livery. (Author's collection)

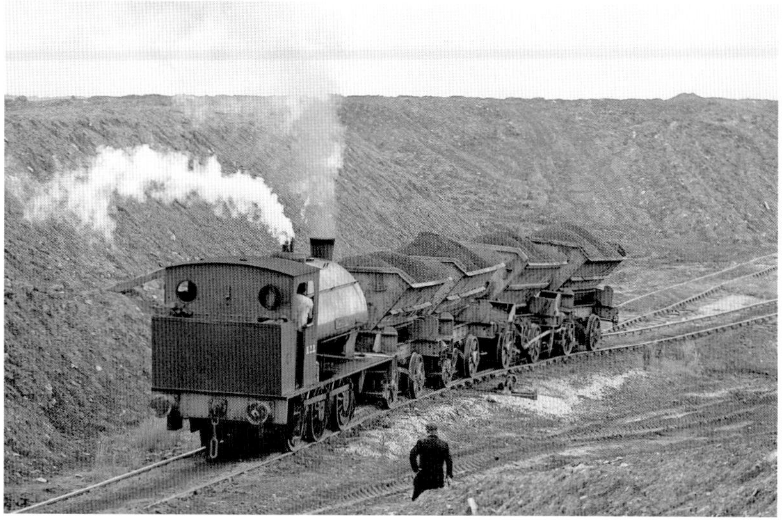

Above: The same working as shown on the left passes over the points, which allowed access to different areas of the tip. (Richard Stevens)

Below: Peckfield colliery in Micklefield was the most northerly of the collieries in the Yorkshire coalfield. In the 1970s it normally required the use of two locos per day, although one of them was often a diesel. A major part of both locos' duties was frequently removing waste from the colliery in tipper wagons and working up onto the tip, south of the colliery. On 17 August 1972, Hunslet 16 x 22-in. (IC) 0-6-0 saddle tank *Primrose No. 2* (W/No. 3715 of 1952) heads up the bank to the tip with one of the regular loads of spoil. In the background are several loaded MGR wagons ready for collection by BR from the exchange siding adjacent to the Leeds–York/Hull line. (Richard Stevens)

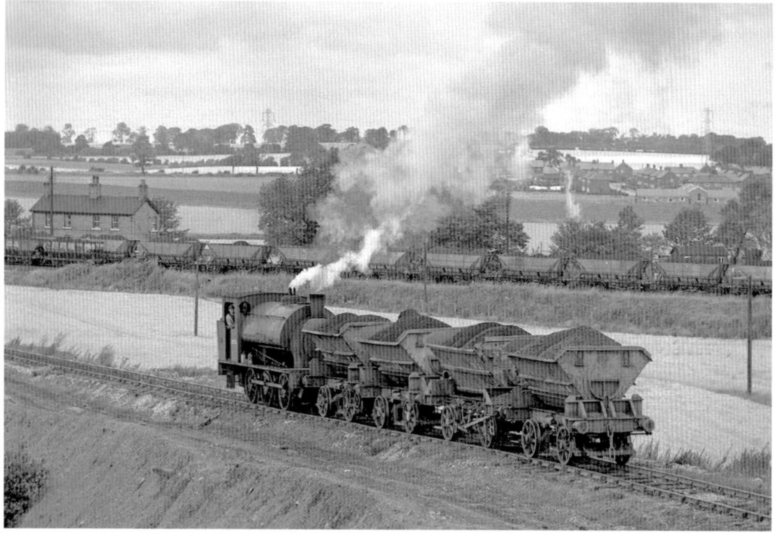

Opposite page: On 23 March 1972, and viewed from the footbridge located at the entrance to the colliery, Hudswell Clarke 16 x 24-in. (OC) PLA Class 0-6-0 tank S100 (W/No. 1822 of 1949) returns empty Hudson side-tipping wagons from the tip. It had served the colliery well on these duties for the preceding decade, but steam activity was to cease at Peckfield at the end of that year. To the left of S100 is the former North Eastern Railway's Peckfield signal box, which controlled movements into and out of the colliery as well as on the main line. (Richard Stevens)

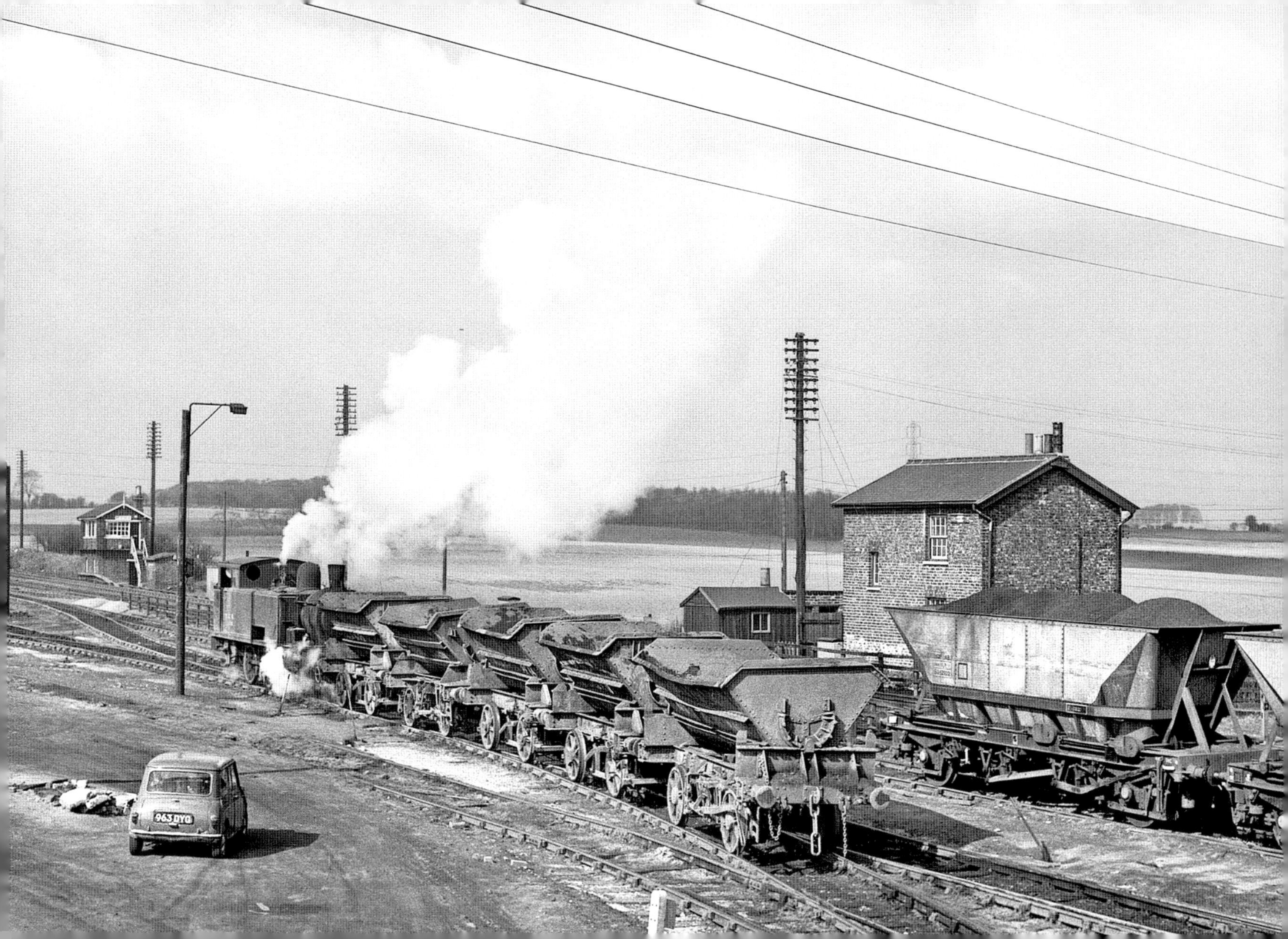
963 DYG

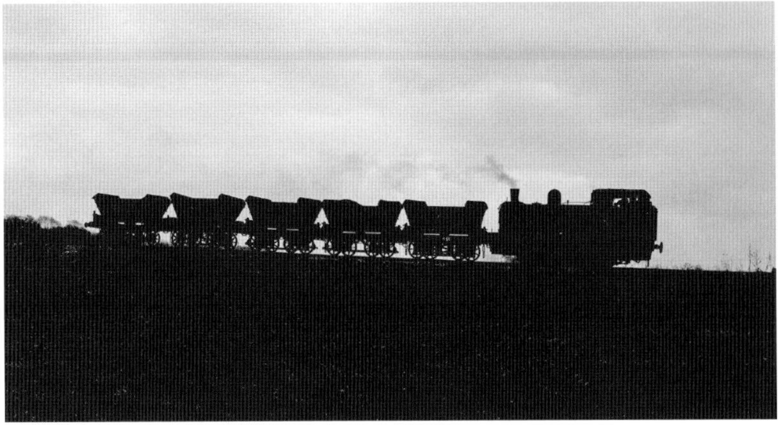

Right: A train of spoil empties returns down the bank from the tip behind Hudswell Clarke S100 on 23 March 1972. As with the Hunslet 0-6-0 saddle tanks, a tapered stovepipe chimney on this type of loco indicated that an underfeed stoker had been fitted, a device fitted to many locos in this area, usually at the Allerton Bywater Central Workshops. (Richard Stevens)

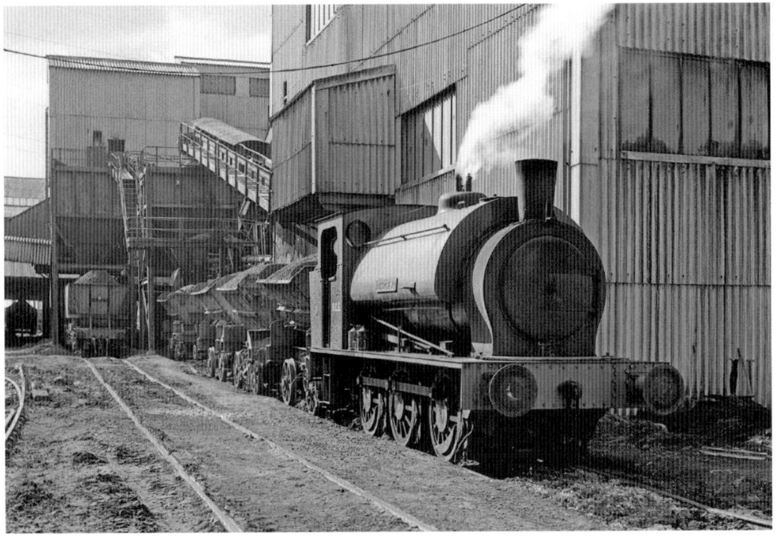

Left: Hunslet *Primrose No. 2* waits for a worthwhile rake of loaded tipper wagons to gather behind it at Peckfield colliery before setting off for the tip on 17 August 1972. This loco was one of several of this design in the NCB's North Yorkshire area, equipped with the Hunslet patented underfeed stoker and stovepipe chimney. (Richard Stevens)

Opposite page: Although the sun was still quite high in the sky at Peckfield colliery on 17 August 1972 when this photo was taken, it was starting to set on steam working in the NCB's North Yorkshire Area, with a brand-new diesel just out of the photo to the right, and several similar locos already in place or being built for neighbouring pits by Yorkshire locomotive manufacturers the Hunslet Engine Company Ltd of Leeds and Thomas Hill (Rotherham) Ltd of Kilnhurst. Rather ironically, the diesels at Peckfield were to work for only eight years, the colliery ceasing to wind coal in December 1980. (Richard Stevens)

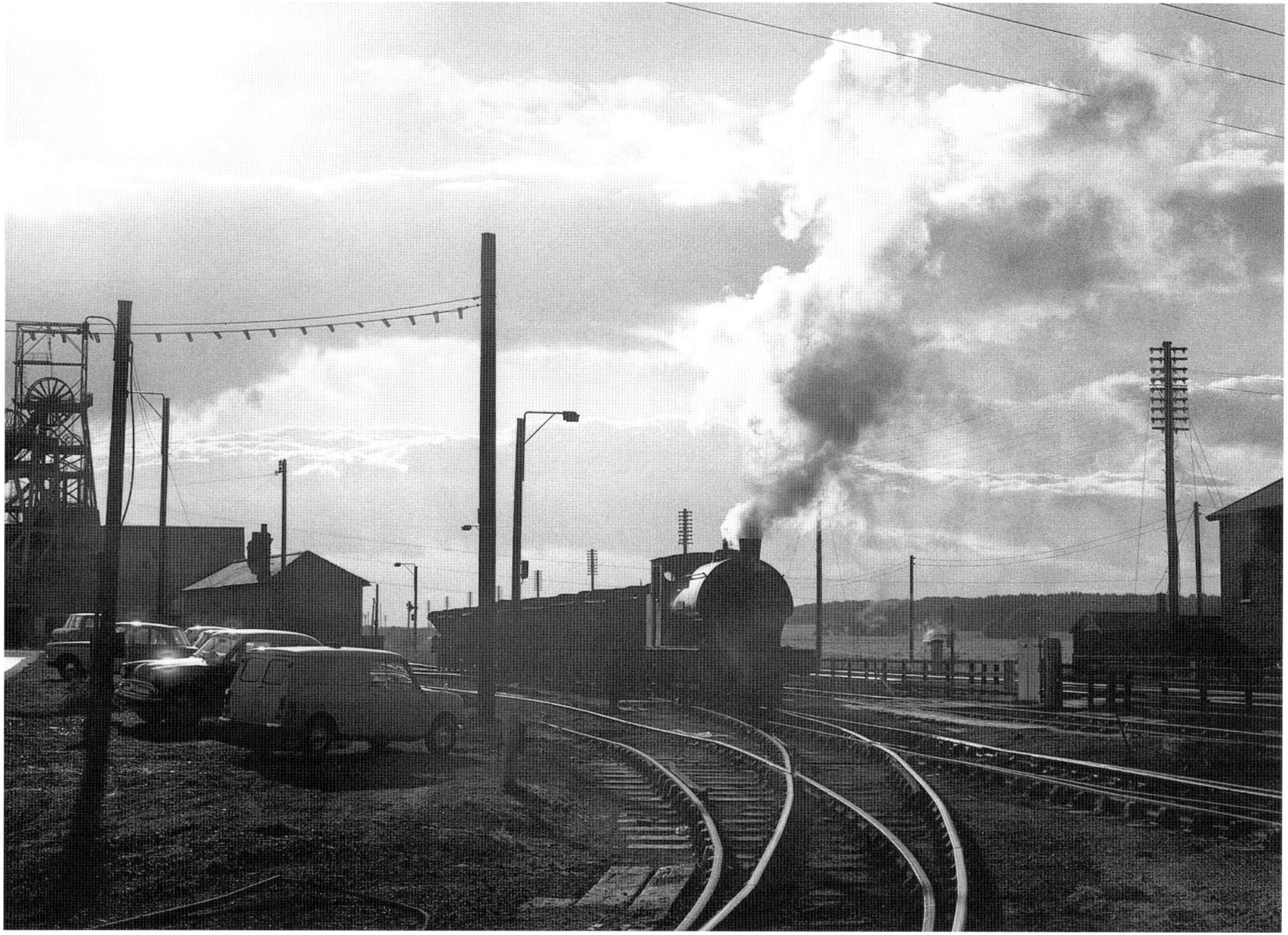

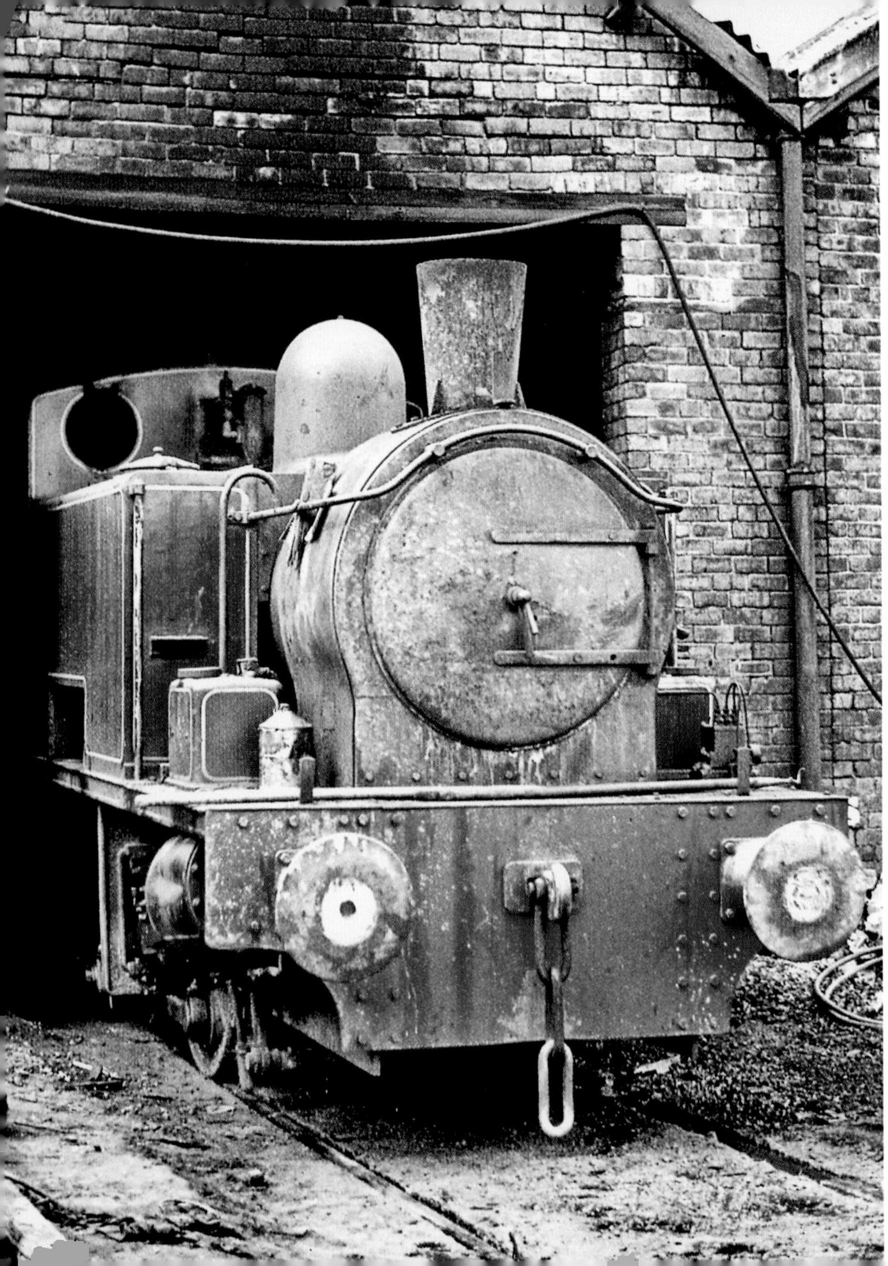

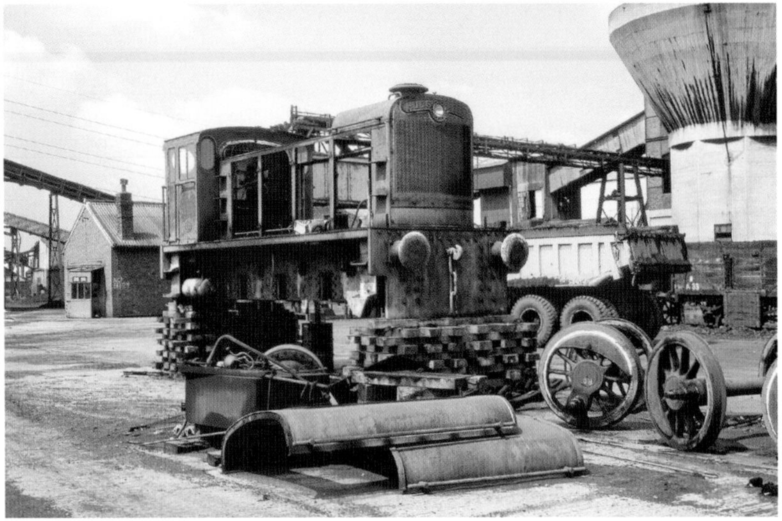

Left: Hudswell Clarke S100, taking a weekend break from its routine tipping duties, simmering on Peckfield colliery shed on Saturday 24 June 1972. It was to survive into preservation and passed to the Yorkshire Dales Railway at Embsay just one year later, in July 1973. (Author)

Above: Hudswell Clarke 260 hp 0-6-0 diesel-mechanical *NCB No. 3* (W/No. D974 of 1957) on blocks with its engine and wheels removed at Peckfield on 15 July 1972. Whether it saw further service at the colliery or was just being stripped for spares is unclear, but it was certainly scrapped on site by Wakefield Metal Traders around 1975/1976. Following the demise of steam at the colliery around 1973, standard-gauge diesel traction continued to serve the pit until its closure in December 1980, and the coal preparation plant until September 1982, when all surface rail traffic ceased at Peckfield. A narrow-gauge line ran from Ledston Luck colliery and this served the coal preparation plant's requirements after Peckfield colliery's closure (see page 119). Peckfield's coal preparation plant eventually closed in October 1986. (John Sloane)

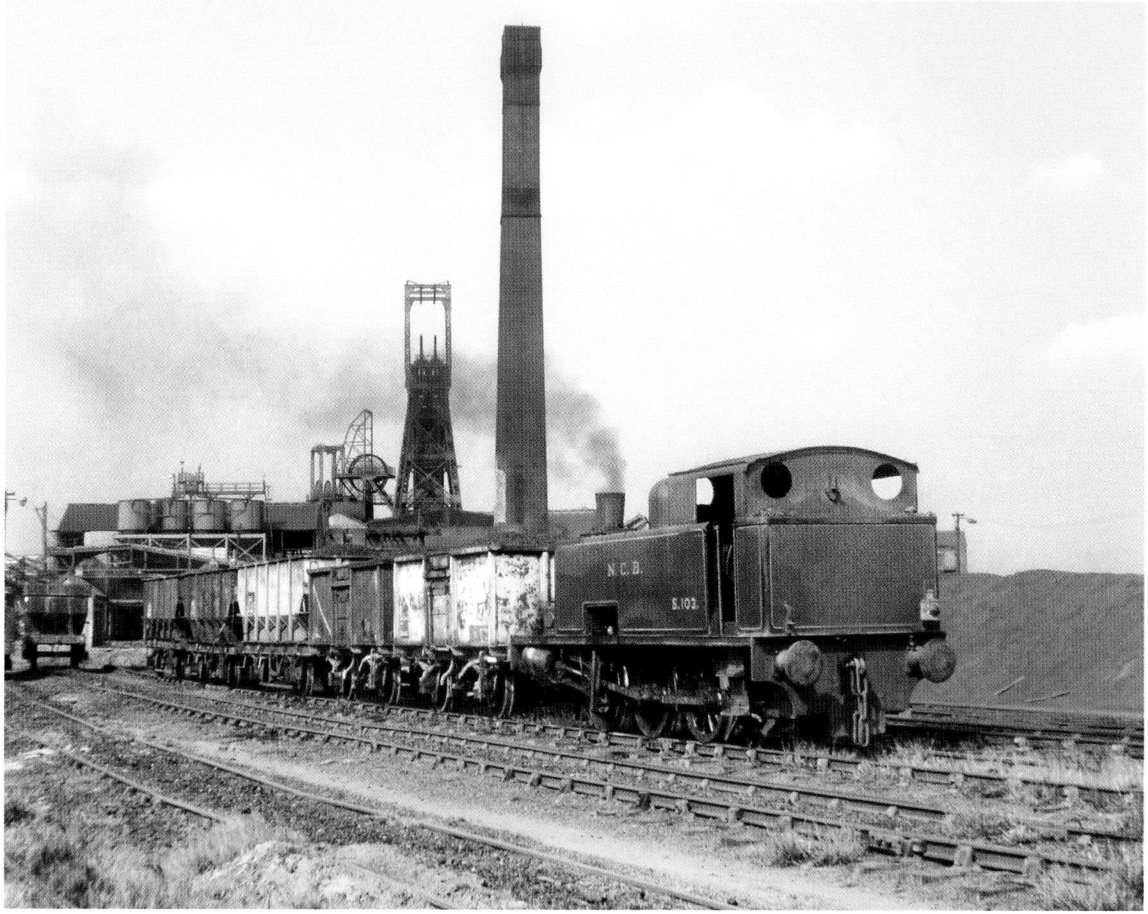

Glasshoughton colliery at Castleford, one of the largest in the area, was effectively two locations on one site – a colliery and a coking plant, connected by internal railway systems. It was the only Castleford area pit unable to despatch coal by water. Arguably the ugliest loco ever built usually worked at the coking plant (see page 64), but in complete contrast this splendid Hudswell Clarke 16 x 24-in. (OC) PLA Class 0-6-0 tank S103 (W/No. 1864 of 1952) was, on 8 September 1969, positioning loaded BR 16-ton mineral and 21-ton hopper wagons. The colliery was to close in March 1986. (John Sloane)

3

COAL BY-PRODUCTS & CHEMICALS

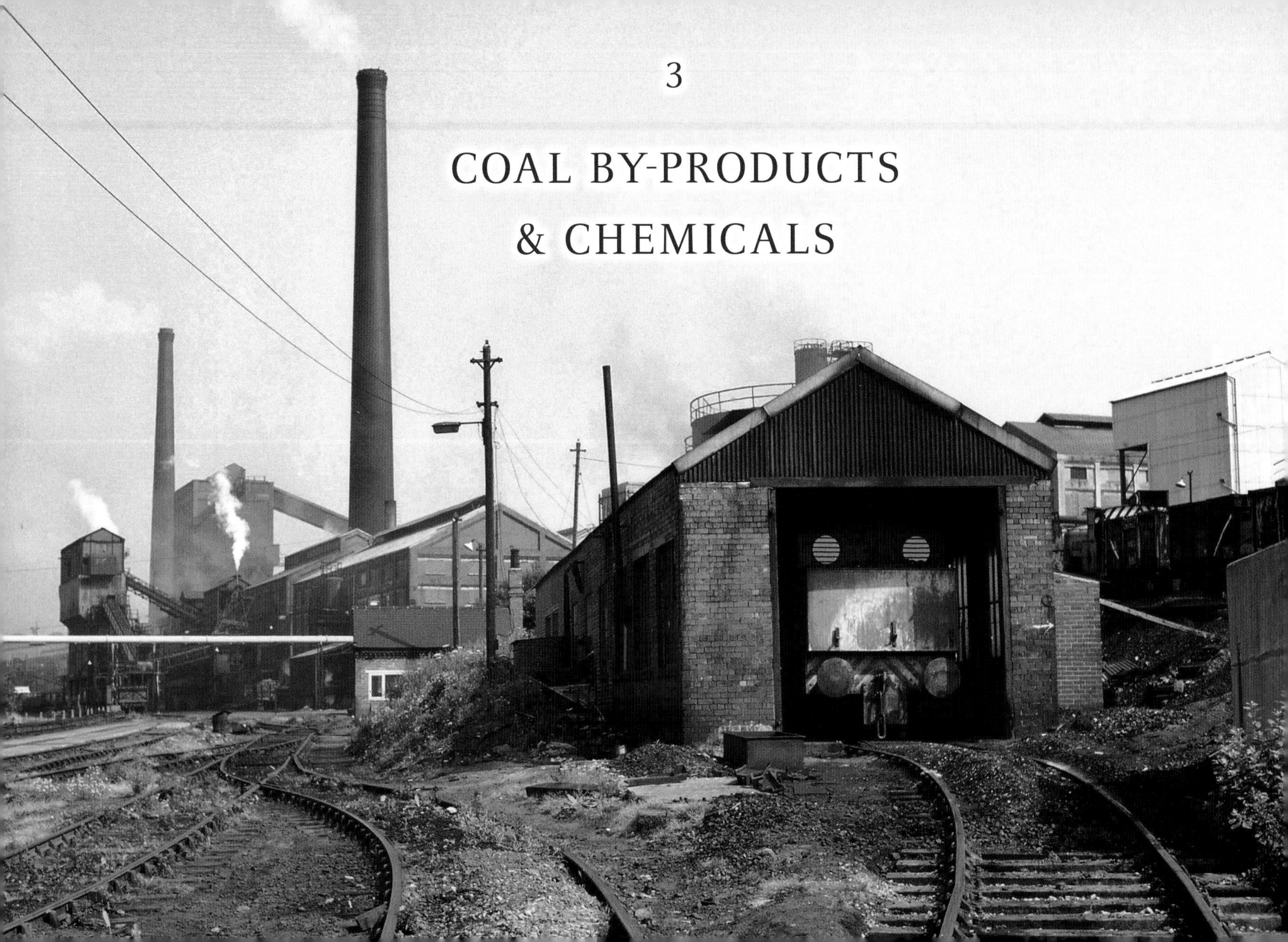

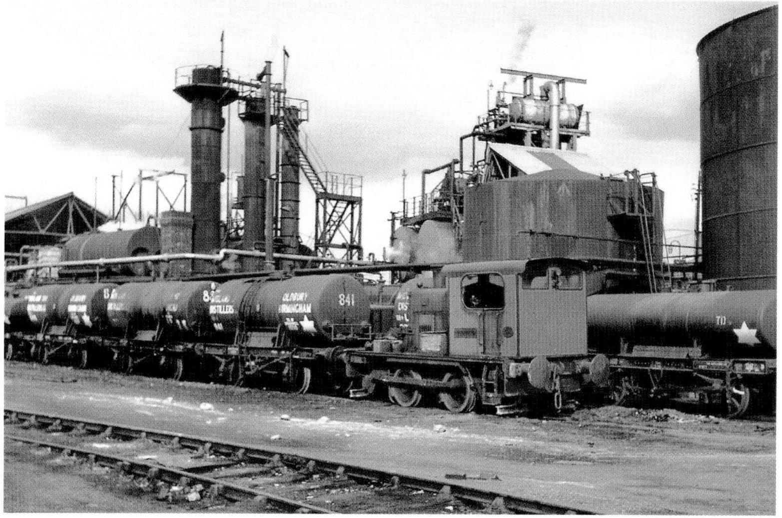

Opposite page: Several coke manufacturing plants administered by the Coal Products Division of the NCB were located adjoining or close to the Yorkshire collieries. The National Smokeless Fuels Smithywood coking plant was one such place and for many years was fuelled by coal conveyed for several miles by aerial ropeway. On 15 July 1972, Hunslet Austerity *SWCP No. 2* (W/No. 3192 of 1944 and rebuilt by Hunslet W/No. 3888 of 1964), one of two then present, takes a break between its duties on shed. (John Sloane)

Right: This Andrew Barclay 'Pug' 0-4-0 saddle tank (W/No. 2217 of 1947) spent its entire industrial working life at the Kilnhurst works of Yorkshire Tar Distillers, near Swinton in Rotherham, before being made redundant just after the occasion of this 28 July 1971 visit. It was replaced by the John Fowler diesel transferred from Oldbury. Following over three decades of private storage at Tinsley in Sheffield, it was moved to the Ecclesbourne Valley Railway in Derbyshire in 2005, where it is now a working loco and named *Henry Ellison*. (Roy Burt)

Left: Yorkshire Tar Distillers, Kilnhurst Works, in 1974 with John Fowler 80 hp Class 6A 0-4-0 diesel-mechanical *H. W. Robinson* (W/No. 4100003 of 1946). It had worked from new at the Midland Tar Distiller's Oldbury works until rail traffic ceased there in 1971, when it was transferred to the Kilnhurst plant for further work, replacing the Andrew Barclay steam loco illustrated below. (Author's collection)

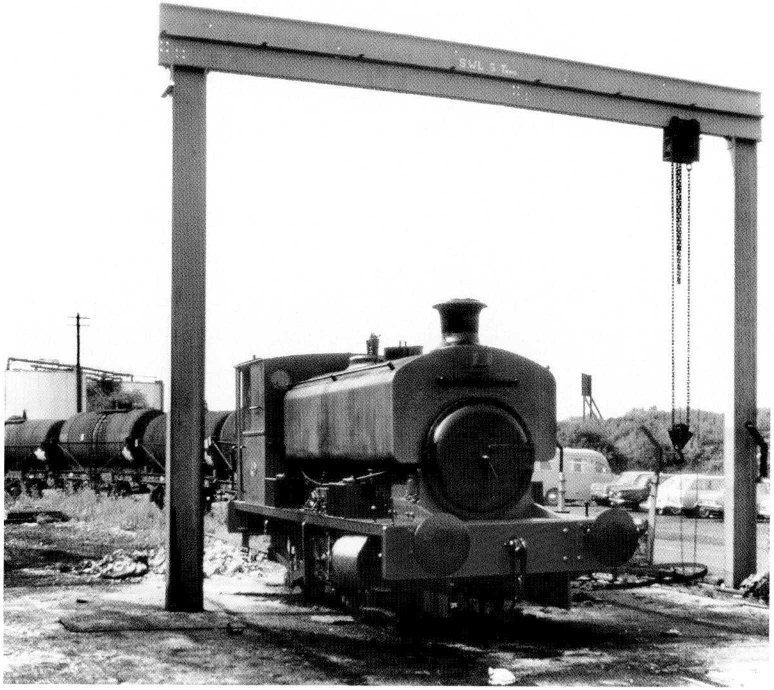

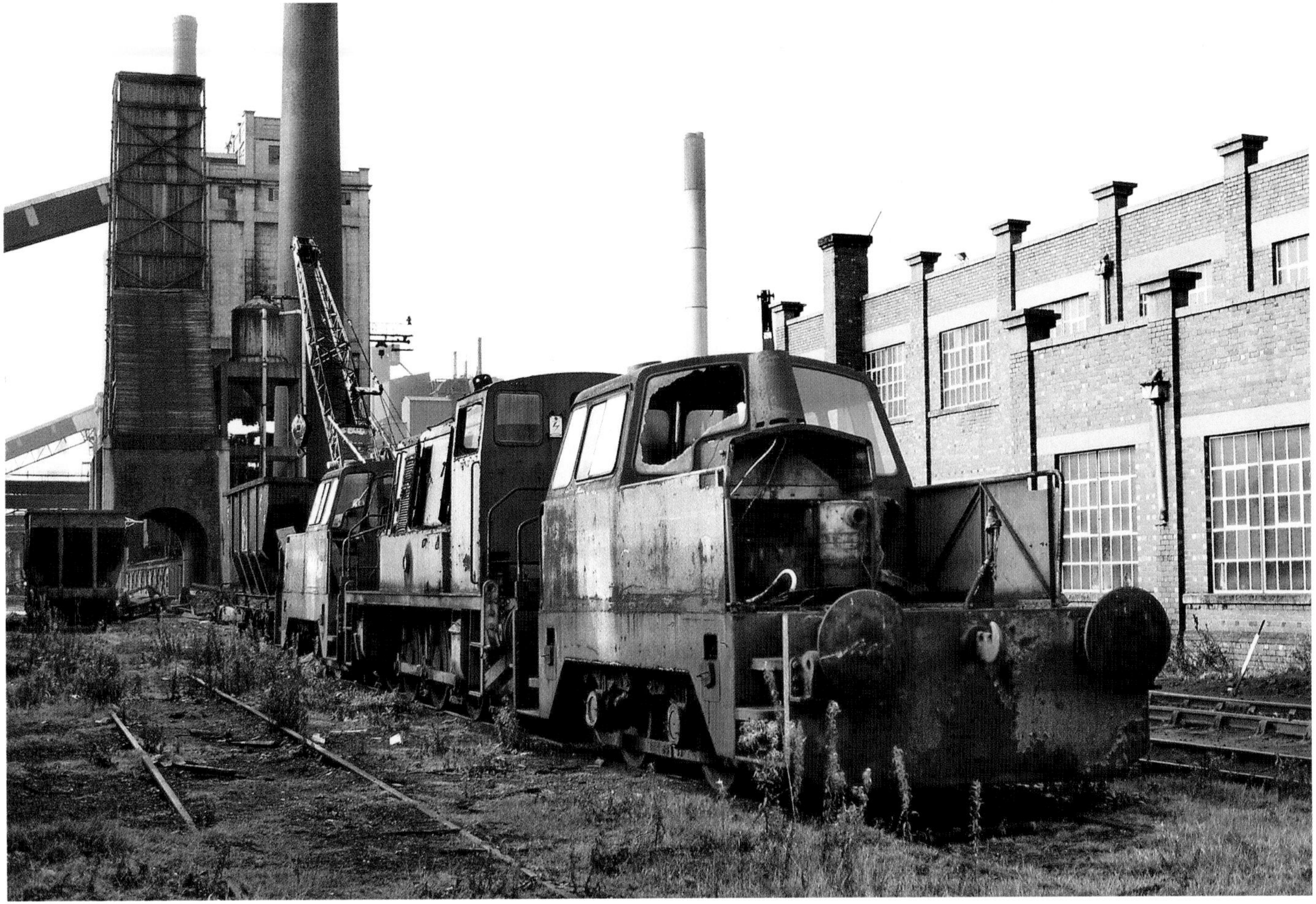

Dereliction at the British Steel Corporation's Orgreave Coke & Chemical works on 17 November 1985, with the abandoned remains of Rolls-Royce four-wheel diesel-hydraulic No. 4044-22 (W/No. 10246 of 1966), a Yorkshire Engine 0-6-0 diesel-electric (W/No. 2528 of 1953) and Rolls-Royce four-wheel diesel-hydraulic No. 4044-21 (W/No. 10245 of 1966). (Author)

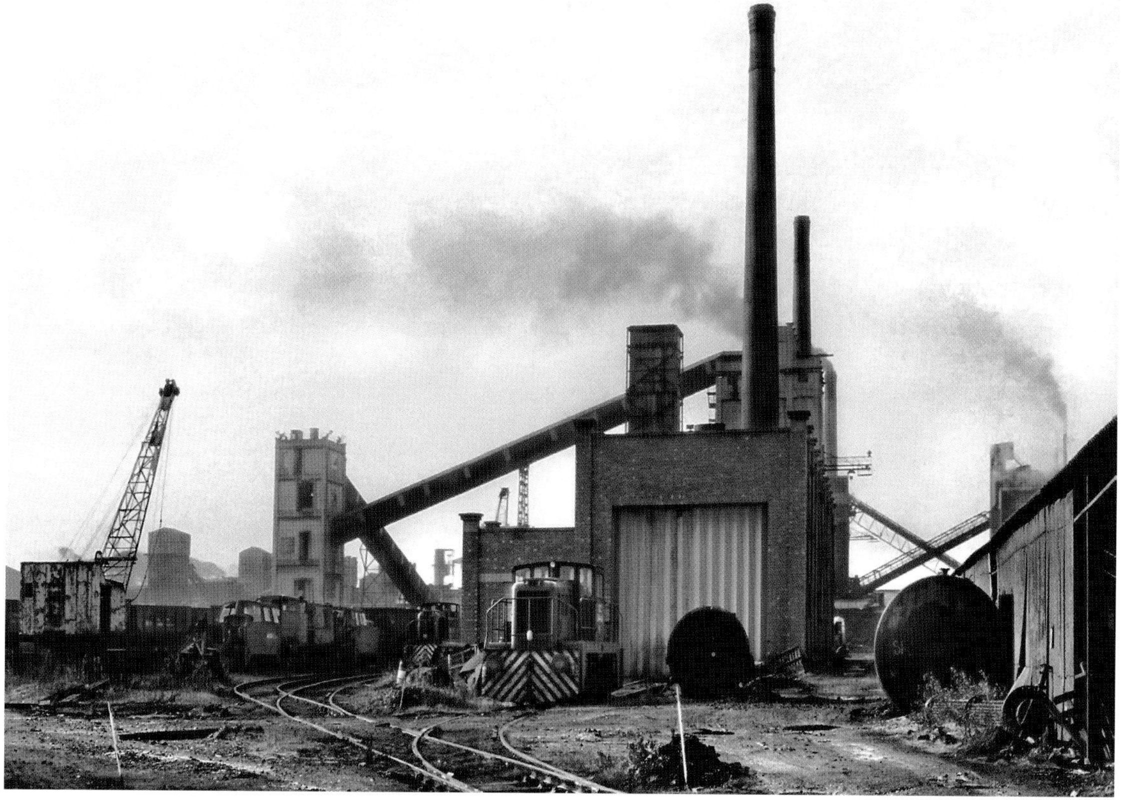

An early morning scene at the British Steel Corporation's (BSC) Orgreave Coke & Chemical works on 17 November 1985, with Yorkshire Engine 0-6-0 diesel-electric No. 2444/16 *No. 1* (W/No. No. 2753 of 1959), one of two operational works shunters at that time, outside the loco shed. At nationalisation the mining and coking operations at Orgreave were split, but the coal processing and chemicals interests remained with United Steel Companies under their subsidiary, the United Coke & Chemical Company. The nearby NCB collieries, at Orgreave and Treeton, were linked underground and the coal drawn by these collieries was fed by conveyor to the washery at Orgreave coal preparation plant, and then fed by conveyor again, to BSC's coking plant. Orgreave colliery ceased winding in October 1981 but coal from Treeton colliery continued to be transported by the overland conveyer, for washing at the surviving Orgreave washery. The washery, along with the adjoining coking and chemical plant, was closed in 1990. (Author)

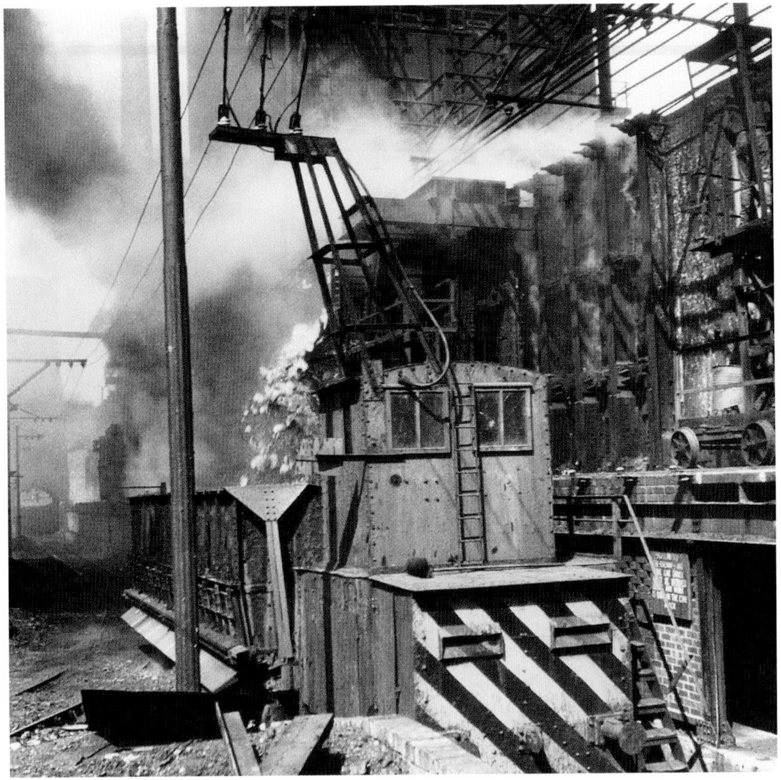

Left: The Barnsley District Coking Company coke ovens at Barrow, in full swing on 30 July 1971, with coke being discharged into the bespoke hopper wagon prior to being propelled to the quencher in the background by the semi-permanently coupled Wellman, Smith Owen Engineering Corp. Ltd standard gauge steeple-cab 0-4-0 overhead electric coke oven loco. The coke ovens were located approximately half-way along a three-quarter-mile branch line between Barrow colliery and the BR main line, south of Dovecliffe station. (Roy Burt)

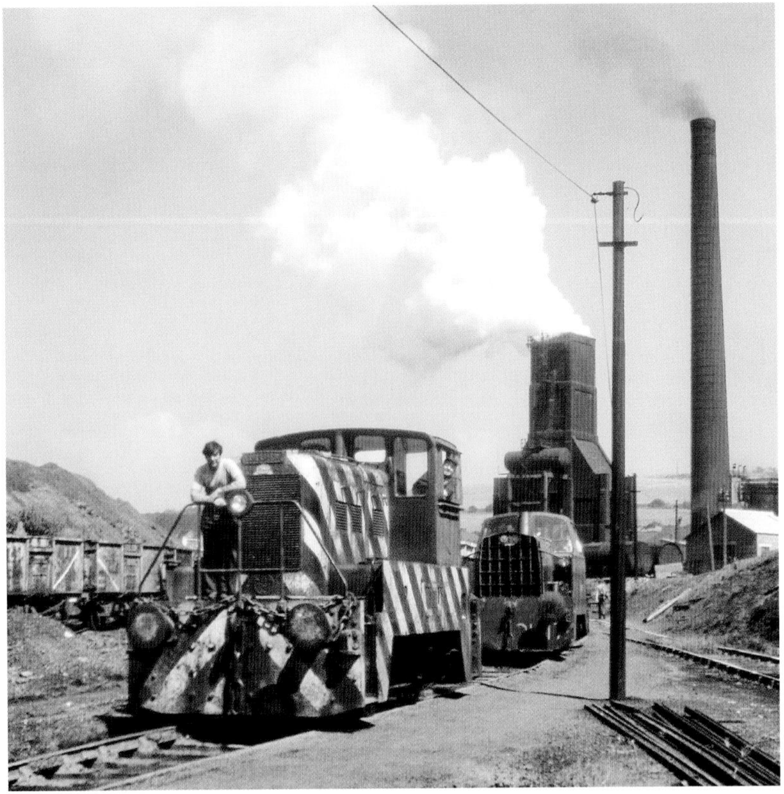

Right: A Yorkshire Engine Company 200 hp 0-4-0 diesel-electric (W/No. 2729 of 1958) and Sentinel 230 hp four-wheel diesel-hydraulic No. DH17 (W/No. 10176 of 1964) returning along the branch to work in tandem on trains between Barrow Colliery and Barnsley District Coke Works at Worsborough on 30 July 1971. The Yorkshire Engine was acquired by Smithywood coking plant in October 1976, but the Sentinel was not so fortunate, being despatched for scrap at C. F. Booth of Rotherham in April 1986. (Roy Burt)

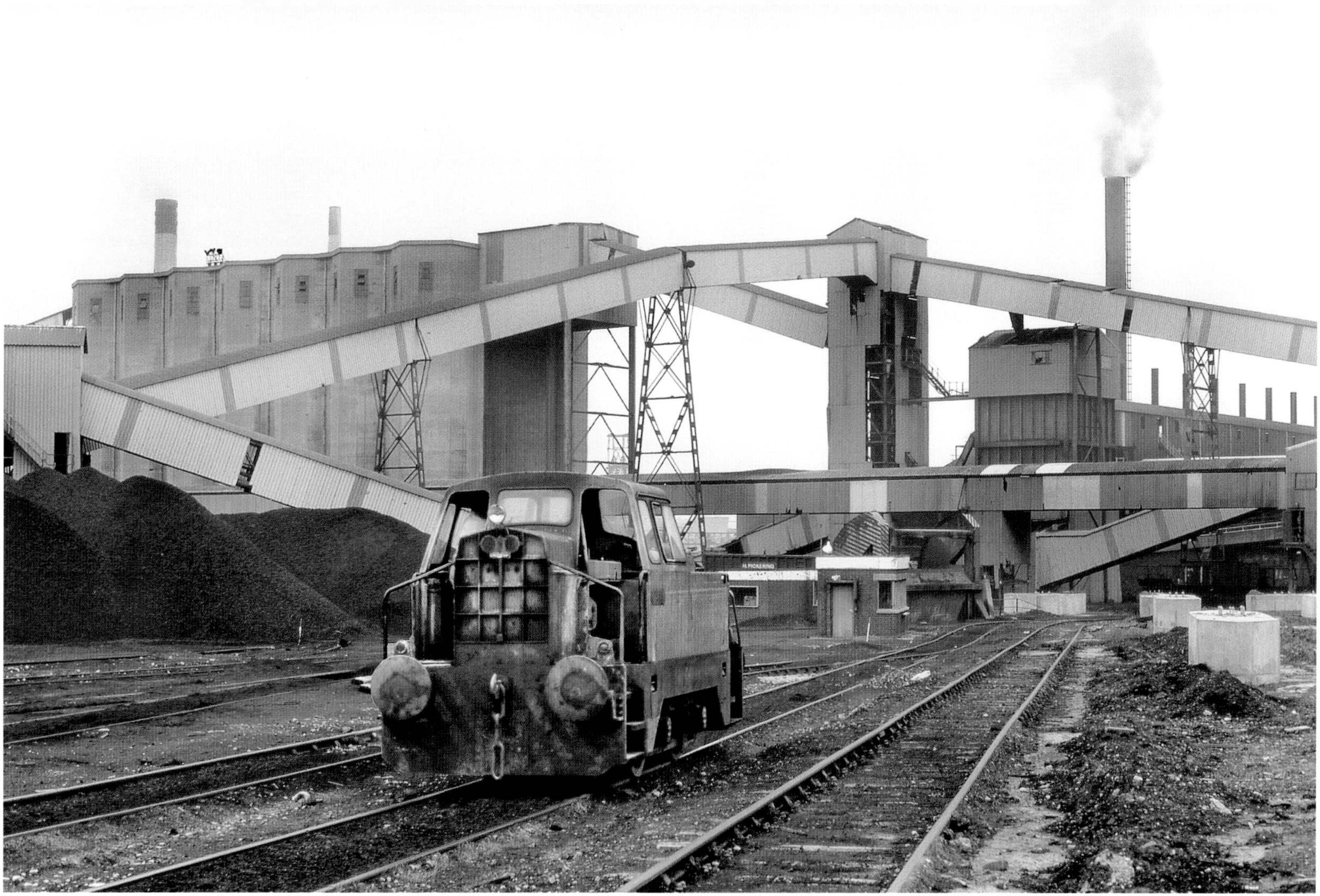

Rolls-Royce Sentinel 325 hp four-wheel diesel-hydraulic No. 1 (W/No. 10258 of 1966) at Coalite & Chemical Products Ltd, Grimethorpe, near Barnsley on 5 May 1983. The plant closed in 1994 due to a fall in demand for coke. (Roy Burt)

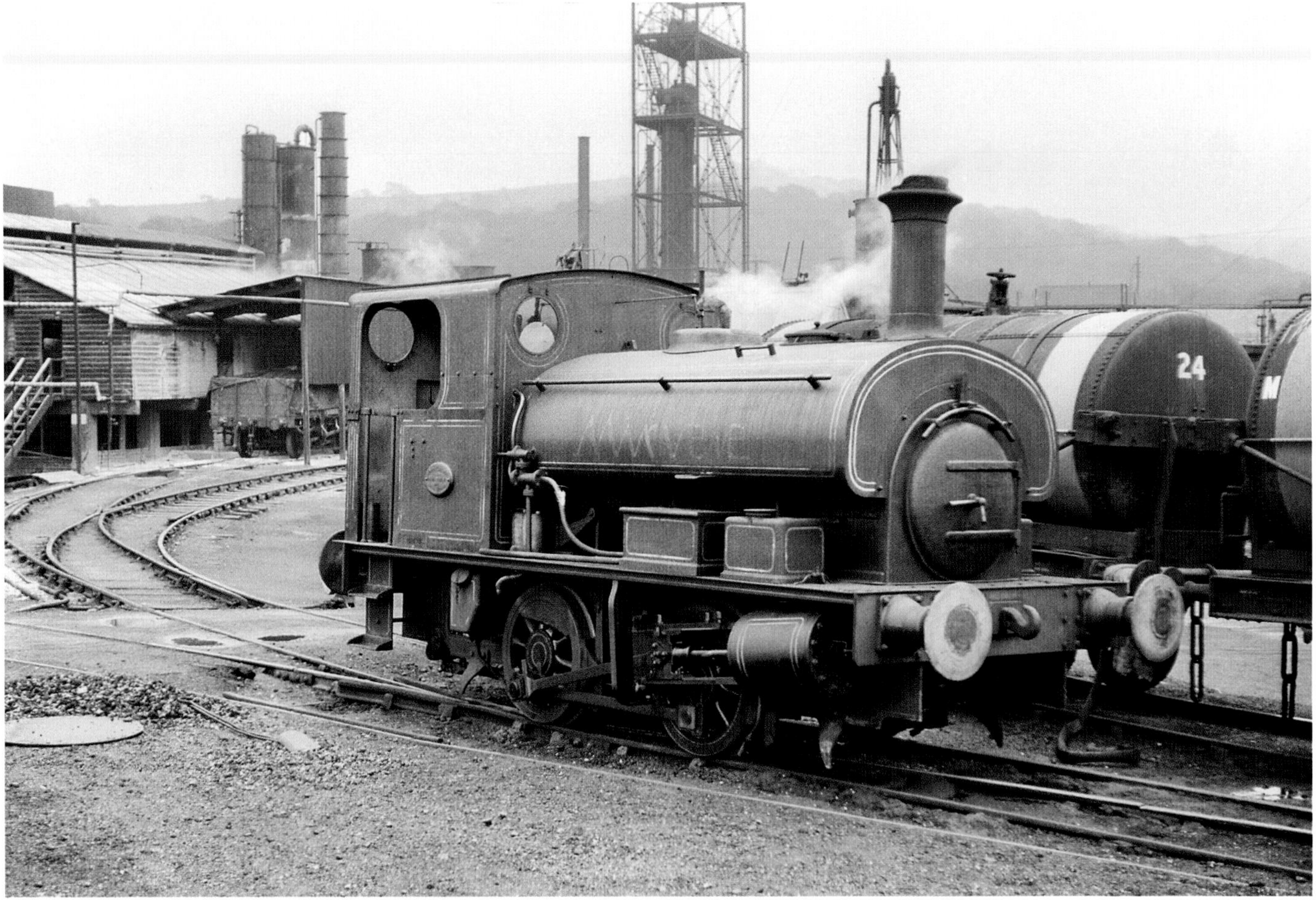

Hudswell Clarke 13 x 18-in. (OC) 0-4-0 saddle tank *Mirvale* (W/No. 1882 of 1955) at the Mirvale Chemicals Ltd works at Mirfield on 21 October 1964. This loco holds the distinction of being the first to work on the heritage North Yorkshire Moors Railway at the beginning of 1969, shortly after arriving from the chemical works, where it worked its entire commercial industrial career. (Peter Eckersley – author's collection)

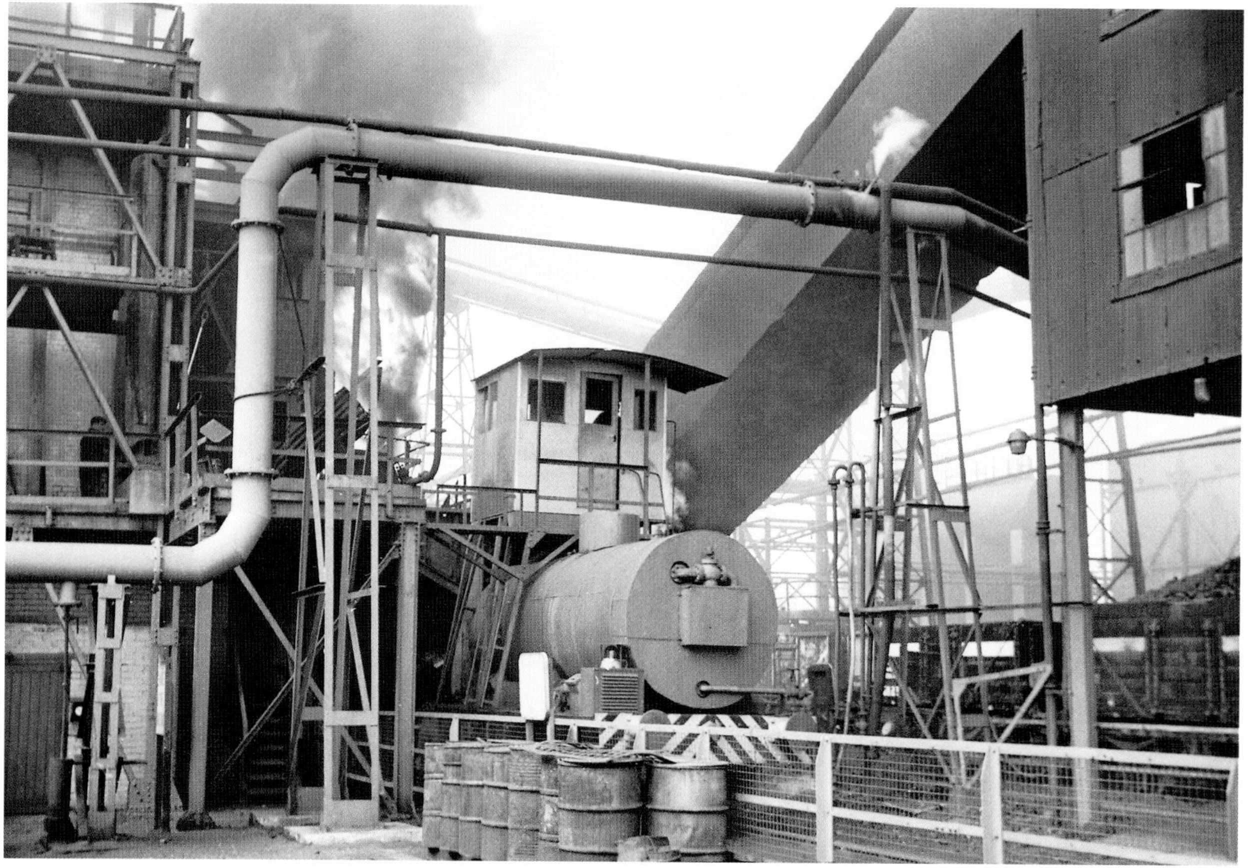

The NCB Coal Products Division coking plant at Glasshoughton near Castleford had a most unusual, yet ugly, loco to position a coke car beneath the coke ovens, as seen here on 23 July 1966, almost looking like a fixture of the plant itself. This blue-liveried 0-6-0 fireless loco held the distinction of being the last 'steam' locomotive, albeit unconventional, to be built by the famous Robert Stephenson & Hawthorns Company Ltd at their Newcastle works (W/No. 8082 of 1958). A standard design of fireless locomotive with 20 x 18-in. outside-cylinders, it was fitted with an elevated cab to enable the driver to see the operation of the coke car. It did not have a particularly lengthy existence for such a bespoke piece of industrial plant machinery, and was replaced by an electric-operated coke car, being scrapped on site in November 1971. (Author's collection)

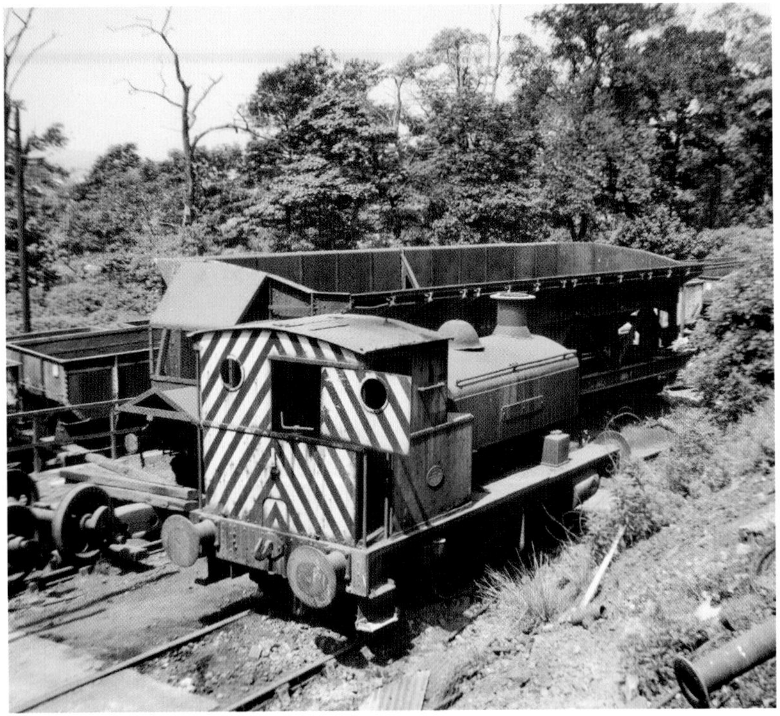

Opposite page: Around the late 1970s, the regular working steam loco at Smithywood coking plant was Hunslet Austerity *SWCP No. 2* (W/No. 3192 of 1944, rebuilt No. 3888 of 1964), but by the early 1980s it was maintained purely on standby to diesel traction. Surprisingly, *SWCP No. 2* (rebuilt by Hunslet W/No. 3888 of 1964) was found to be at work on Sunday morning 25 July 1982, a time when the sight of steam traction working in industry in Britain was an experience to be savoured, especially during a weekend! The coking plant had been in operation since 1929, converting coal into coke for use in blast-furnaces, the process consuming around 400,000 tons of coal per annum. The by-products plant also extracted oil, producing the well-known household Izal disinfectant product, gas for the Sheffield Gas Company, ammonium sulphate, crude benzole and tar. The continuous operation at Smithywood had the use of a battery of fifty-nine coke ovens, of which one would have been charged and discharged every twenty minutes. Until the 1960s, an aerial ropeway system provided much of the coal from Smithywood, Rockingham and Thorncliffe collieries, and conveyed coke to the Thorncliffe ironworks of Newton Chambers & Co. Ltd. Prior to nationalisation at Smithywood, Thorncliffe Coal Distillation Ltd, a subsidiary of this ironworks, provided the original structural ironwork for the construction of the coke and by-products plant. Smithywood closed in 1986 and was quickly demolished during the following year. The site has now been landscaped and redeveloped as a business park. (Roy Burt)

Above: Hawthorn Leslie 0-4-0 saddle tank No. 9 (W/No. 2454 of 1900) dumped out of use at the NCB Coal Products Division Smithywood Coking Plant, Chapeltown, on 6 June 1970. (John Sloane)

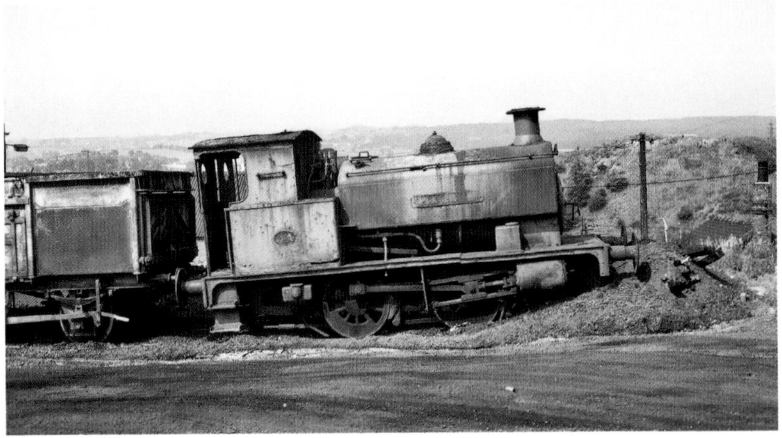

Right: By this return visit on 15 July 1972, No. 9 had been moved to the end of a siding, in the company of some crippled wagons, and its future didn't look bright – in fact the 14 x 20-in. (OC) four-coupled saddle tank was despatched for scrap at Steel Breaking & Dismantling Ltd's Chesterfield scrapyard in September 1972. Before arriving at Smithywood in January 1964, it had previously seen use at Rotherham Main and Handsworth Nunnery coking plants. (John Sloane)

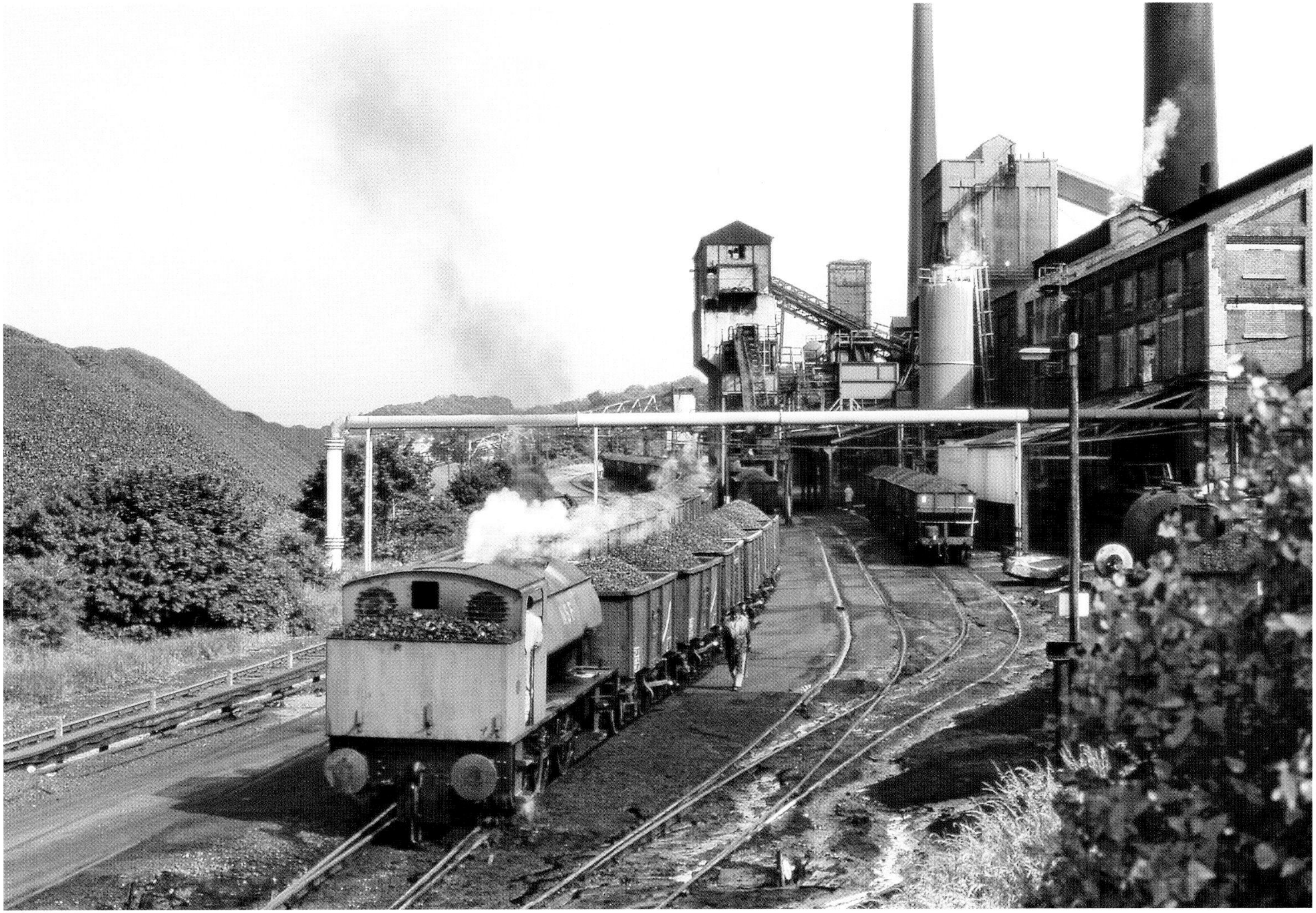

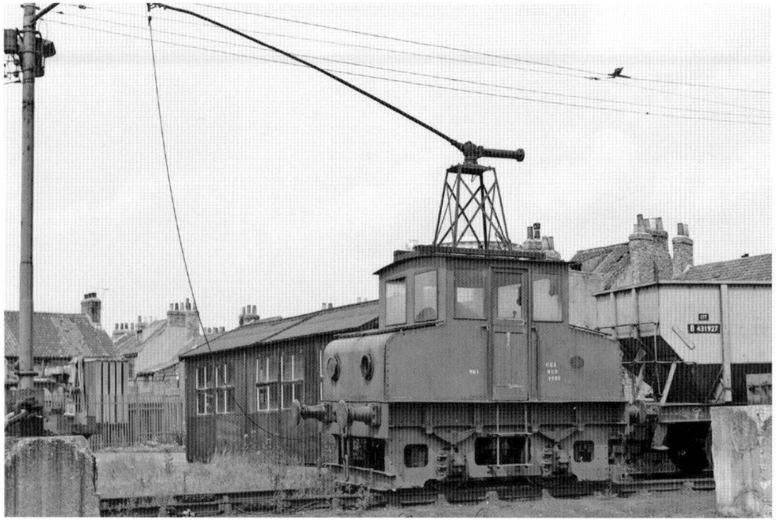

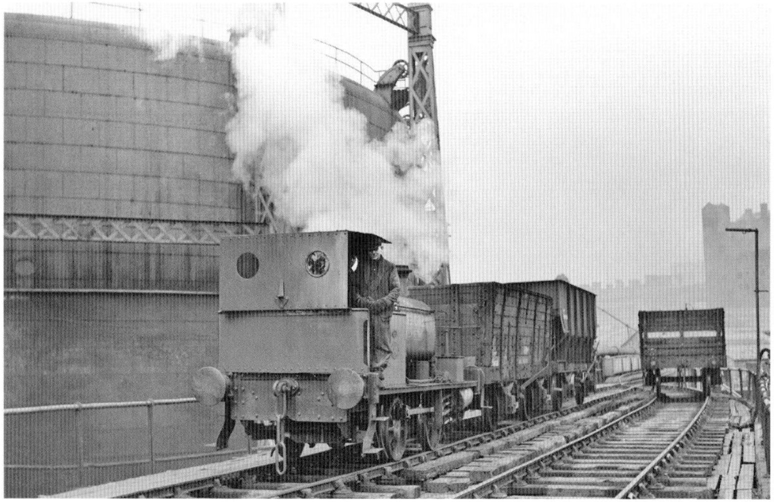

4

GAS & ELECTRICITY

Left: Still bearing the initials of the North East Division of the Central Electricity Authority, Kerr Stewart four-wheel 500-volt overhead electric No. 1 (W/No. 1269 of 1912) with BR 21-ton coal hoppers at Central Electricity Generating Board (CEGB), Foss Islands power station, York, on 7 August 1961. The power station was connected to the Derwent Valley Light Railway at Layerthorpe. (Harry Townley – IRS collection)

Below left: A Hudswell Clarke 0-4-0 saddle tank (W/No. 448 of 1895) at North Eastern Gas Board (NEGB), York, in the early 1950s. (Harry Townley – IRS collection)

Opposite page: Peckett 0-6-0 saddle tank No. 2 (W/No. 2050 of 1944) standing with internal patent Sheffield Twinberrow side-tipping bogie wagons at the weighbridge serving NEGB Harrogate works on 4 July 1949. The 2-foot gauge line was first installed between 1907 and 1908 and conveyed coke from the NER/BR exchange sidings at Bilton to the New Park gas works, located on the northern perimeter of the town. The railway's first loco was a 0-6-2 saddle tank built by Thomas Green & Son Ltd of Leeds and now preserved on the South Tynedale Railway. The NEGB subsequently acquired a surplus War Department Light Railways (WDLR) Hunslet 4-6-0 tank in 1920, but this was replaced by this new-build Peckett. Dieselisation came in 1949 in the form of a Baguley-Drewry 0-6-0 diesel-mechanical, relegating the Peckett to standby duties. All locos had cut-down cabs and boiler mountings to enable them to clear the 800-yard-long tunnel on the line, quite an amazing structure for this unique narrow-gauge railway. The Harrogate gas works railway closed in 1956 and the Peckett, now bearing the name *Harrogate*, is preserved on the private Statfold Barn Railway in Staffordshire. (Harry Townley – IRS collection)

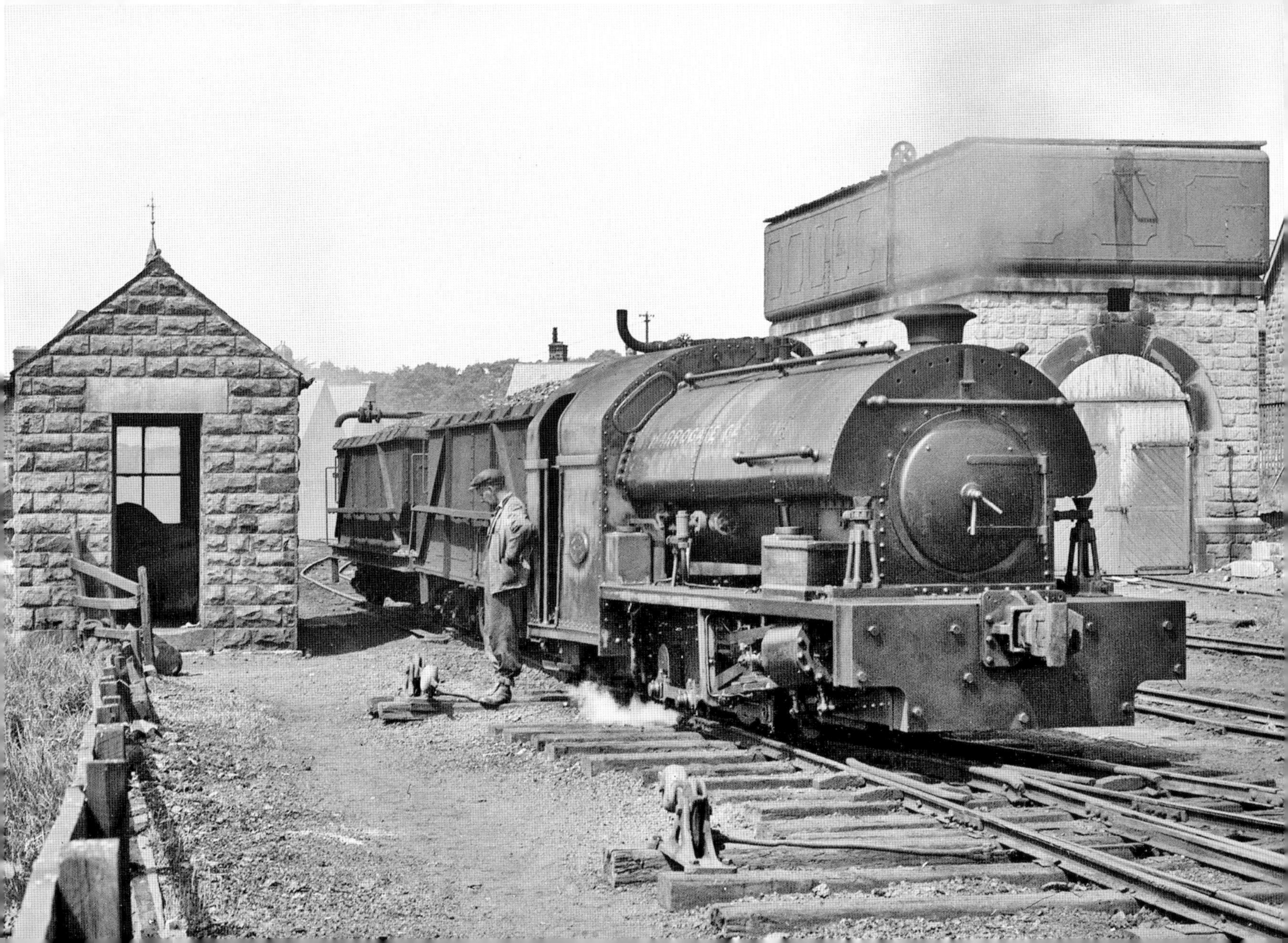

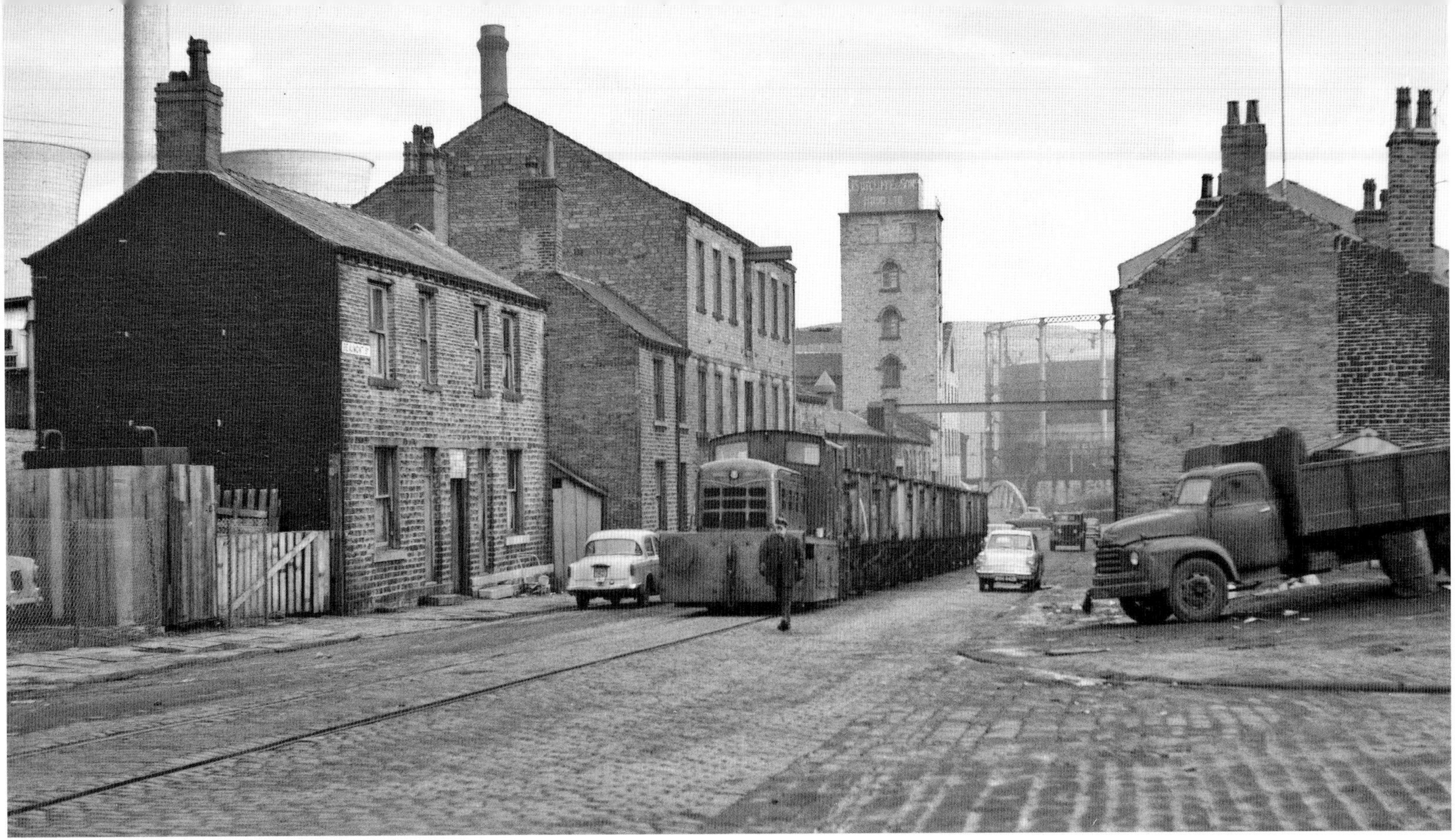

NEGB John Fowler 0-4-0 diesel-mechanical No. 3 (W/No. 4210041 of 1951) running along Beaumont Street in Huddersfield with empty BR 16-ton wagons for the exchange sidings. The quarter-mile branch line connected with the Newtown goods yard. Rail traffic ceased in March 1966. (Brian Webb – IRS collection)

5

LIFE AFTER THE MAIN LINE

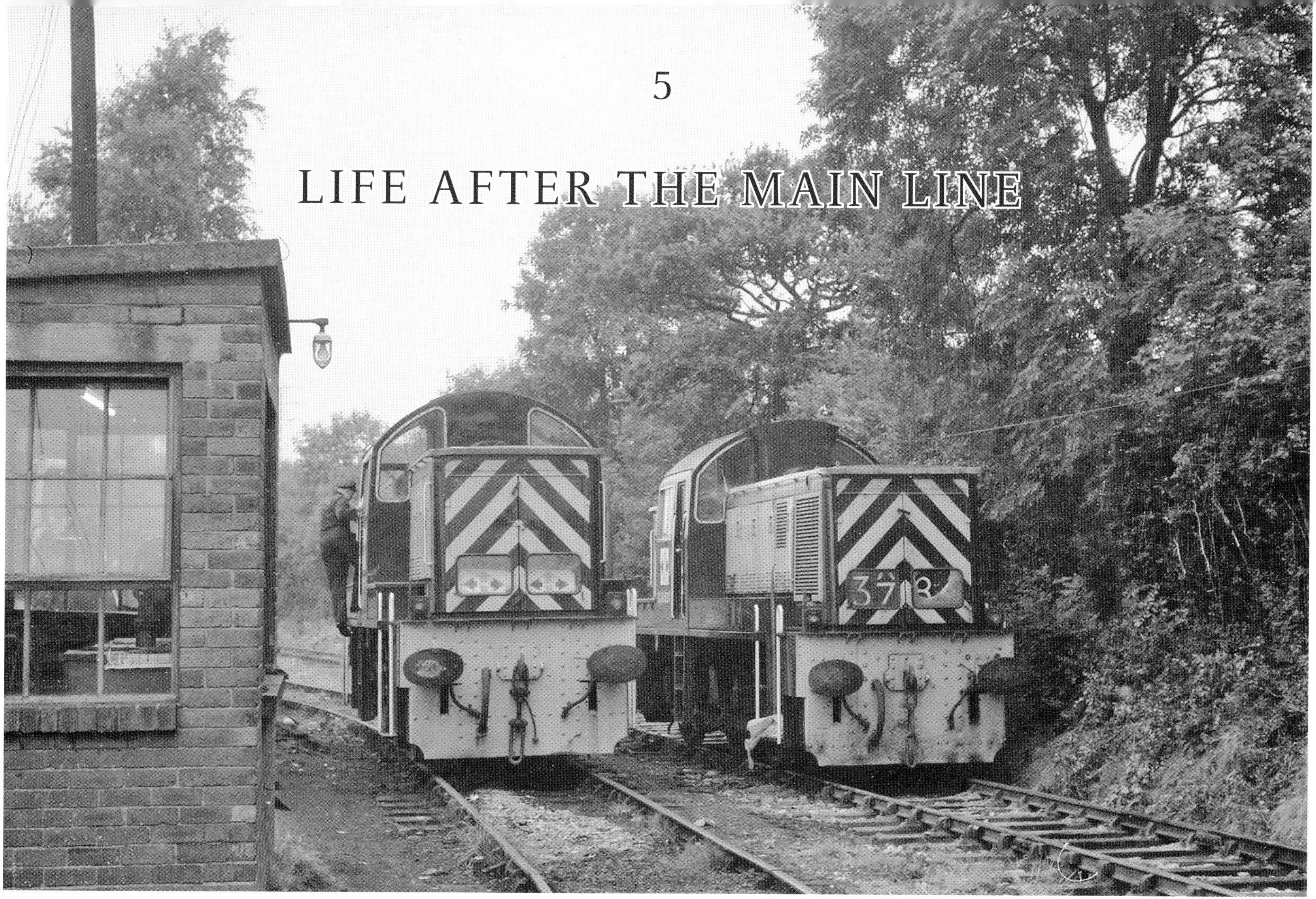

Former BR Swindon-built Class 14 Paxman 650 hp 0-6-0 diesel-hydraulic locos Nos D9531 and D9513 at the NCB British Oak Disposal Point at Crigglestone, possibly in summer 1969, both having served less than five years' service with BR. (Kevin Lane collection)

Right: A Hunslet 170 hp 0-6-0 diesel-hydraulic (W/No. 1724 of 1934) at Bullcroft colliery on 8 November 1969. It was originally supplied new to the London, Midland & Scottish Railway (LMS), who were exploring the use of diesel traction in the early 1930s, evaluating products from a variety of builders. It had mechanical transmission and was initially equipped with a Davey Paxman 180 hp diesel engine and allocated running number 7054. Subsequent experience led the LMS to invest in production series locos of a greater horsepower, and it was sold on to the military for service at home during wartime. Following cessation of hostilities, it was returned to Hunslet and was eventually sold on to the NCB and in April 1953 it was first put to work at Brodsworth colliery. It was later rebuilt, at Hunslet in 1962, with hydraulic transmission and fitted with a Rolls-Royce C6NFL diesel engine, as fitted to the BR Class 02 locos. It subsequently spent time at Bullcroft colliery, where it was photographed, and Hickleton colliery, where it was scrapped on site around 1974/1975. (John Sloane)

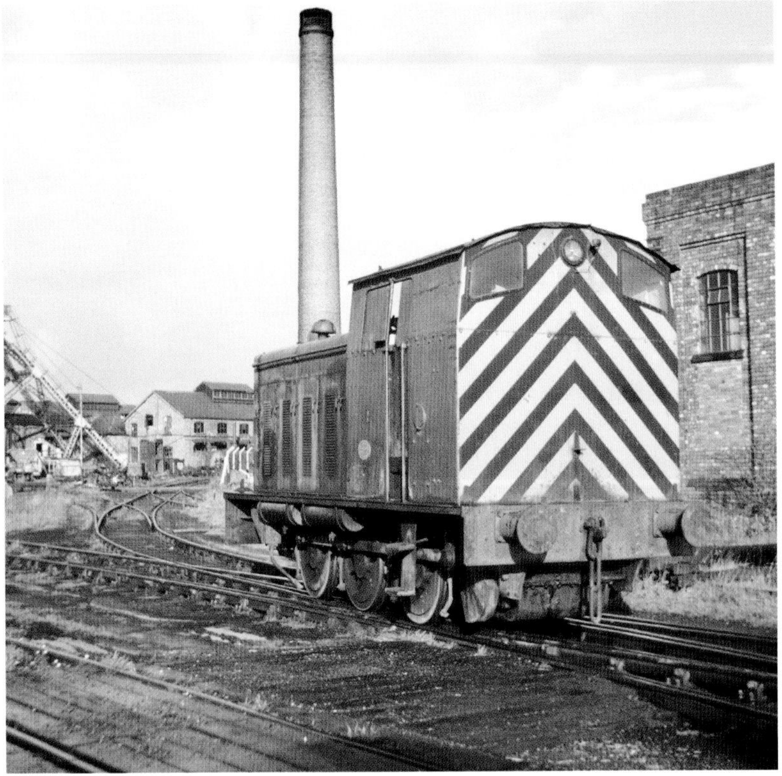

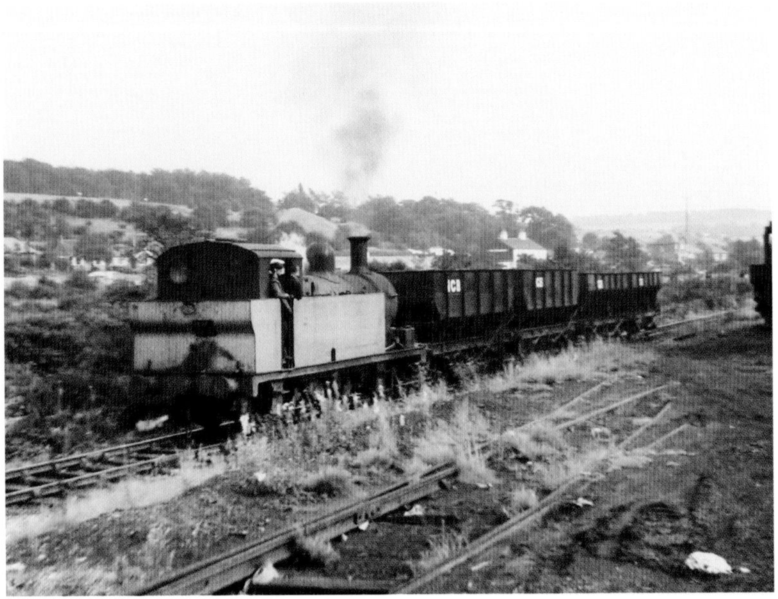

Left: Former BR Jinty Class 0-6-0 tank No. 47445 (built by Hunslet W/No. 1529 of 1927) in service at NCB British Oak Disposal Point at Crigglestone on 8 September 1969. It had been transferred from BR in May 1966, having been withdrawn from Crewe South depot during the previous month. Its post-BR service in industry assured its survival, and in July 1970 it passed to the Midland Railway Project, then based at BR Derby locomotive works. It was the last steam loco to work at Crigglestone, being replaced by ex-BR Class 14 locos (see previous page). (John Sloane)

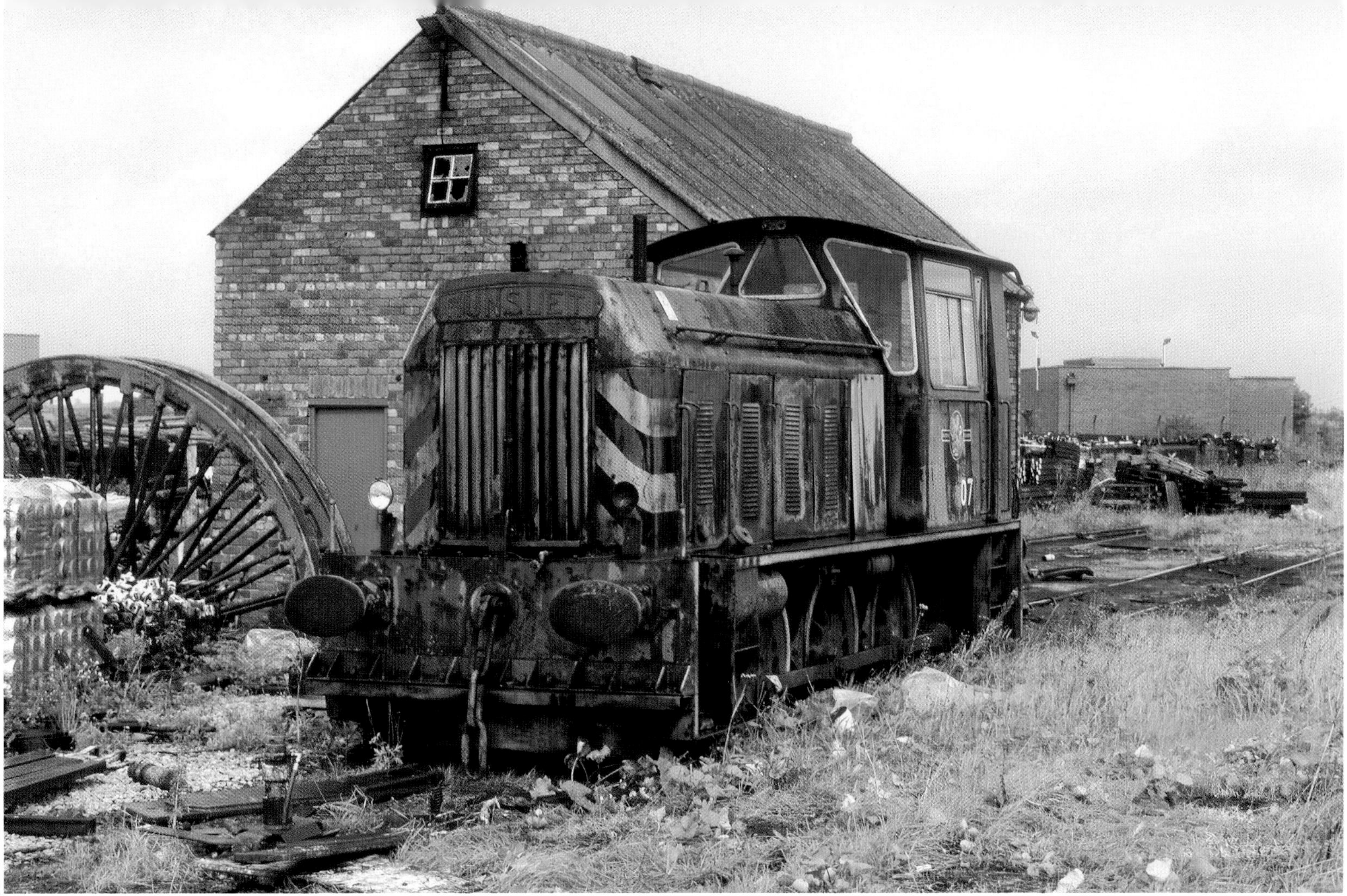

A Hunslet 0-6-0 diesel-mechanical, former BR No. D2607 (W/No. 5656 of 1960), at Steetley colliery on 22 August 1982. The 204 hp Class 05 loco was withdrawn from BR service in December 1967. Although located in Nottinghamshire, the colliery fell under the jurisdiction of NCB South Yorkshire Area, therefore qualifying for inclusion herein! (John Sloane)

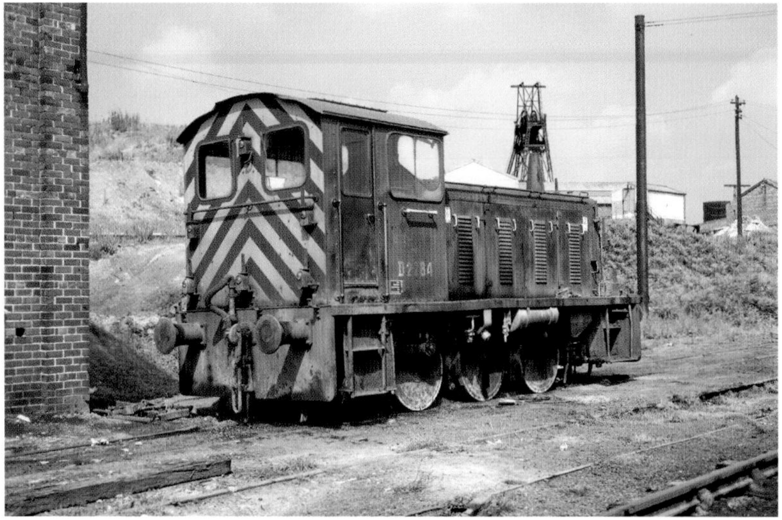

Right: Former BR Drewry 204 hp Class 04 No. D2284 at North Gawber colliery on 15 July 1972. Supplied new to BR Southern Region in March 1960, it was allocated to Guildford depot. It was withdrawn from BR service at Colchester in April 1971, when it was acquired by the NCB. It is now preserved by the Heritage Shunters Trust at Rowsley. (John Sloane)

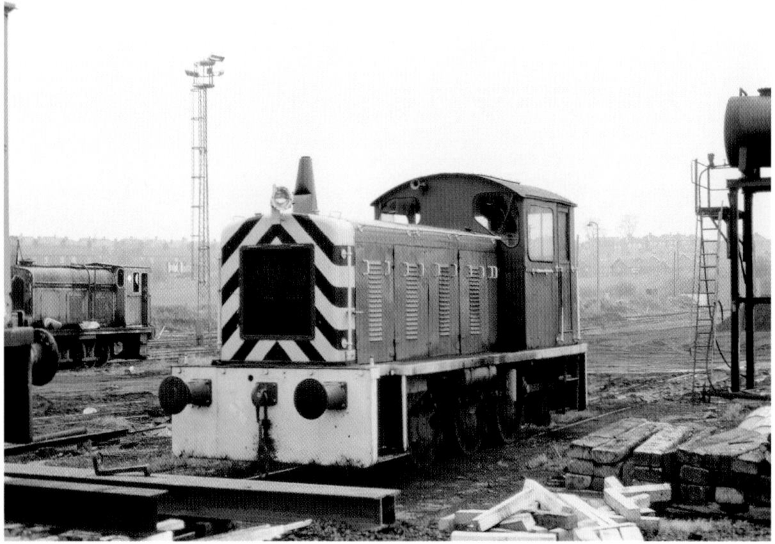

Left: Former BR 204 hp Class 04 Drewry No. D2328 at Kiveton Park colliery on 16 March 1983. Delivered new to BR Tyne Dock shed in August 1961, it was withdrawn from BR service at Thornaby in September 1968. Sold on to the NCB, it became No. 31 in the South Yorkshire Area fleet. After this photograph was taken, it was moved to Cortonwood Colliery and finally scrapped in 1986. (Roy Burt)

Opposite page: Coming under the South Yorkshire Area of the National Coal Board, although just in North Nottinghamshire, Manton Colliery near Worksop possessed an ex-BR Drewry Class 04, and No. D2229 was representative of several ex-BR Class 04 shunters that found their way into Yorkshire collieries. It was photographed on 14 June 1987 in the BR exchange sidings serving the colliery alongside No. 20 *Manton*, a Hudswell Clark 0-6-0 diesel-mechanical (W/No. D1121 of 1958). No. D2229 had been withdrawn from BR service at Thornaby in December 1969 and was sold to the NCB, initially working at Orgreave and Brookhouse collieries before moving on to Manton. (Author)

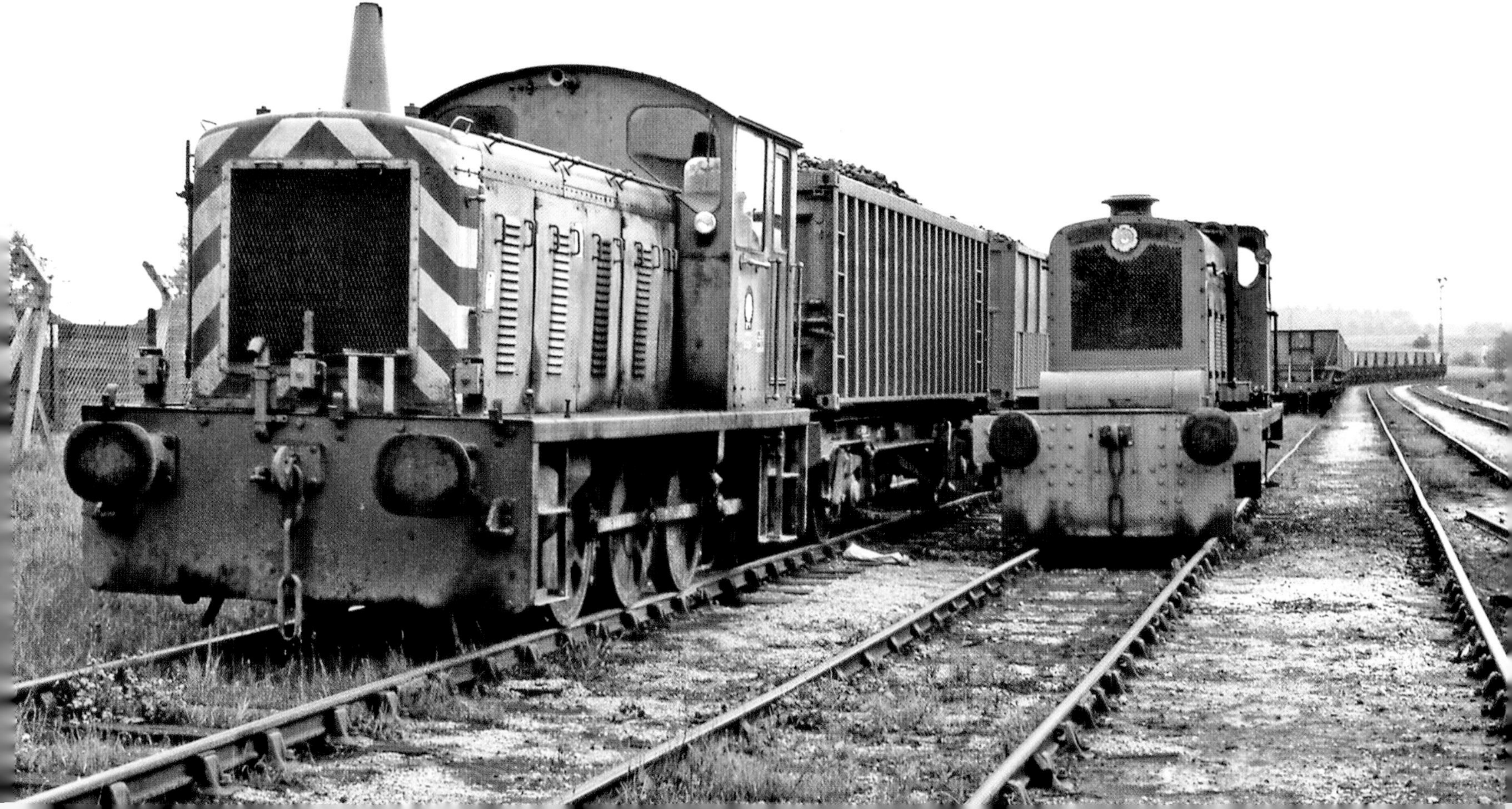

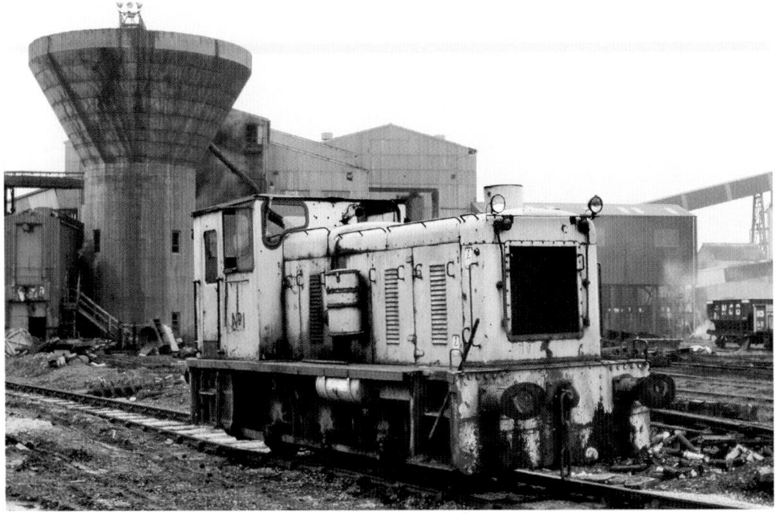

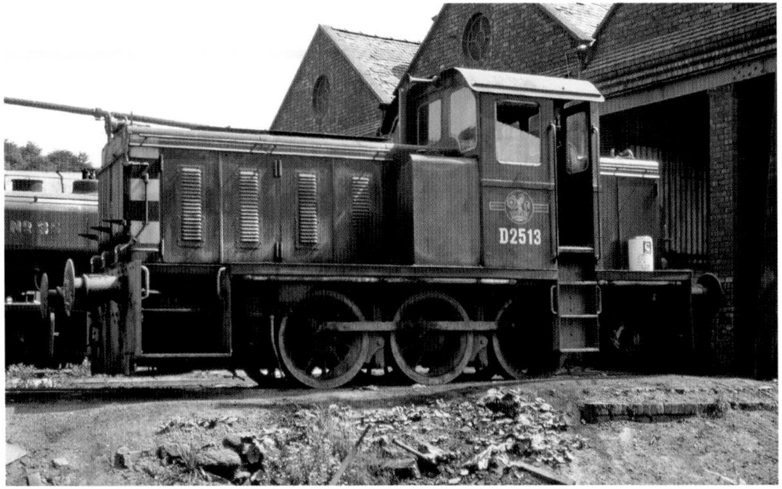

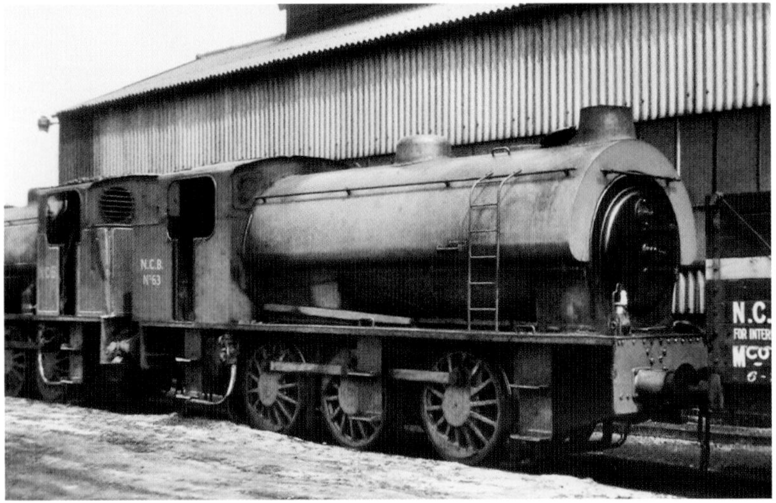

Above left: Withdrawn from BR service at Thornaby depot in September 1972, Doncaster 1959-built Class 03 No. D2057 is seen at Grimethorpe colliery on 5 May 1983. Along with sister No. D2093, also allocated to Thornaby depot and withdrawn in October 1971, they had both been converted by Hunslet in 1967 and fitted with exhaust scrubbers for working the exchange sidings of Teesside-area chemicals plants. (Roy Burt)

Above: Former BR Hudswell Clarke 204 hp 0-6-0 diesel-mechanical No. D2513 (W/No. D1204 of 1961) at Cadeby colliery, Conisbrough, on 15 July 1972. It had been withdrawn from BR service at Barrow-in-Furness in December 1968. Its NCB service proved to be short-lived, being scrapped on site in October 1975. (John Sloane)

Left: Hudswell Clarke Austerity No. 63 (W/No. 1792 of 1946) outside the running shed at Manvers Main on 14 June 1969. Before NCB acquisition, in February 1963, it was BR J94 Class No. 68067 based at Langwith Junction depot. It was fitted with the Hunslet underfeed stoker system in 1964, identified by the anti-vacuum valve on the smokebox and fibreglass chimney cowling. Having lost its BR identity, it was put to work at Manvers Main, but was scrapped on site in September 1971. (John Sloane)

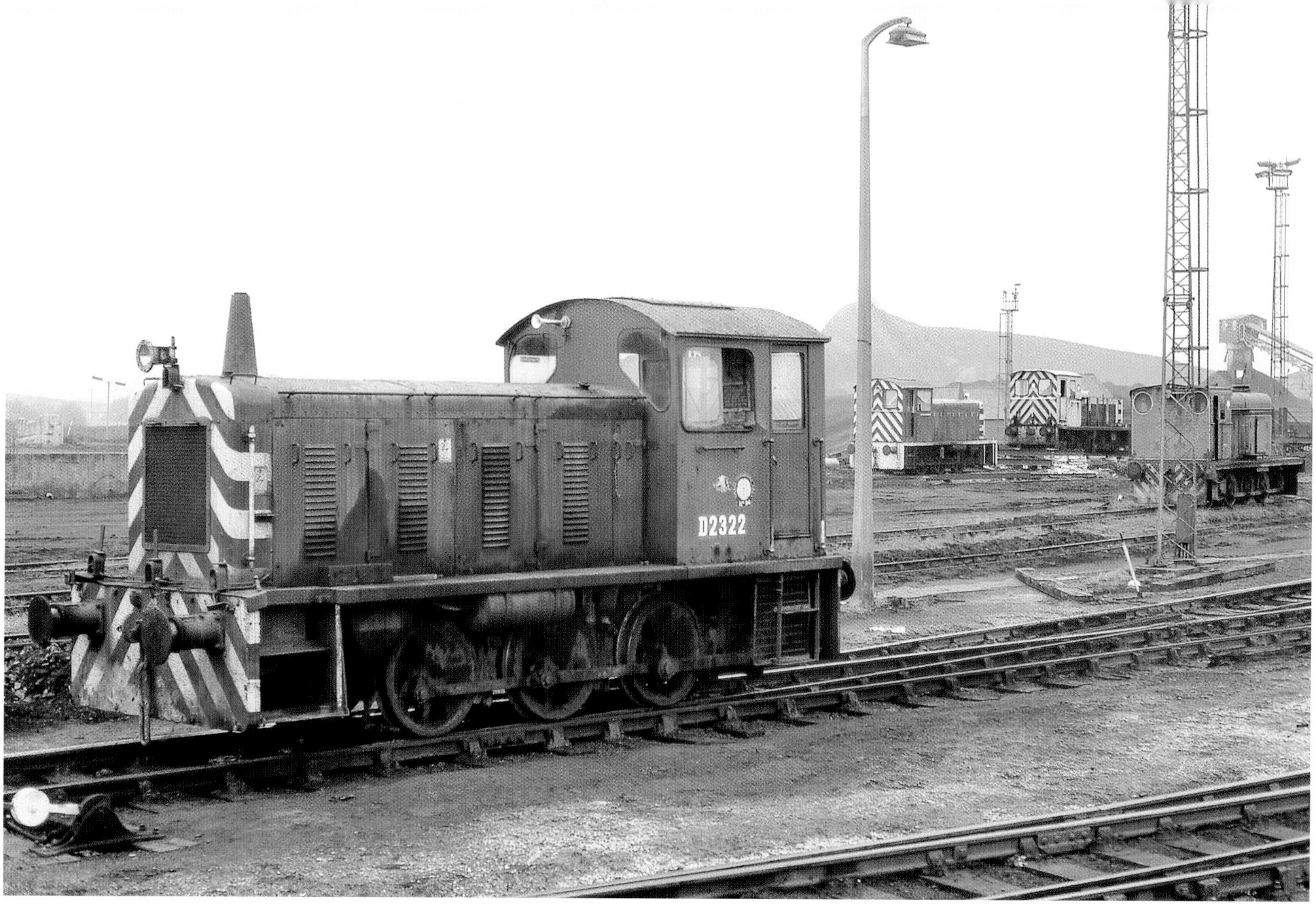

Former BR Class 04 No. D2322 at Kiveton Park colliery on 16 March 1983, with sister ex-BR Class 04s Nos D2328 and D2209 partly dismantled, and Hudswell Clarke 0-6-0 diesel-mechanical No. 15 (W/No. D1174 of 1959) in the background. (Roy Burt)

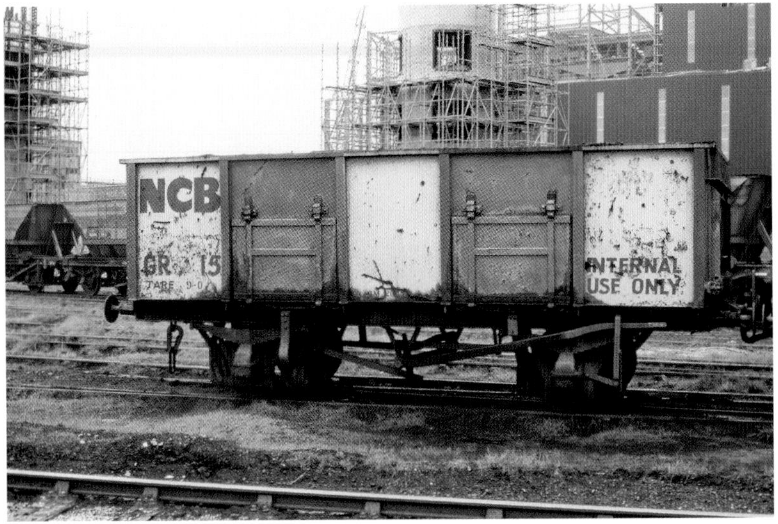

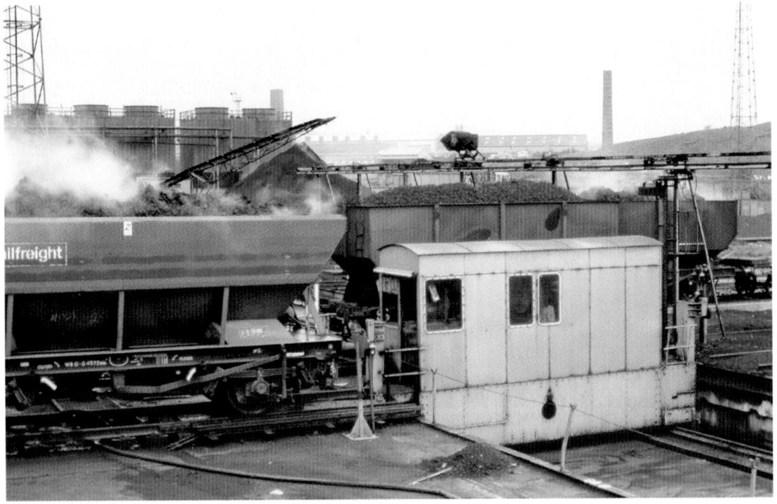

6

WAGONS ROLL

Above left: Grimethorpe wagon fleet number GR15, one of the many 9-ton tare internal-use-only coal wagons employed at Coalite & Chemical Products Ltd, Grimethorpe works, near Barnsley on 5 May 1983. This was a steel-bodied two-door conversion from a BR 21-ton gross clasp-brake wagon. The Grimethorpe Coalite plant was built adjacent to the colliery in 1966, producing fuel for the home household markets. Coalite is a low temperature coke used as a smokeless fuel, ideal for open domestic fire grates. The Coalite plant was supplied with coal from Houghton Main colliery, wound at Grimethorpe. The solid fuel business began to shrink in the 1980s due to a falling demand as the availability of cheaper natural gas became widely available for domestic heating. The resultant downturn in the demand for the product forced the Coalite plant to close during 1994.

Below left: A loaded BR HEA Class wagon on the traverser at Coalite & Chemical Products Ltd, Grimethorpe works, on 5 May 1983. Almost 2,000 of these wagons were built at BR's Shildon works between 1975 and 1979, intended to become the standard general-purpose hopper wagon. Originally classified as HBA, they were rebuilt with improved suspension and reclassified HEA and in the 1980s were in widespread use conveying household coal in block trains to coal concentration depots and yards around the country. A standard BR 21-ton coal hopper, originally of LNER design, is behind the traverser control hut.

Opposite page: An abandoned veteran eight-plank internal-user coke hopper wagon of unknown origin and a standard BR 16-ton wagon languish in the 'cripples siding' at National Smokeless Fuels Ltd, Smithywood coking plant, on 14 September 1986, just around the time of the plant's closure. (All Roy Burt)

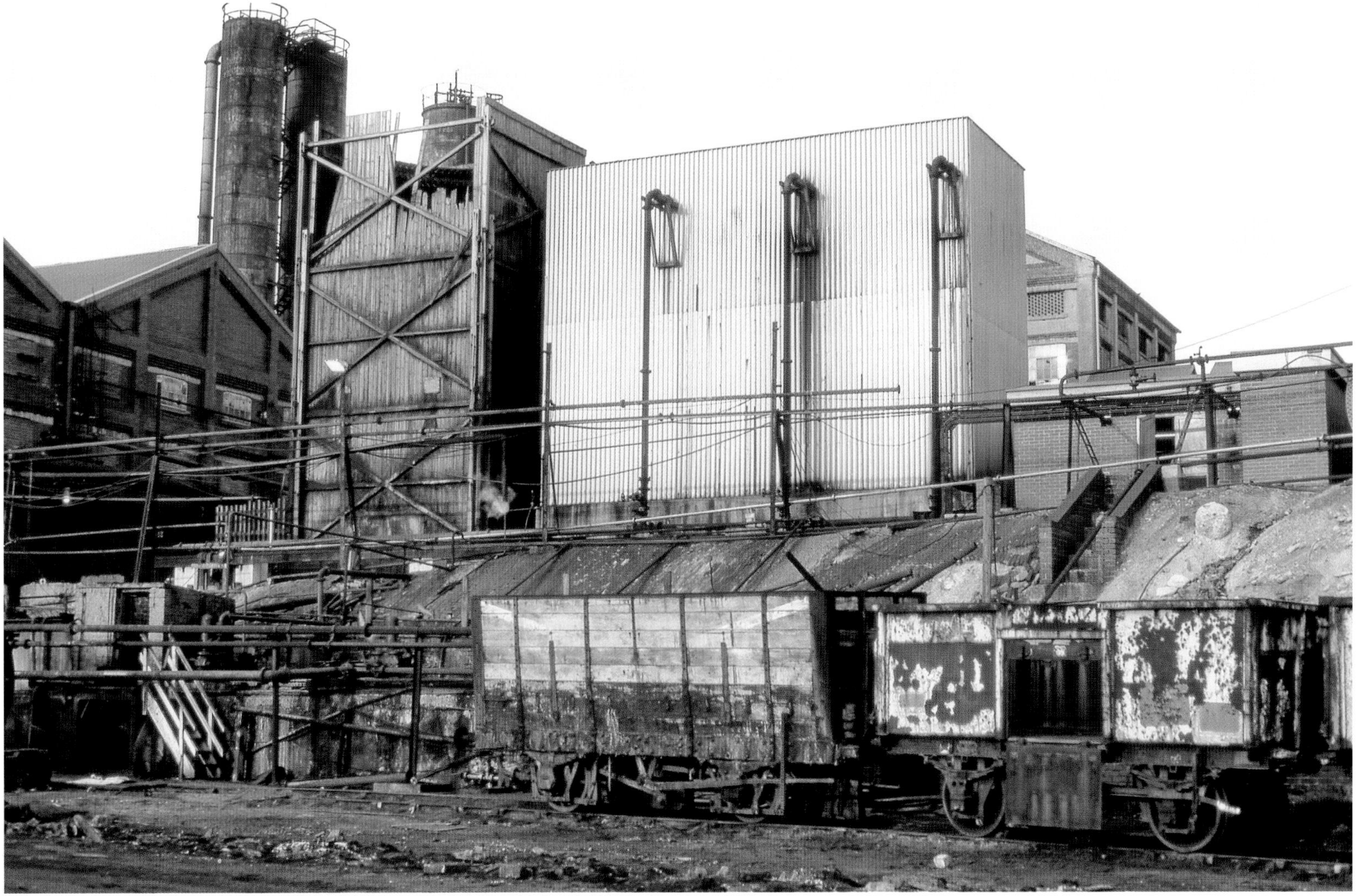

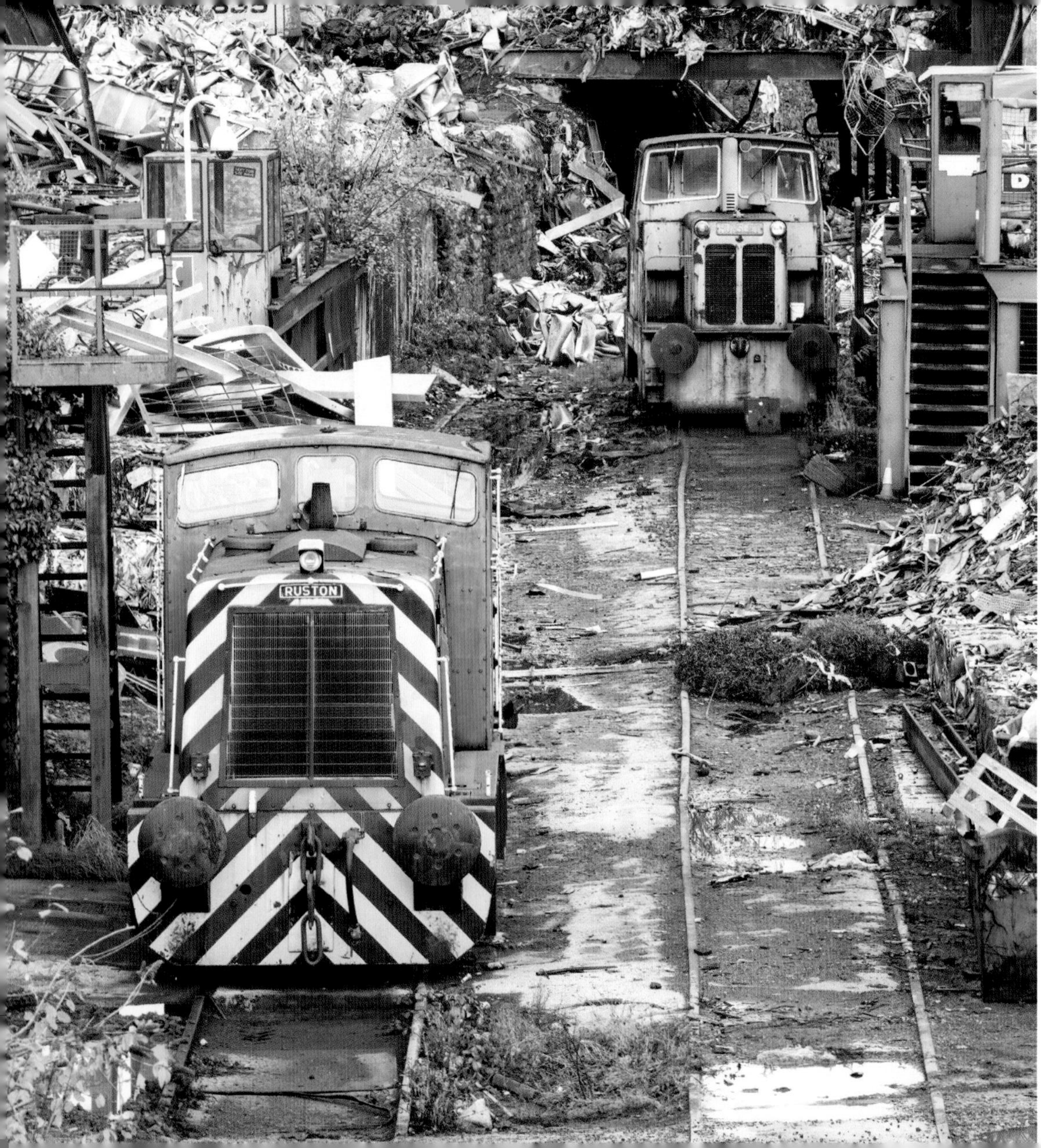

7

SCRAP

Left: Two of the five industrial locomotives on the books of metal processors Crossley Evans Ltd at Shipley on 24 November 2016. The LSSH Class Ruston & Hornsby 0-6-0 diesel-hydraulic (W/No. 459519 of 1961) was originally Army Department No. 425 and had previously worked on the Marchwood Port Military Railway, while the blue Hunslet 179 hp 0-4-0 diesel-hydraulic (W/No. 7159 of 1969) had previously been employed at Bradford Corporation's Esholt Sewage Works (covered on pages 108–112). (Author)

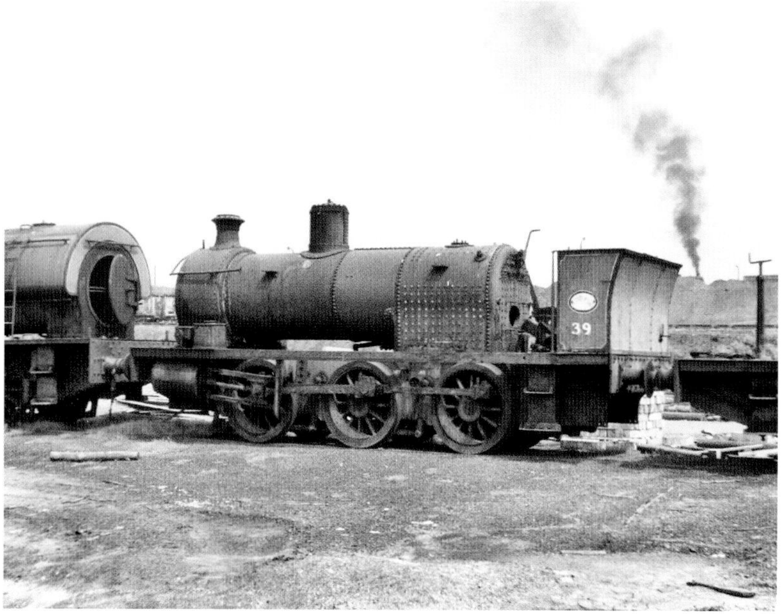

Left: The forlorn remains of Hawthorn Leslie 0-6-0 tank No. 39 *Frederick* (W/No. 3676), delivered new to Dalton Main Collieries Ltd in 1927, in a line of redundant locos, including a Hunslet Austerity (W/No. 3832 of 1955), at the workshops of the extensive Manvers colliery and coal preparation plant complex at Wath-on-Dearne on 14 June 1969. The remains of the 16 x 24-in. (OC) side tank loco had been disposed of on site between January and April 1970. The penultimate steam loco constructed from new for British industry (also see page 125), Austerity 0-6-0 (IC) saddle tank No. 65 (W/No. 3889 of 1964), is seen shunting in the background, maintaining a solitary working steam presence at Manvers Main at this time, but all too soon this residual steam activity would be no more there. (John Sloane)

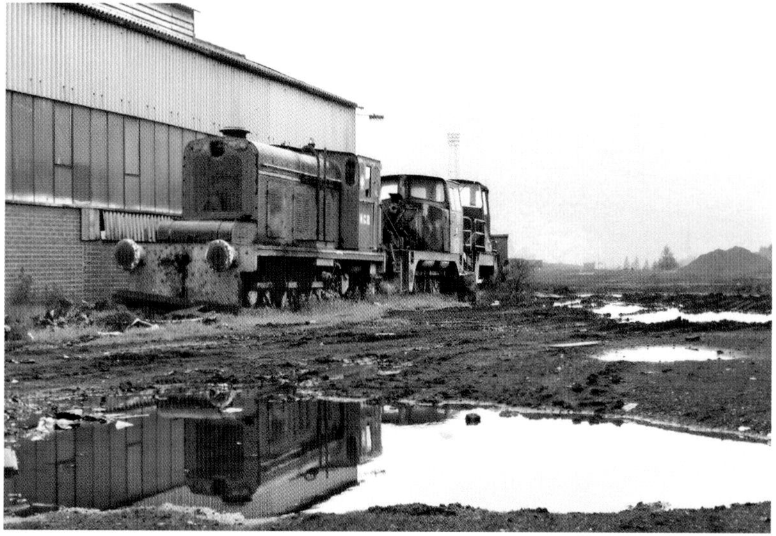

Right: Almost twenty years on from the photo above, on 14 June 1987, Hudswell Clarke 204 hp 0-6-0 diesel-mechanical No. 21 (W/No. D1154 of 1959) awaits collection for scrap, along with two other heavily cannibalised and damaged locos, a Yorkshire Engine 0-6-0 diesel-hydraulic (W/No. 2939 of 1965) and a Hunslet 0-6-0 diesel-hydraulic (No. 7422 of 1976), on what, at first sight, appears to be a desolate part of the Manvers Main complex, but in fact was alongside the main running shed for the complex. All three locos were despatched to C. F. Booth at Rotherham for scrap on 8 April 1988. Despite the apparent desolation, the colliery at Manvers was not to close until the following March, and the coal preparation plant survived for just a short while longer, until March 1989. (Author)

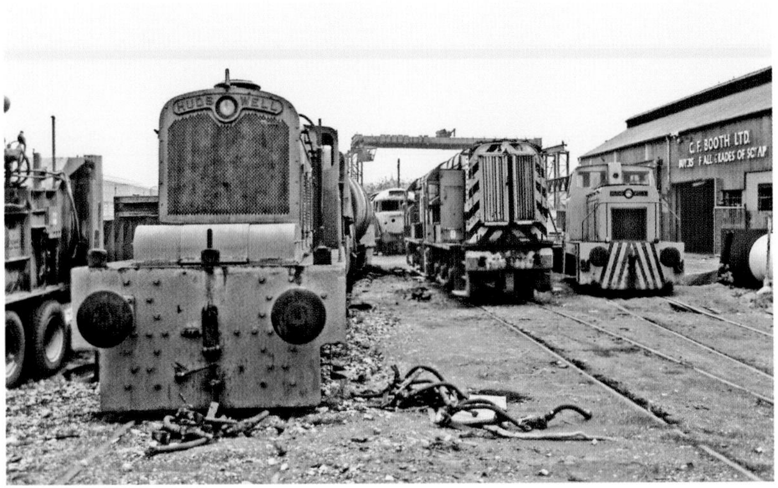

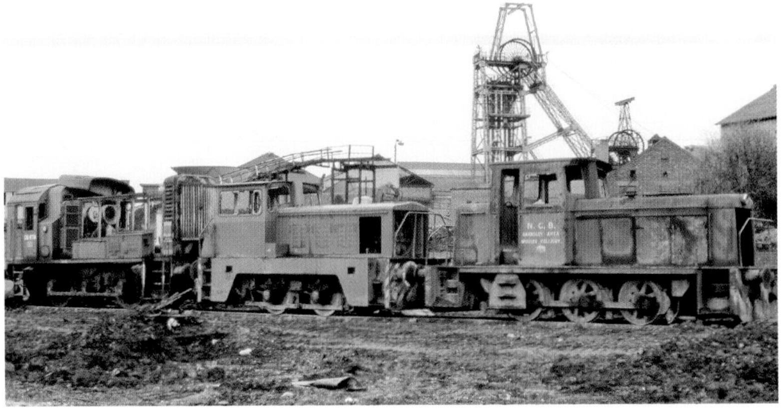

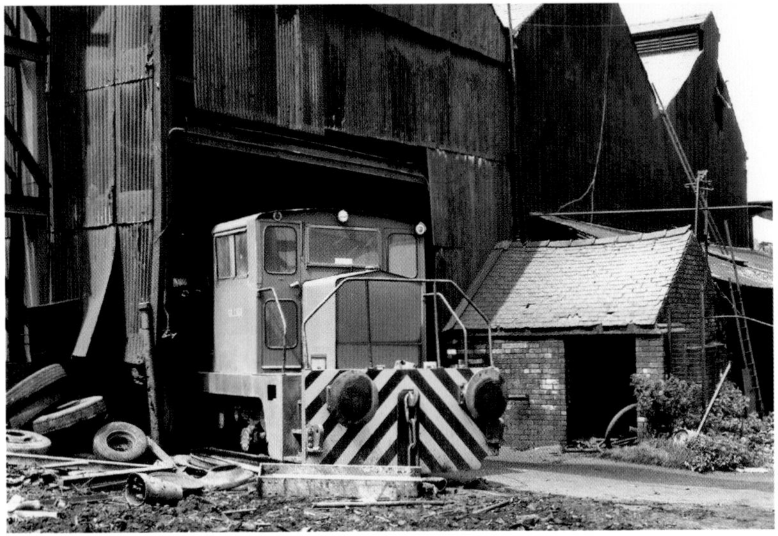

Above left: Innumerable locomotives and rail vehicles of both BR and industrial origin have been disposed of at the Booth Roe (formerly C. F. Booth) Rotherham scrapyard. Offering a flavour of the diversity to be found on visits to the site during the time of this photo, when ex-BR and industrial loco disposals arguably were jointly at their zenith, the line-up on 12 February 1993, viewed from the rather useful public access thoroughfare bisecting the scrapyard, was *Enterprise*, a former prototype 0-6-0 diesel-mechanical built by Hudswell Clarke in 1953 (W/No. D810), BR Class 47 No. 47456, Class 08 No. 08334 and an ex-NCB Shirebrook colliery Hudswell Clarke 0-4-0 diesel-hydraulic (W/No. D1344 of 1965). (Author)

Left: C. F. Booth had a habit of using the best of its industrial loco acquisitions for their own shunting requirements before selling them on for further use in industry or, if they finally refused to turn a wheel, were unceremoniously scrapped without further ado. Thomas Hill Vanguard four-wheel diesel-hydraulic *Gillian* (W/No. 182V of 1967), a former resident of NCB Gedling colliery, was one of the more fortunate examples to visit the Rotherham scrapyard; photographed there on 22 May 1989, she was eventually sold on for further use at the Cardiff Maindy wagon works of Powell Duffryn Ltd. (Author)

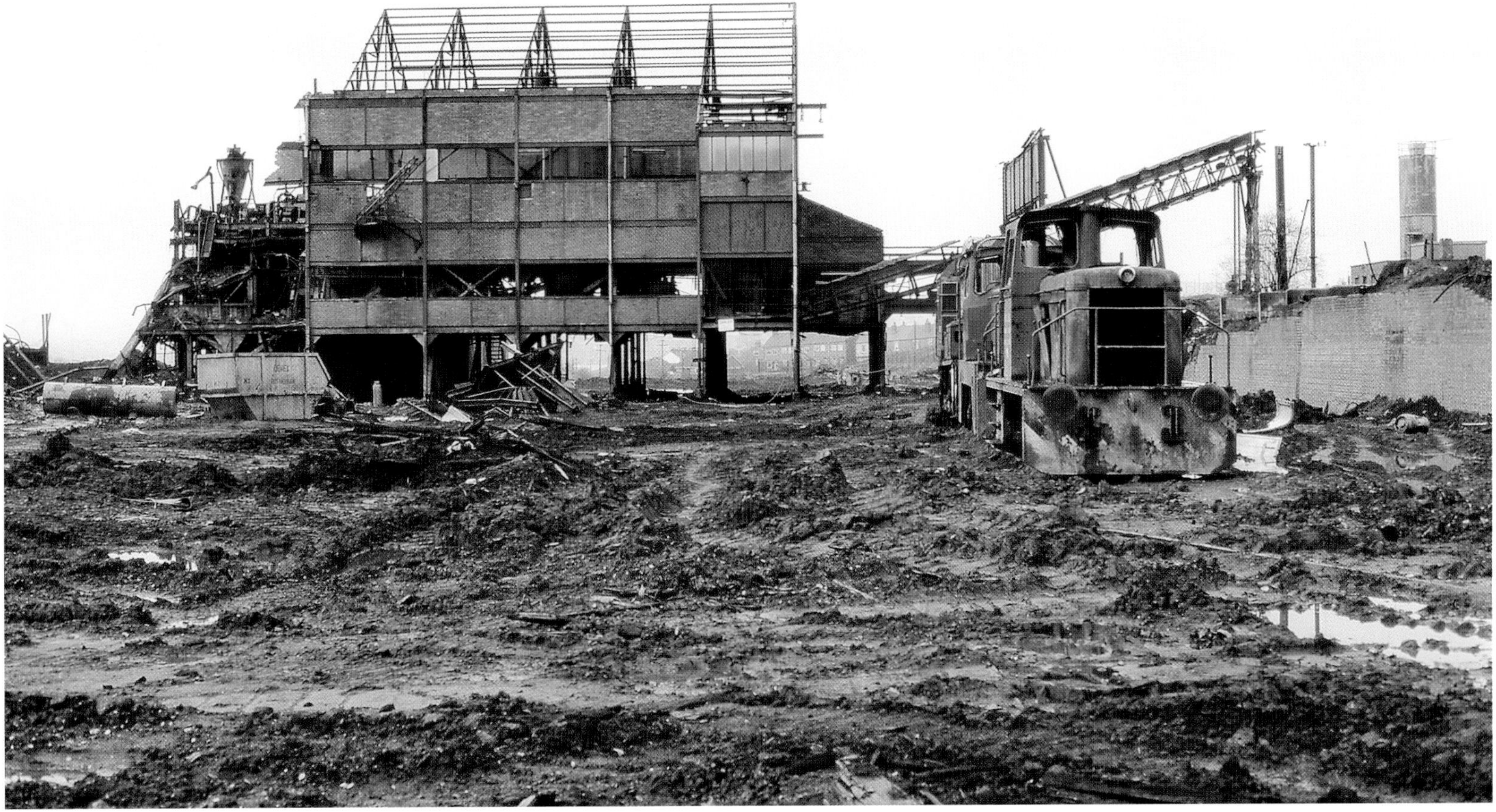

Above and opposite page top right: North Gawber colliery has been featured in Chapter 2, but a visit on 12 April 1986 found the demolition and site clearance process already well in hand following the colliery's output then being wound at Woolley colliery, from January 1986. In this desolate scene are Andrew Barclay 375 hp 0-6-0 diesel-hydraulic *Woolley No. 1* (W/No. 553 of 1969), Thomas Hill 311 hp 4-wheel diesel-hydraulic (W/No.142C of 1964, rebuilt using a frame of a Sentinel vertical boiler steam loco) and former BR 350 hp 0-6-0 diesel-electric No. 08679. All three locos were moved to Booth's at Rotherham during the following week and were to be no more by the end of May 1986. (Roy Burt)

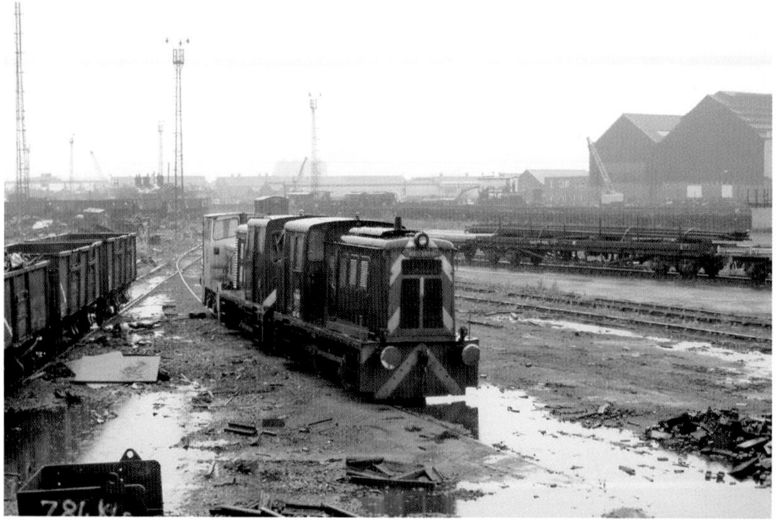

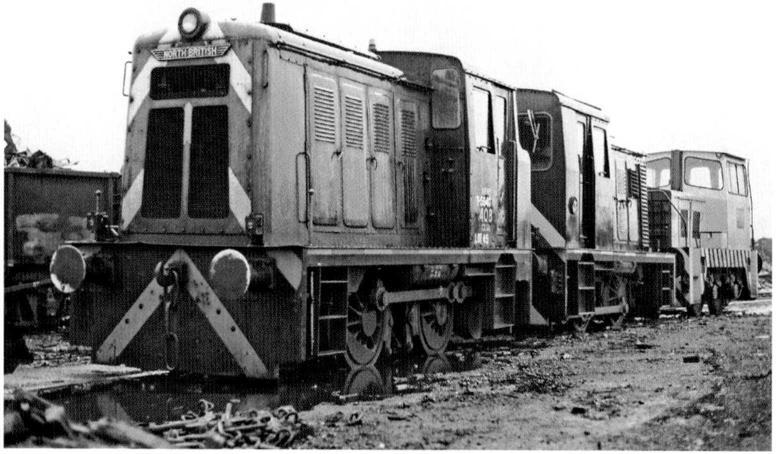

Above and below left: The 'Final Parade' – at 7.00 on the drenching wet morning of 5 June 1985, a visit to the Attercliffe scrapyard of Marple & Gillott Ltd found several former Ministry of Defence Army Department locomotives awaiting disposal. In this line-up are two North British 0-4-0 diesel-hydraulics, Nos 408 (W/No. 27429 of 1955) and 409 (W/No. 27644 of 1959), in the company of the yard shunter of the time, a Thomas Hill Vanguard four-wheel diesel-hydraulic (W/No. 140V of 1964). The scrapyard operations were undertaken on the site of what was originally the Attercliffe Goods Yard of British Railways and at this time the large BR Eastern Region blue rectangular enamel sign was still affixed to the office building at the entrance. (Author)

Opposite page: These massive Andrew Barclay 0-8-0 diesel-hydraulics had seen service on the Kineton and Bicester Military Railways following their ex-works delivery by rail from their Kilmarnock manufacturer between 1964 and 1966. Six of these large 61-ton locos, each equipped with two Cummins NT400 310 hp diesel engines, were supplied to the Ministry of Defence Army Department, who classified them as Class D3SA. The Army Railway Organisation deemed them surplus to requirements just two decades later and no interest in these long wheelbase locos was shown by industry, other than purchase for scrap. Shortly after removal to the Sheffield scrapyard, again by rail and by then with most traces of their former identification painted over, in the line-up awaiting their ultimate fate were: No. 624, formerly named *Royal Pioneer* (W/No. 504 of 1965) and still bearing a wreath from its final day in operation with the military; No. 622, formerly named *Greensleeves* (W/No. 502 of 1965); No. 620, formerly named *Sapper* (W/No. 500 of 1964); and No. 623, formerly named *Storeman* (W/No. 503 of 1965). (Author)

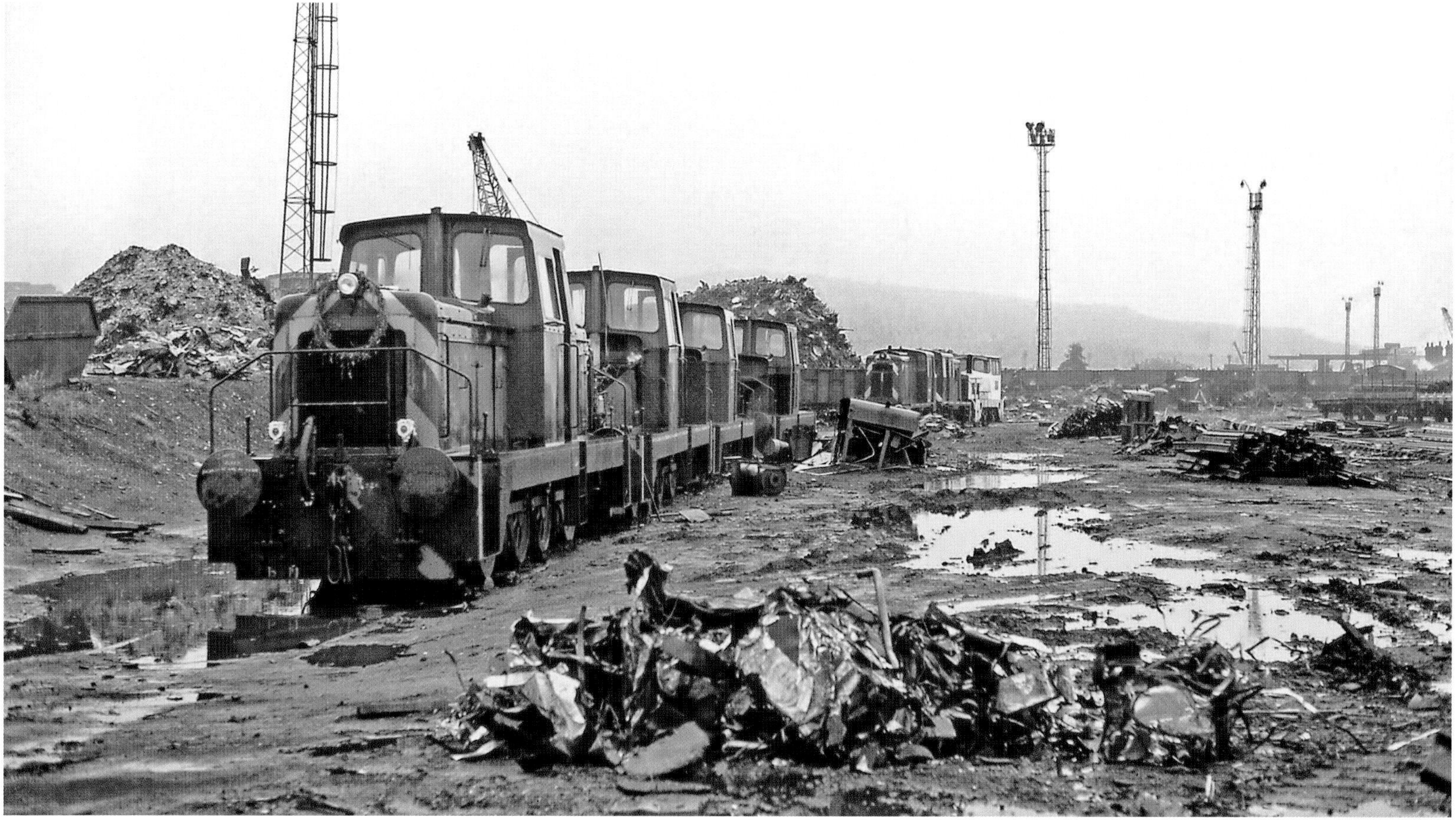

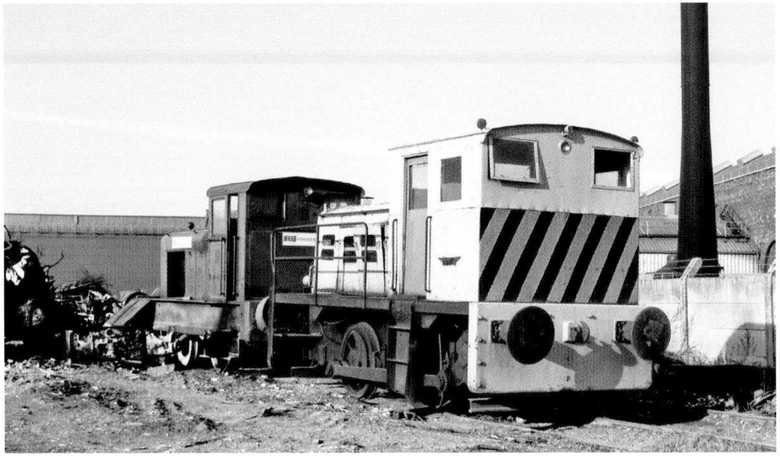

Right: A John Fowler 0-4-0 diesel-mechanical (W/No. 4210056 of 1951), ex-CEGB Barrow-in-Furness power station, and a Ruston & Hornsby 88DS Class four-wheel diesel-mechanical (W/No. 458952 of 1960) at T. W. Ward's scrapyard, Tinsley, on 24 April 1985. (Author)

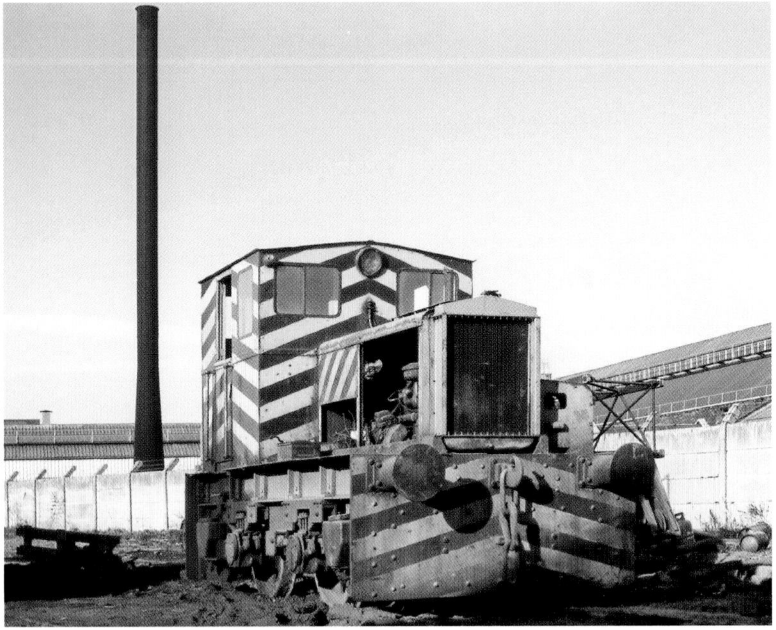

Left: Also languishing at the Tinsley scrapyard premises of T. W. Ward during the same visit on 24 April 1985 was a Frank Hibberd 77 hp Planet four-wheel diesel-mechanical (W/No. 3677 of 1954) on hire from the adjacent Tinsley Wire Industries Ltd factory. (Author)

Opposite page: The wholesale decimation of the mining industry in Britain during the 1980s is only too evident in this scene of these former NCB shunters awaiting the cutter's torch at the Roe Brothers Meadowhall, Sheffield, scrapyard on 17 November 1985. All originated from North Derbyshire Area collieries, and in the line-up awaiting their fate were English Electric Vulcan Works 0-4-0 diesel-hydraulic No. DL19 (W/No. D922 of 1965) from Bolsover colliery, Ruston & Hornsby 0-4-0 diesel-hydraulic No. DL8 (W/No. 468047 of 1962) from Renishaw Park colliery, English Electric Vulcan Works 0-6-0 diesel-hydraulic No. DL21 (W/No. D1196 of 1967) from Pleasley colliery, Ruston & Hornsby 0-4-0 diesel-hydraulic No. DL6 *Whitwell Warrior* (W/No. 466620 of 1962) from Whitwell colliery, Sentinel four-wheel diesel-hydraulics Nos DL23 (W/No. 10163 of 1963) and DL22 (W/No. 10141 of 1962), both from Arkwright colliery, and English Electric Darlington Works 0-4-0 diesel-hydraulic No. DL20 (W/No. 8448 of 1963) from Bolsover colliery. The company's yard shunter, a Thomas Hill Vanguard (W/No. 158C of 1965), is on the right. (Author)

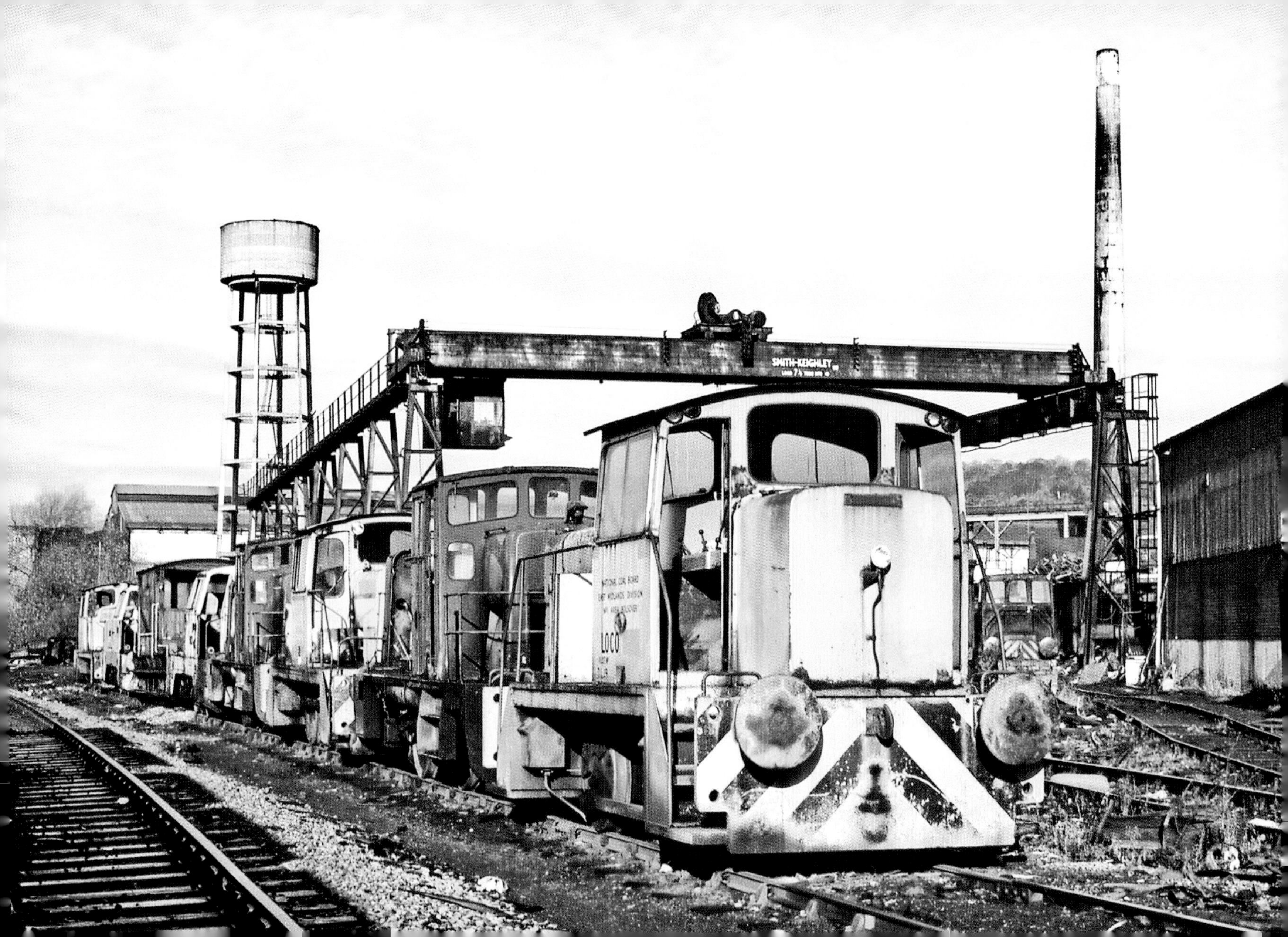
SMITH-KEIGHLEY
NATIONAL COAL BOARD
EAST MIDLANDS DIVISION
LOCO

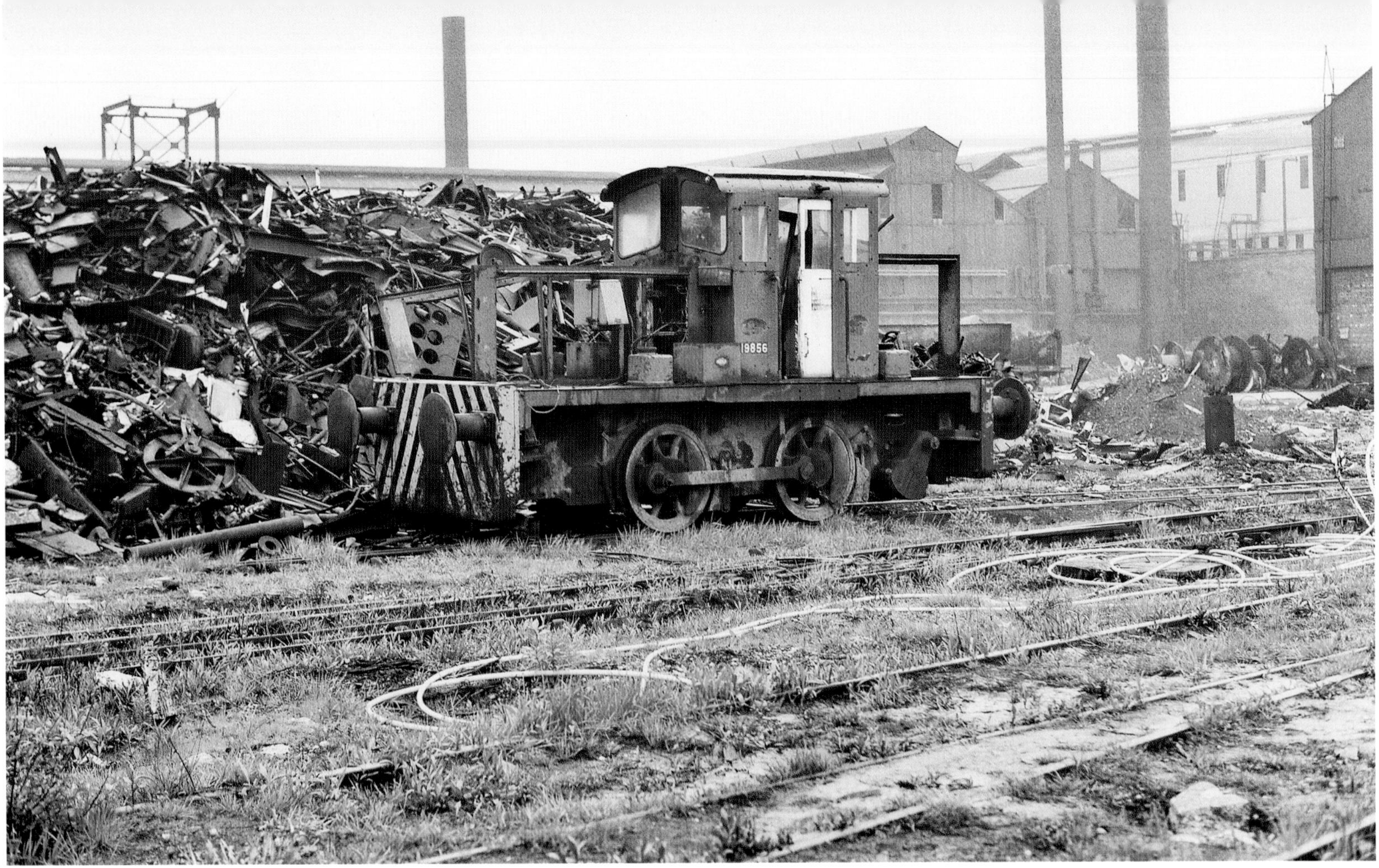

The dismantled remains of John Fowler 0-4-0 diesel-hydraulic No. 19856 (W/No. 4200007 of 1946) at Hadfields Ltd, East Hecla Works, Tinsley, Sheffield, on 10 May 1981. This loco had been subject to a rebuild at Thomas Hill's Kilnhurst works in 1962, being allocated their works number 116C when turned out. Hadfields, founded in 1869, was renowned for its quality castings for wheels, axles, cylinders and other machinery used on the railways, and steel shells for military munitions. The over-capacity of the British steel industry in the 1980s forced the, by then much-contracted, Hadfields business to finally close in 1983. Most of the former site is now covered by the Meadowhall retail shopping complex. (John Sloane)

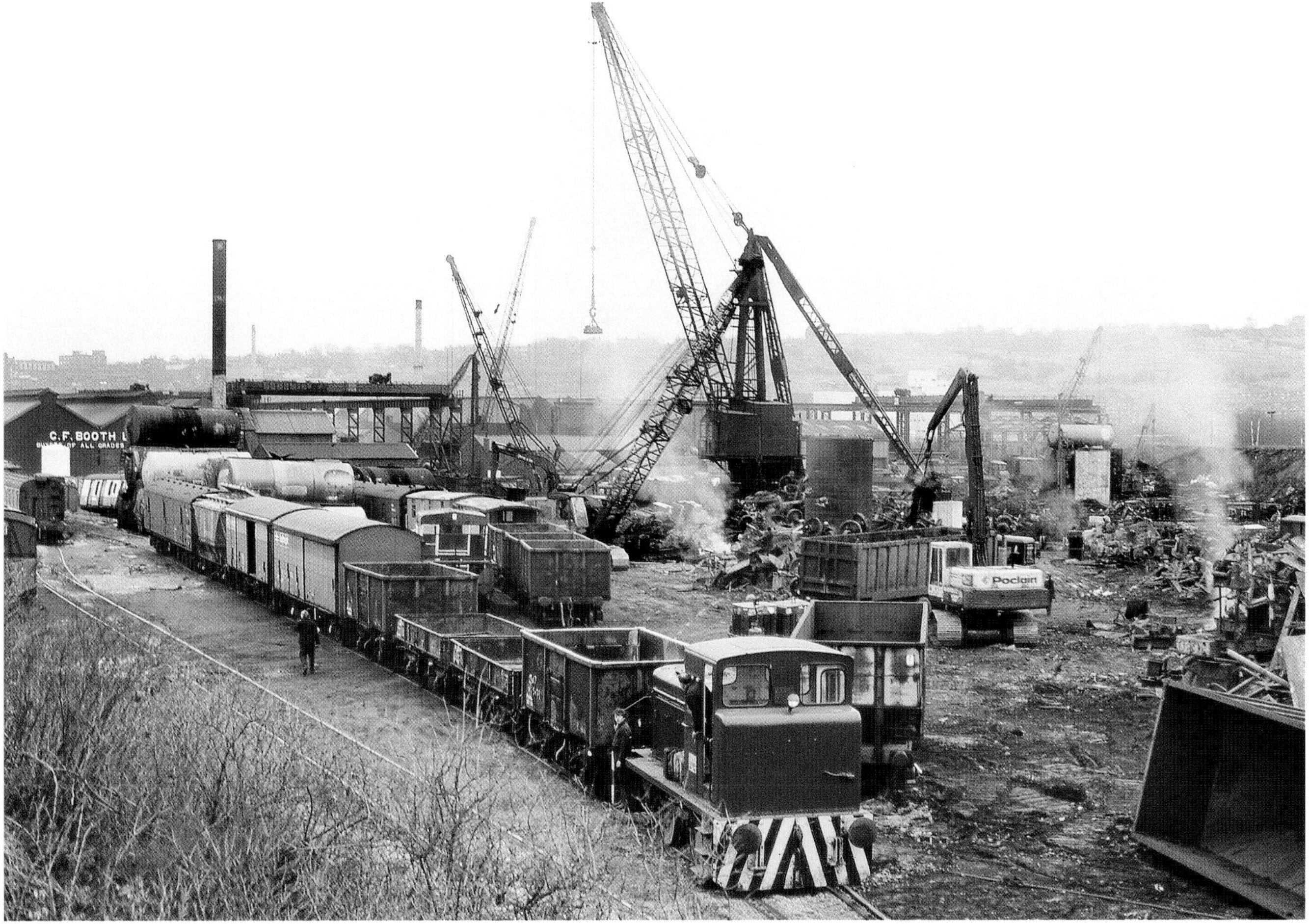

C. F. Booth's scrap business has been much referred to in this publication, the company having disposed of many surplus main line and industrial railway locos and rolling stock, and even continues to do so today. An elevated viewpoint of their extensive Rotherham scrapyard site on 18 November 1988 found an Andrew Barclay 0-4-0 diesel-hydraulic (W/No. 478 of 1963) moving a variety of ex-BR rolling stock into position for disposal. (Roy Burt)

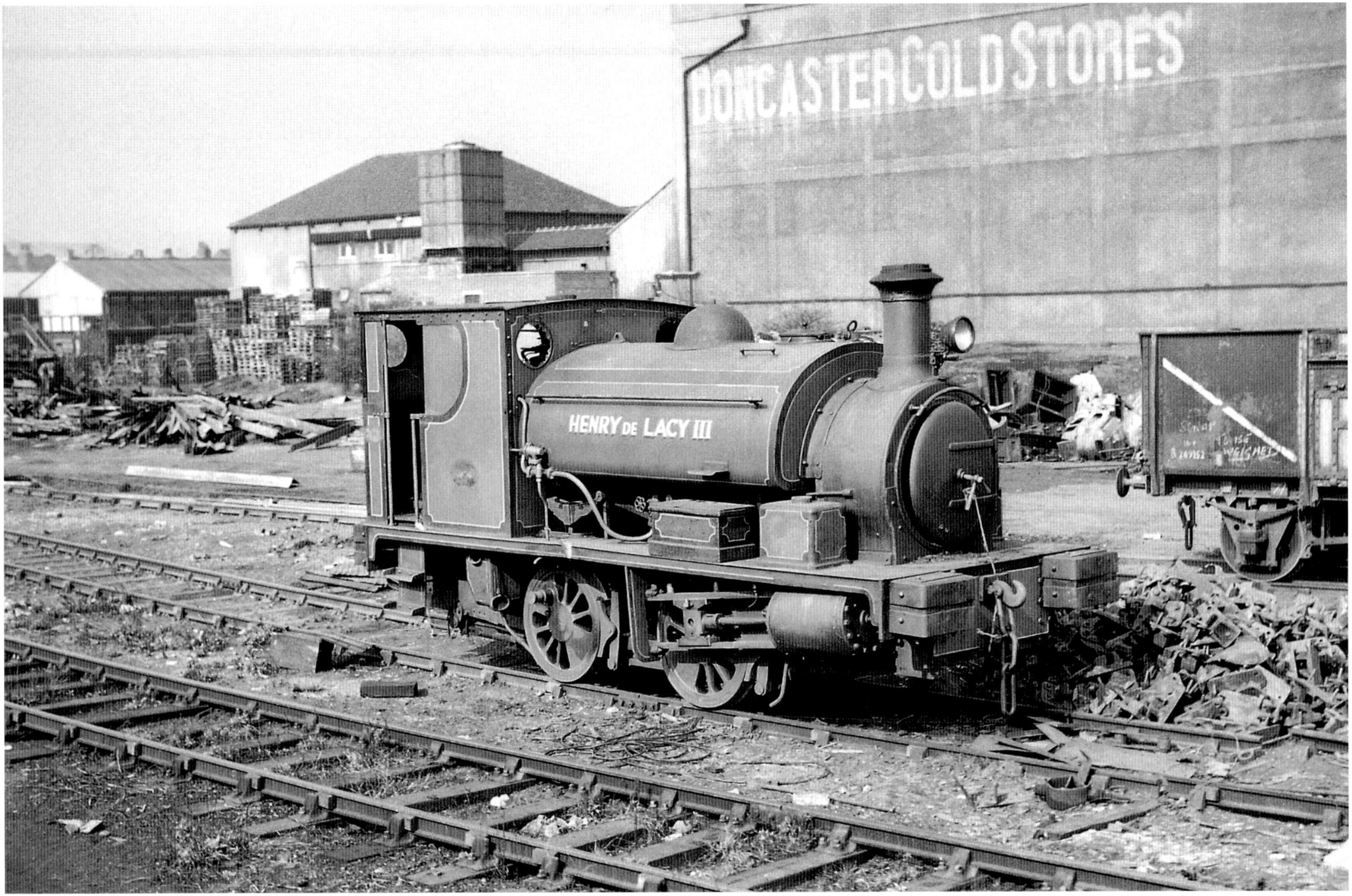
DONCASTER COLD STORES
HENRY DE LACY III

8

IRON, STEEL & ENGINEERING

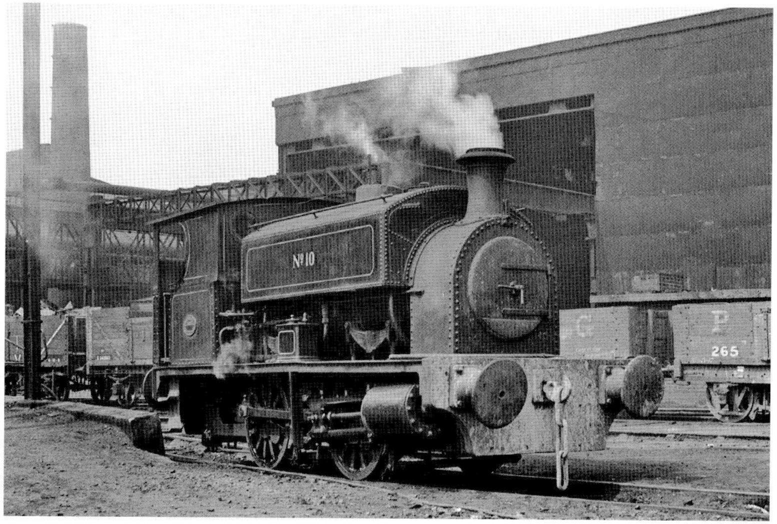

Opposite page: Hudswell Clarke 14 x 20-in. (OC) 0-4-0 saddle tank *Henry de Lacy III* (W/No. 1716 of 1940) awaiting cutting up at the Cherry Tree depot of Thos. W. Ward Ltd at Doncaster in April 1968. It was supplied new to Kirkstall Forge Engineering Ltd near Leeds, and worked alongside an older sister Hudswell Clarke, which has survived into preservation at the heritage Middleton Railway. (Author's collection)

Right: Markham 14 x 21-in. (OC) 0-4-0 saddle tank No. 10 (built in 1909) at Park Gate Iron & Steel Co. Ltd, Rotherham. Markham (and their predecessors, Olivers) built only nineteen locos between 1889 and 1914, eight going to Yorkshire collieries and steelworks. No. 10, along with her two sisters, No. 11 and No. 12, were the last three built by this small Chesterfield manufacturer, working exclusively at the Rotherham steelworks alongside other better-known four-coupled products from Manning Wardle, Andrew Barclay, Avonside and Sentinel. No. 10 was unceremoniously scrapped in February 1961, although happily one example built for the Staveley Coal & Iron Company in 1894 is extant today, on static display at the Midland Railway Centre at Butterley. The former Park Gate works is the site of today's Aldwarke works of Liberty Steel, producing high-quality speciality steels. (Kevin Lane collection)

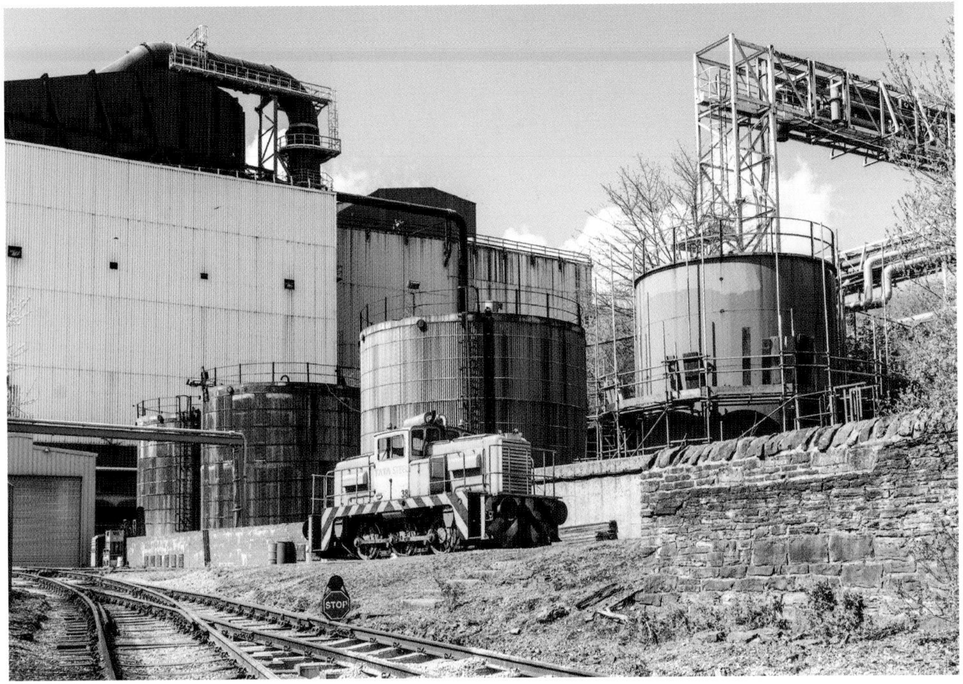

The heavy steel industry in South Yorkshire, traditionally having been centred around Sheffield and Rotherham, is sadly but a shadow of its former self; in fact, the industry countrywide employs just one tenth of its 1960s workforce. Following a near collapse in 2016, due to a combination of a flood of imports, an unfavourable exchange rate and high energy costs at home, happily the future is now looking brighter for the British steel industry. Gone are the heavy mills with their extensive internal rail systems and locomotive fleets, such as at Tinsley Park, River Don, Ickles and Templeborough works, but happily Aldwarke and Stocksbridge have weathered the storm and, now in the hands of Liberty Speciality Steels, continue to produce high-value speciality steels chiefly for the aerospace and oil and gas exploration markets, relying on traditional rail transport for their logistical supply chain solutions. Although steelmaking ceased at Stocksbridge in July 2005, much of the original works has been retained as a finishing plant for the high-value steels. Consequently, the original Stocksbridge Railway connection remains in use to this day, connected to the former Woodhead route at Deepcar. This is an essential link, accepting traffic from the main line rail freight operator at the Ellen Cliffe exchange loop, in the form of steel produced at the company's Aldwarke works, for finishing at Stocksbridge.

This page: TATA Steel's 440 hp Janus Class 0-6-0 diesel-electric No. 38 (W/No. 2798 of 1961) stands on the Bessemer Top line at the north end of the Stocksbridge works in April 2015. Samuel Fox & Co., the original owners of the steelworks, purchased their first Janus loco in 1957, and by 1961 the last steam locos had been displaced by several of these Yorkshire Engine diesels. They remain the choice of Liberty Steels' motive power in the twenty-first century, both at Stocksbridge and Aldwarke, although at the time of this visit, in the ownership of TATA, just three were required at the Stocksbridge works, with two usually seeing daily use. The locos are rotated between Stocksbridge and Aldwarke, the latter works being where all heavy repairs are carried out. This Janus was the final loco to be allocated specifically to the Stocksbridge Railway duties between 1986 and the late 1990s, when the rail company was finally dissolved. It is believed to have been equipped with the additional roof-mounted exhaust baffles, which it still carries, during this period of service. (Author)

Opposite page: Also in April 2015, TATA's blue and white sign said it all – 'Total Quality'. Shortly before the company was happily acquired by Liberty Speciality Steels, Yorkshire Engine 440 hp 0-6-0 diesel-electric (W/No. 2635 of 1957) moves a loaded billet wagon out of No. 2 Melting Shop. This veteran Janus Class loco, claiming over six decades of arduous service in the steel industry in Yorkshire, is the oldest Yorkshire Engine-manufactured diesel loco remaining in British industrial service today. (Author)

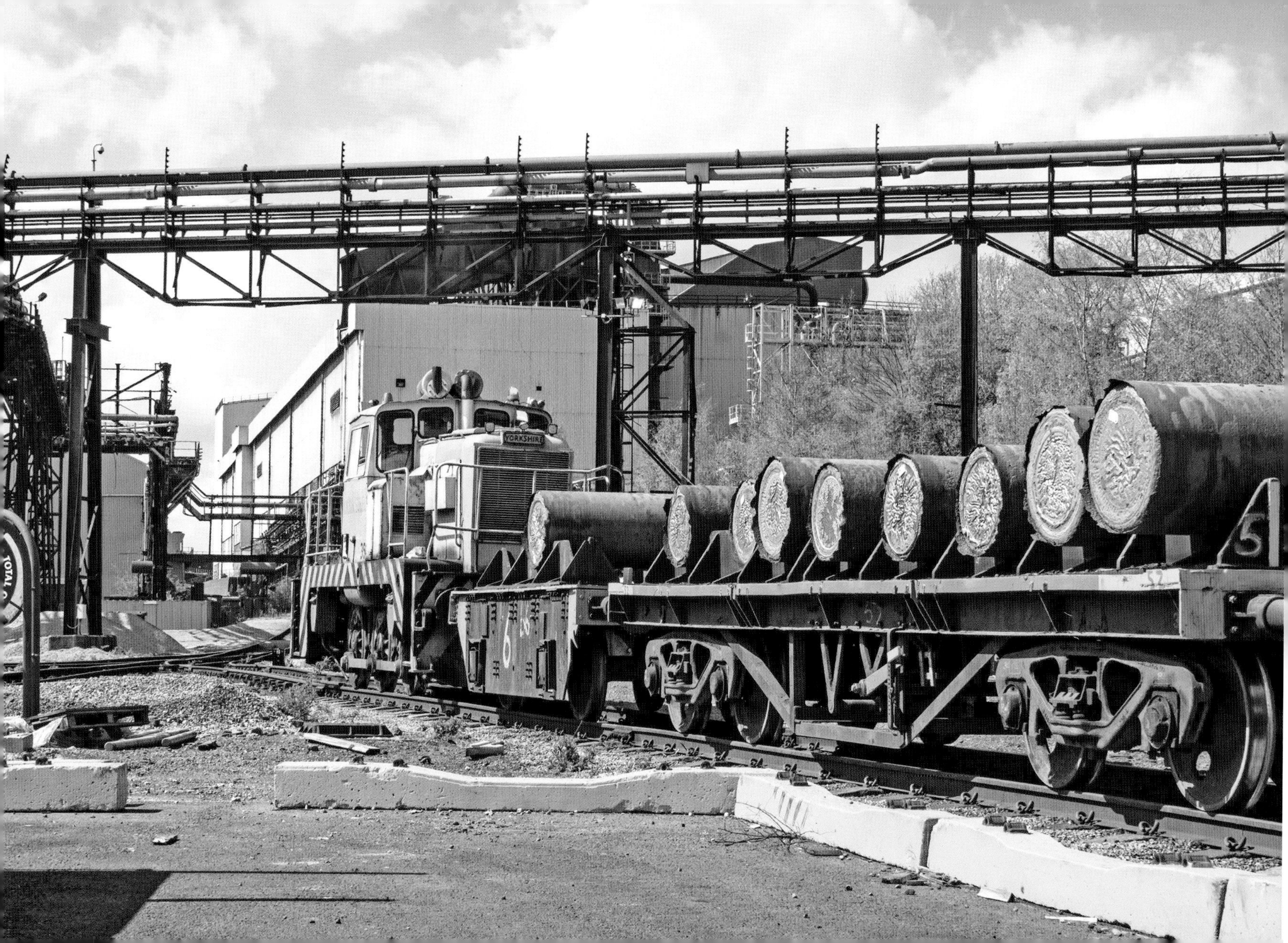
YORKSHIRE

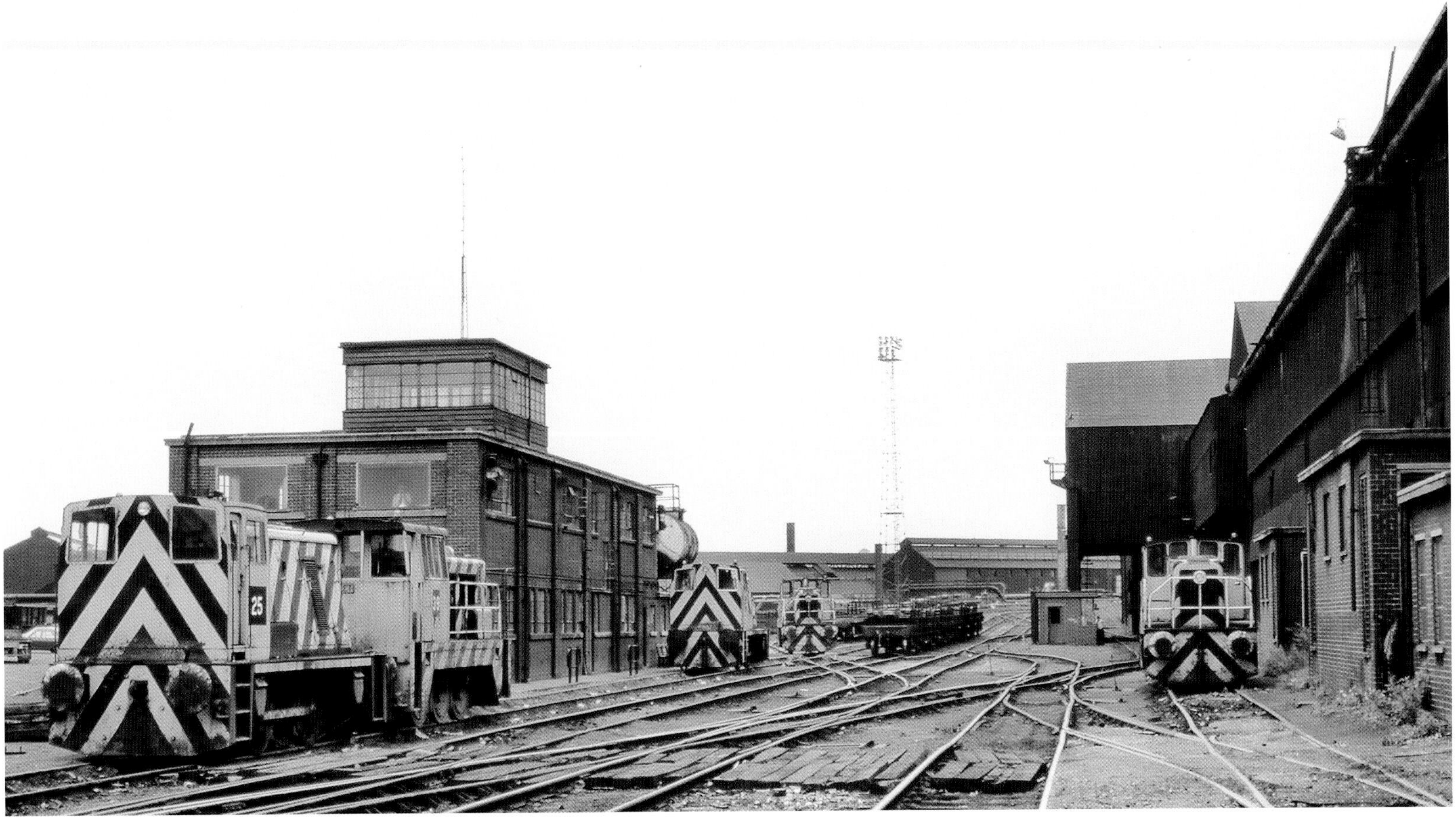

The control tower and main internal railway yard at the British Steel Corporation (BSC) Templeborough works on 23 July 1982. From left to right are Yorkshire Engine 0-4-0 diesel-electric No. 25 (W/No. 2861 of 1962), Hunslet 0-6-0 diesel-hydraulic No. 39 (W/No. 7004 of 1971), Yorkshire Engine 0-4-0 diesel-electric No. 24 (W/No. 2860 of 1962), Yorkshire Engine 0-6-0 diesel-electric No. 31 (W/No. 2904 of 1964) and Yorkshire Engine 0-6-0 diesel-electric No. 32 (W/No. 2935 of 1964). With the fourteen open-hearth furnaces being replaced by six electric-arc furnaces in the 1950s, it became the largest electric-arc steelmaking plant in the world. The steelworks finally closed in 1993 and part of the site has been converted into the Magna Science Adventure Centre. (Roy Burt)

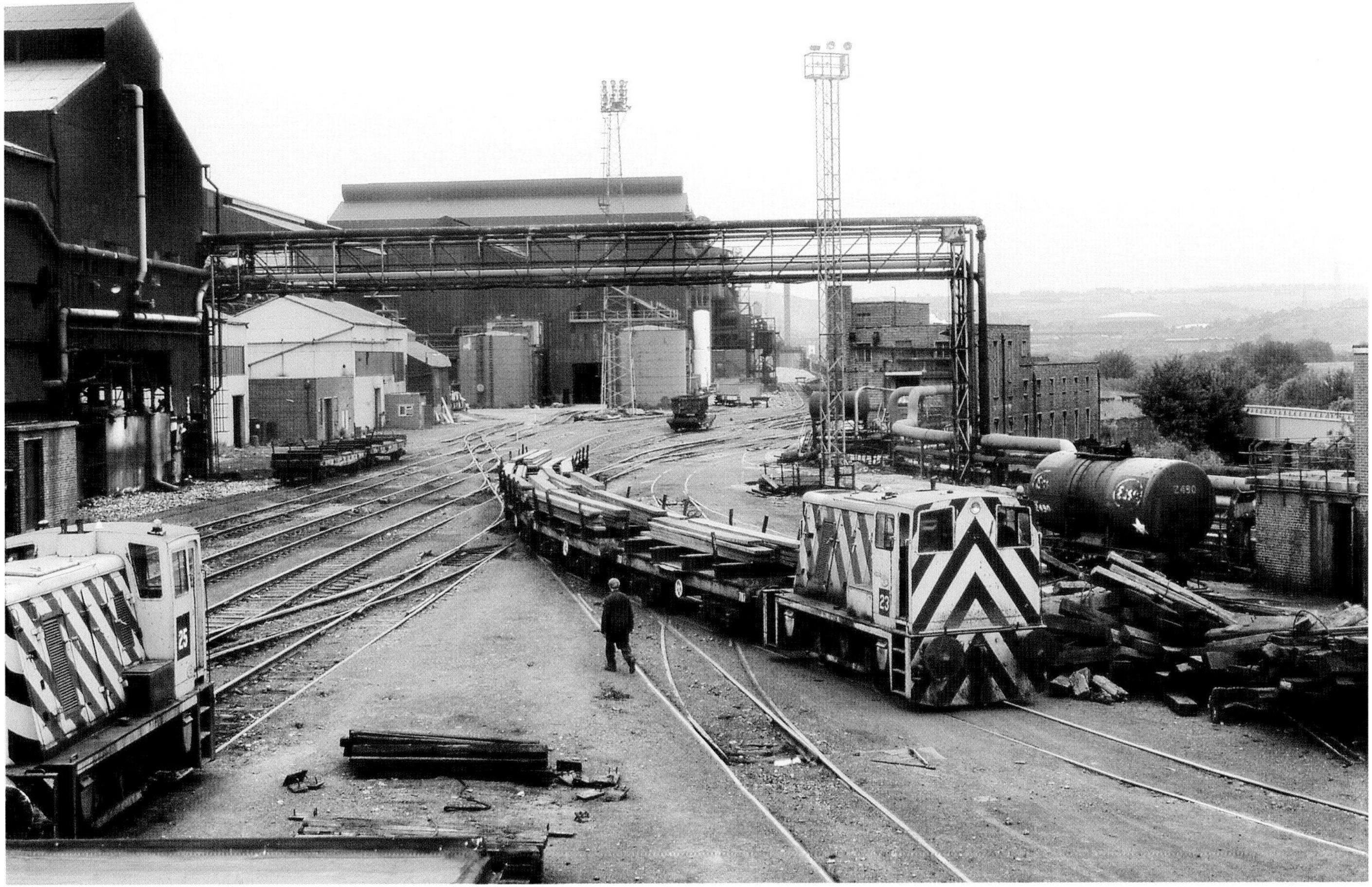

An overview from the BSC Templeborough steelworks railway operations control tower on 23 July 1982, with Yorkshire Engine 0-4-0 diesel-electric No. 23 (W/No. 2786 of 1960) shunting loaded internal bogie-bolster wagons. (Roy Burt)

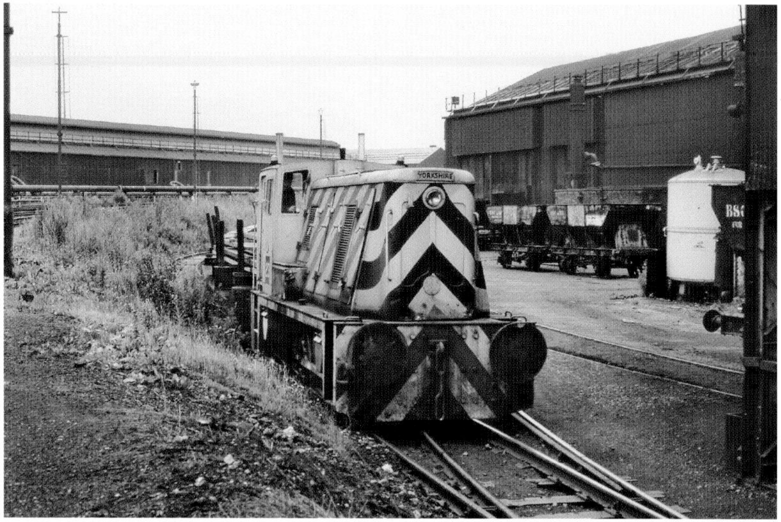

Right: Another view of the classic 275 hp DE2 Class Yorkshire Engine 0-4-0 diesel-electric No. 23 (W/No. 2786 of 1960) stabled between duties at the BSC Templeborough works on 23 July 1982. (Roy Burt)

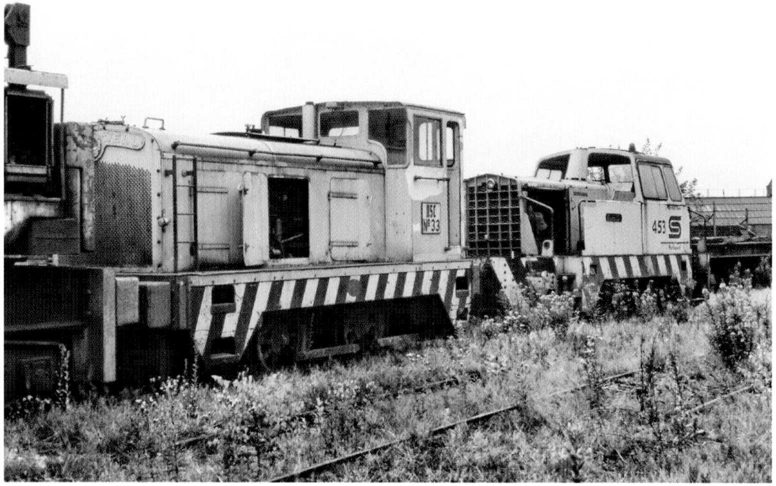

Left: The diesel locomotive products of Hudswell, Clarke & Co. of Leeds were not as commonplace in the Yorkshire steelworks as those supplied by their competitor the Yorkshire Engine Company, perhaps unsurprising with the latter's works located at Meadowhall. The Hudswell Clarke 0-4-0 diesel-mechanical locos at BSC's River Don works, looking somewhat oversized for the four-coupled wheel arrangement, were therefore something of a novelty. By the time of this visit, made on 23 July 1982, *BSC No. 33* (W/No. D817 of 1954) was dumped out of use, along with Sentinel four-wheel diesel-hydraulic No. 453 (W/No. 10025 of 1960).

Opposite page: The final day of rail operations at BSC River Don works, Brightside, Sheffield, on Friday 23 July 1982; Sentinel four-wheel diesel-hydraulic *BSC No. 42* (W/No. 10026 of 1960) crosses Brightside Lane. During 1983 the River Don works of BSC was merged with Firth Brown to form Sheffield Forgemasters, a company specialising in forged cast parts for the engineering, nuclear, petrochemical and process industries worldwide. (Both Roy Burt)

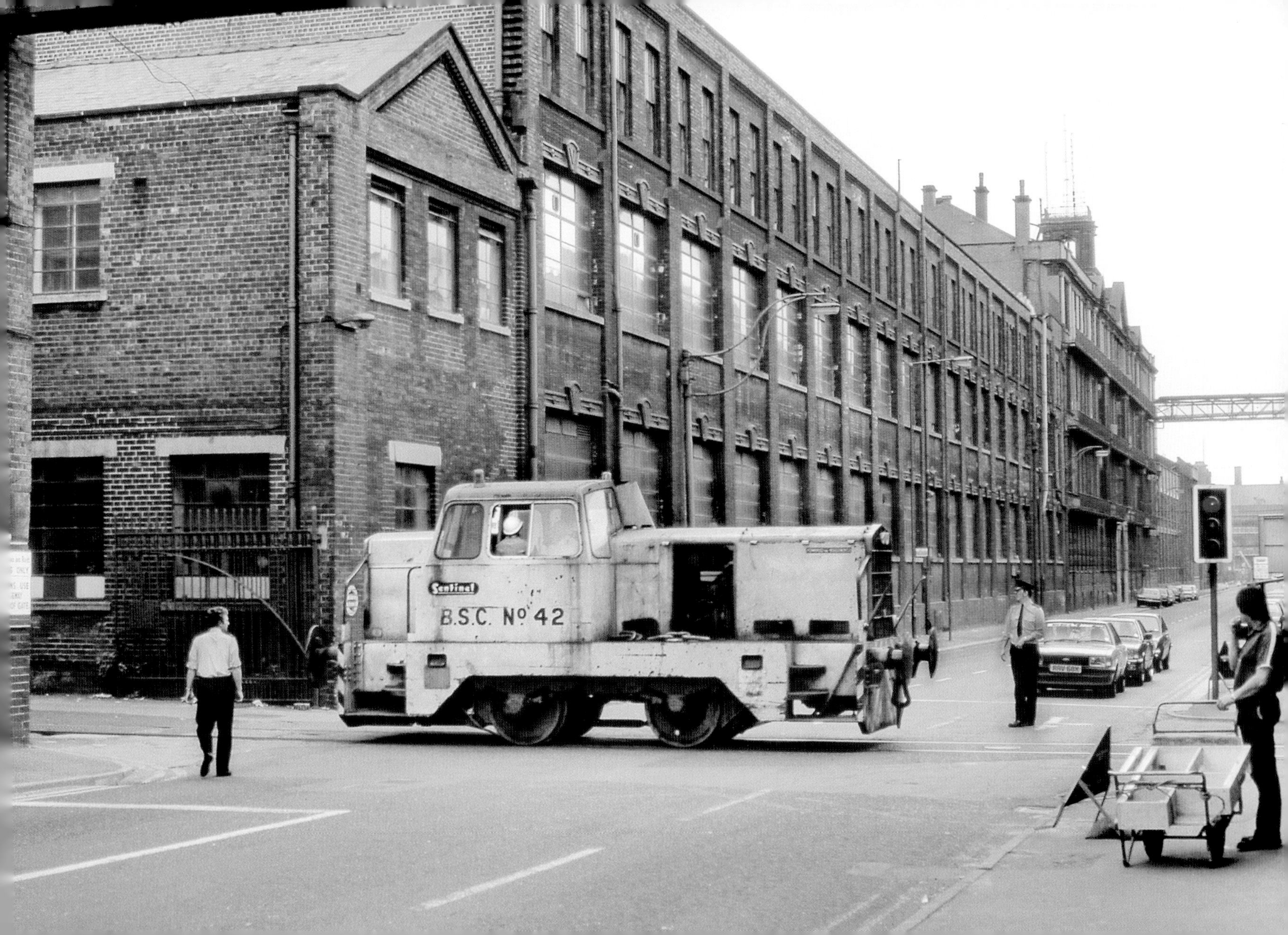
Sentinel
B.S.C. Nº 42

Right: This unique Thomas Hill four-wheel + four-wheel diesel-hydraulic 'master and slave' locomotive (W/Nos 197V and 198V of 1968, for loco and power tender respectively) had been out of use for around three to four years when photographed at BSC Park Gate works on 23 July 1982. The two-section articulated 68-ton chain-drive loco was rated at 2 x 173 hp and was supplied new to the Phoenix works of Steel, Peech & Tozer of Rotherham as a solution for their demand for a powerful loco with an ability to negotiate sharp radius curves. After overhaul in 1973, it was transferred to Park Gate and generally worked between the casting and mould stripping bay with ingot casting flat wagons (see page 99). The solid plate heat shields, to protect the radiators, will be noted fitted to the locos illustrated on these two pages. (Roy Burt)

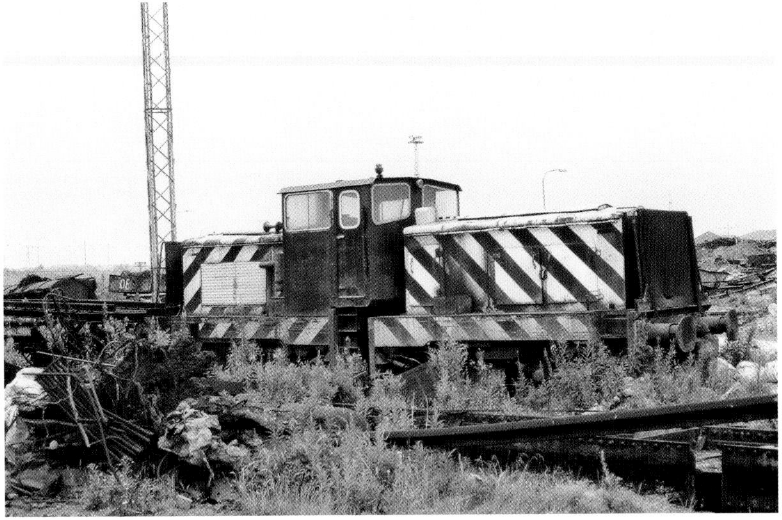

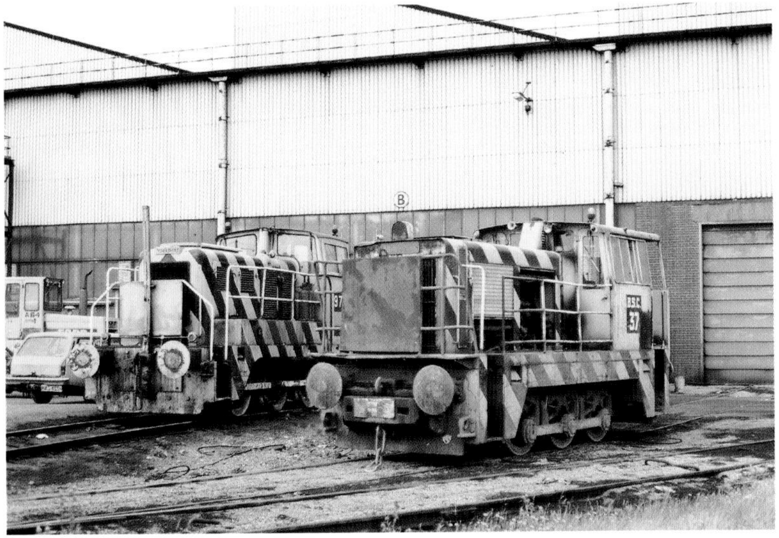

Left: This 1980s scene at Park Gate (now termed the Aldwarke works) is very much the same as that to be found today, apart from these road vehicles! Following several changes of ownership, Aldwarke is now in the hands of Liberty Speciality Steels. The production is closely allied to that conducted at the Stocksbridge works and locos occasionally change location. On 23 July 1982 Yorkshire Engine 0-6-0 diesel-electric No. 97 (W/No. 2906 of 1963), one of the original batch of diesel locos that replaced steam traction at Park Gate, and Hunslet 0-6-0 diesel-hydraulic *BSC 37* (W/No. 7002 of 1971) stand outside the workshop building. Dieselisation came early to the Park Gate Iron & Steel Co. (later BSC), located alongside Rawmarsh junction, when between 1960 and 1968 a fleet of fifteen 230 hp four-coupled Brush/Beyer Peacock diesel-electrics and six Yorkshire Engine 300 hp 0-6-0 diesel-electrics were purchased to replace steam traction. (Roy Burt)

Opposite page: The ingot bay at BSC Aldwarke steelworks on 23 July 1982 with Hunslet 0-6-0 diesel-hydraulic *BSC 41* (W/No. 8805 of 1978), with its barrier wagon, in action with a train of ingots. (Both Roy Burt)

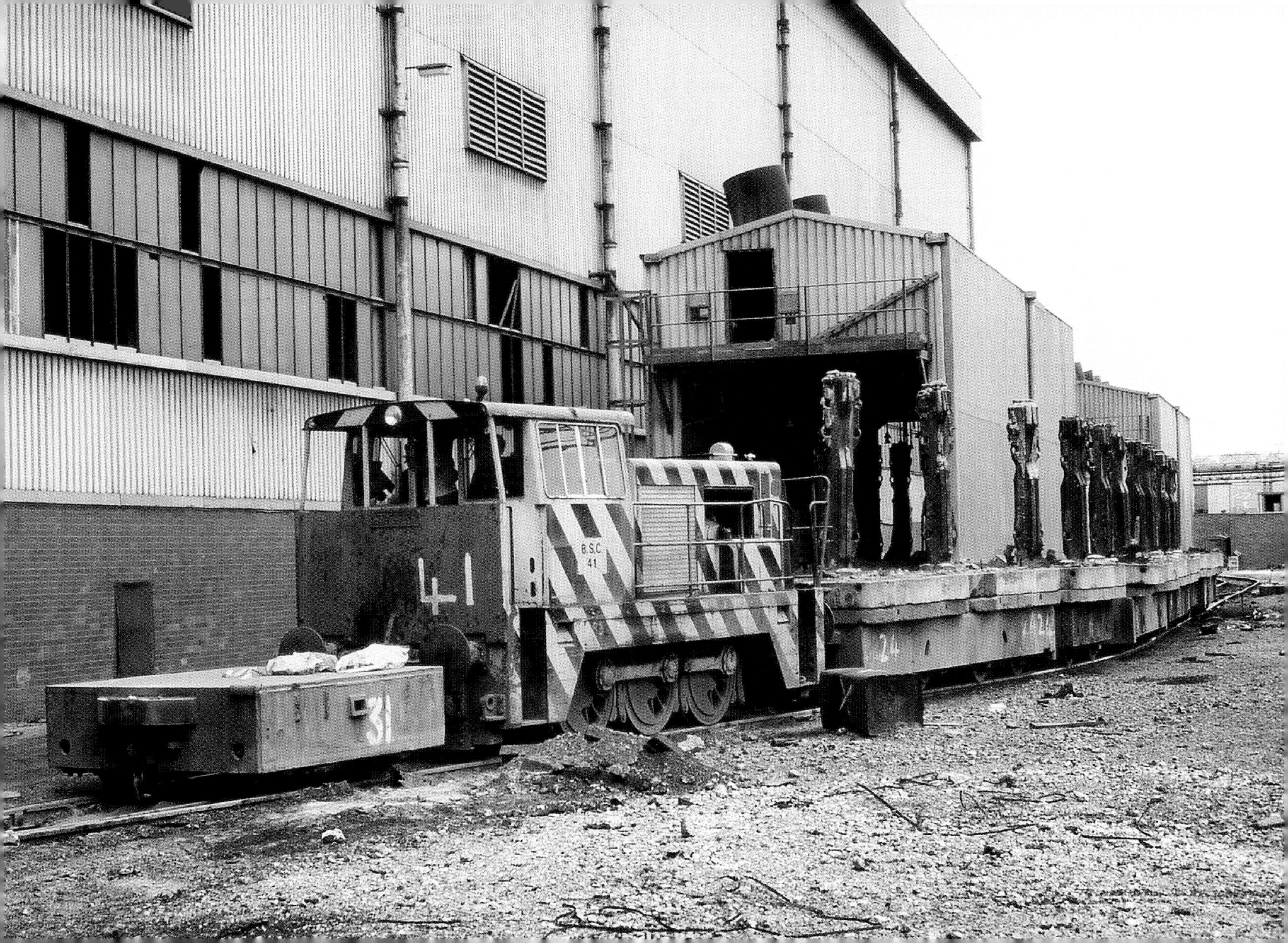
B.S.C.
41
41
31
24

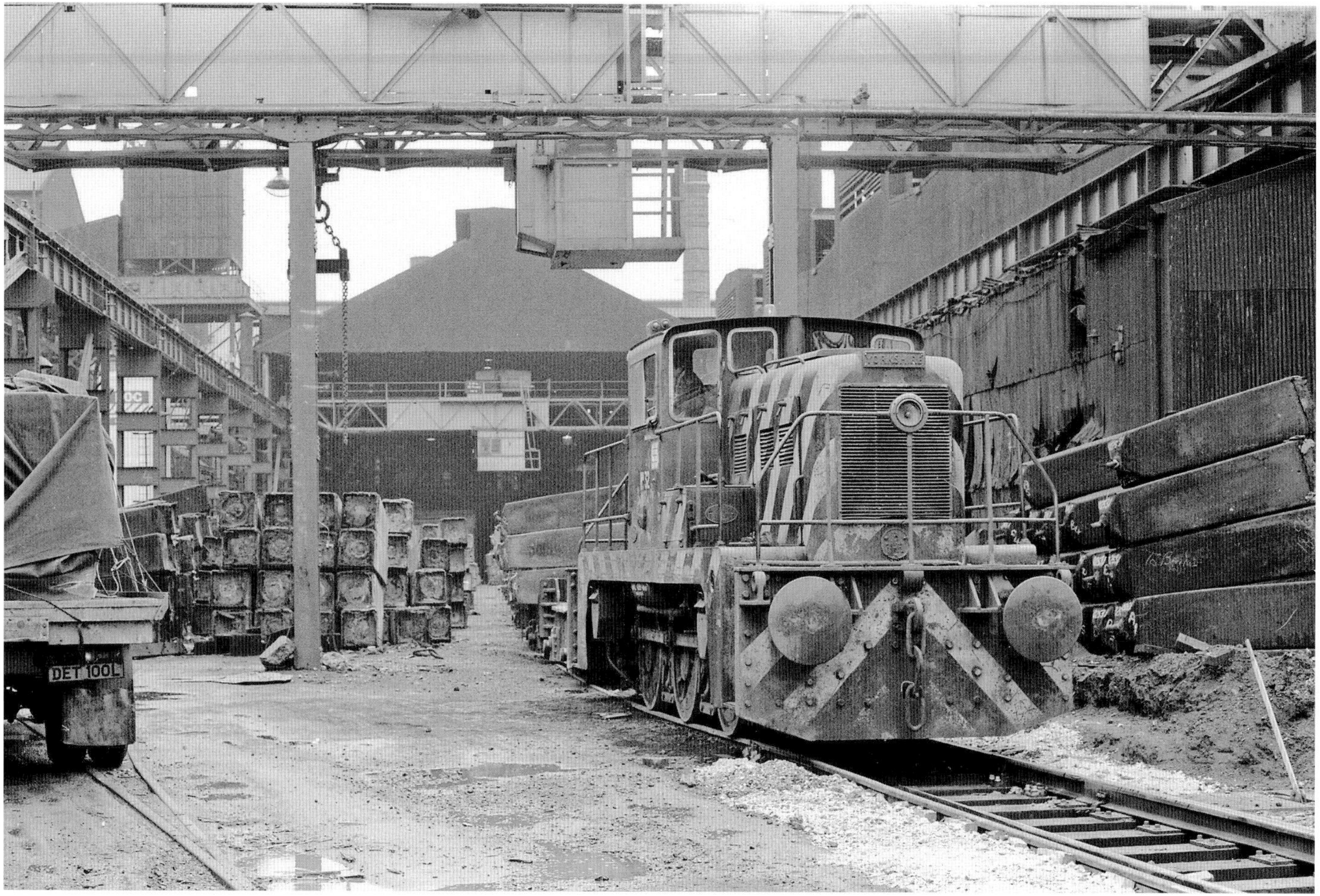

BSC Stocksbridge works on 13 June 1979, with Yorkshire Engine Janus Class 0-6-0 diesel-electric No. 32 (W/No. 2752 of 1959) at work. Today the works, in the ownership of Liberty Speciality Steels, calls on a fleet of just three Janus locos, whereas in the late 1970s sixteen six-coupled locos were to be found at the site. (Kevin Lane)

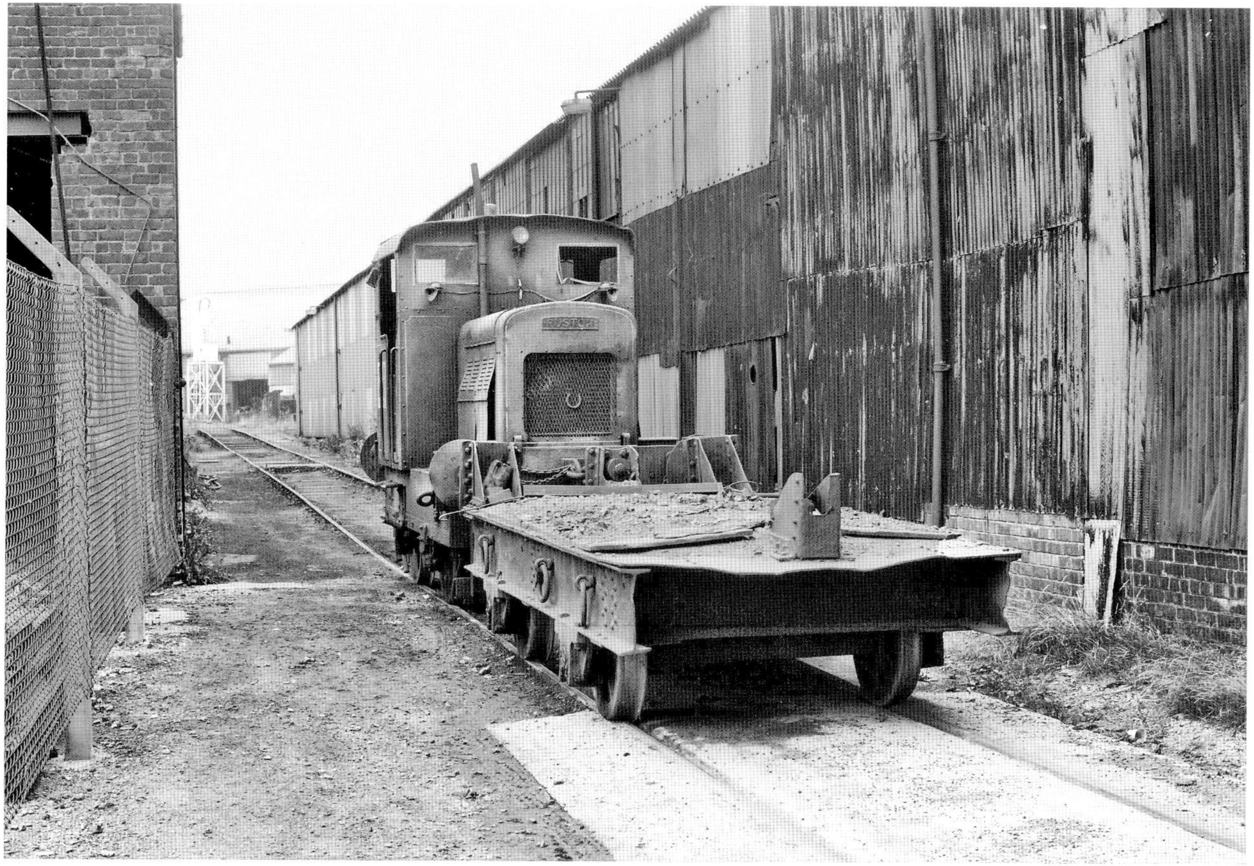

The Blackett Hutton foundry at Guisborough in North Yorkshire had an internal railway system for transporting molten metal in a ladle between the furnace and the foundry. A solitary Ruston & Hornsby 7-ton standard gauge 48DS Class loco (W/No. 265617 of 1948), supplied new to the company, was employed on these duties, and is seen with its solitary flat wagon in September 1986. It is now preserved on the Aln Valley Railway at Alnwick. The foundry commenced work in 1860, initially supplying iron wheels for ore tubs used in the numerous ironstone mines in the area. It closed its doors for the final time in 1997, having in more recent times concentrated on engineering castings, but over the years the foundry had turned its hand to producing such diverse products as First World War mortar shells and castings for bridges, including for the Humber and Forth, as well as work on the Tees Barrage bridge. (Kevin Lane)

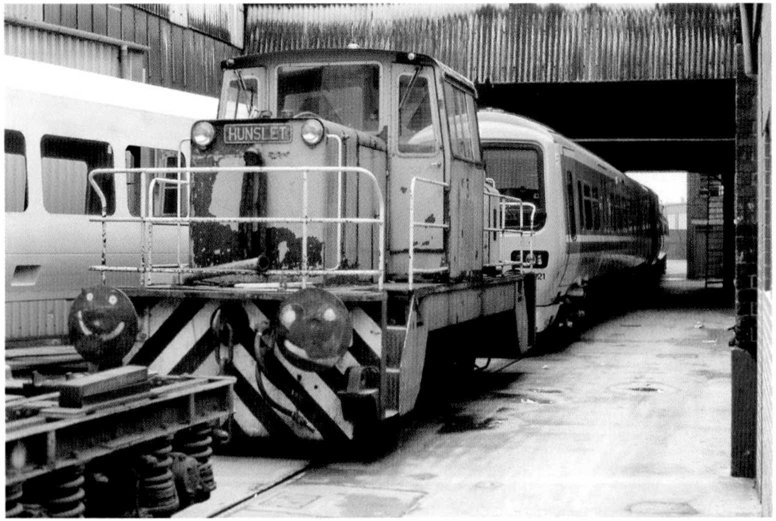

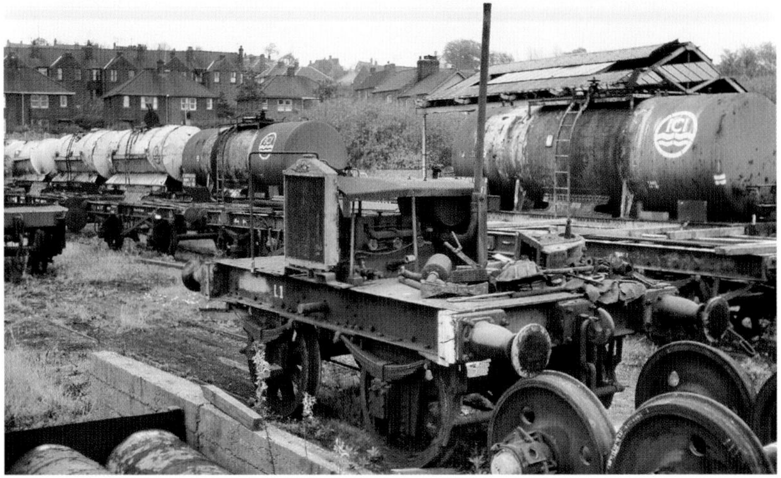

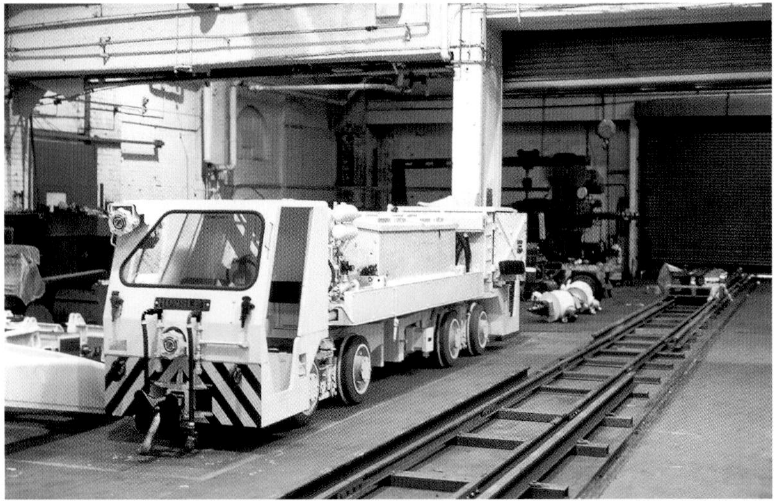

Above left: A former CEGB Carrington power station Hunslet 388 hp 0-6-0 diesel-hydraulic (W/No. 8976 of 1979) as the works shunter at Hunslet TPL, Jack Lane, Leeds, on 21 January 1994. This 388 hp loco, along with its sister from Carrington, are now to be found at the Port of Workington. (Author)

Above: A most unusual contraption, Baguley four-wheel diesel-mechanical No. L1 (W/No. 2082 of 1934), at Wagon Repairs Ltd, Sheepbridge, on 27 October 1977. The dismantled state of the 'tractor locomotive' clearly reveals its six-cylinder 102 hp Albion engine. (Roy Burt)

Left: An Industrial Railway Society visit to Hunslet GMT at Leeds on 21 January 1994 found Hunslet rubber-tyre four-wheel + four-wheel battery-electric *Linzi* (W/No. 9311 of 1992), believed to have been there for repair on behalf of British Coal's Houghton Main colliery. (Author)

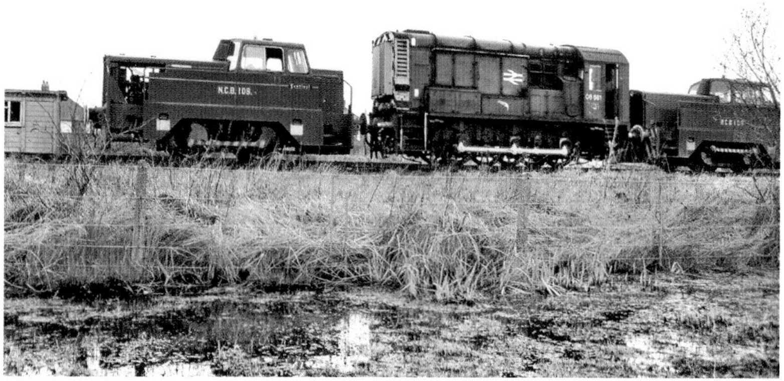

Above: The RFS Engineering Ltd workshops storage siding, alongside the BR Rotherham–Doncaster line at Kilnhurst on 12 February 1993, with 311 hp Sentinel LBH Class 0-4-0 diesel-hydraulic locos from British Coal, Kellingley colliery: *NCB 108* (W/No. 10089 of 1962), *NCB 109* (W/No. 10118 of 1962), and ex-BR No. 08581. Sentinel No. 10089 survives today in industrial service at the Ashford Train Maintenance Centre of Hitachi Rail Europe Ltd in Kent. (Author)

Above right: The compact Thomas Hill (later RFS) works yard at Kilnhurst on 5 August 1971 contained a Frank Hibberd Planet four-wheel diesel mechanical (W/No. 3918 of 1959) from Barium Chemicals Ltd of Widnes, and Sentinel (W/No. 10022 of 1959), en route from APCM Johnson's works in Kent to the company's Dunbar works in East Lothian. BR Class 31 No. D5805 is passing. (Roy Burt)

Right: The RFS yard on 24 January 1990 produced an ex-NCB Baddesley colliery Rolls-Royce Sentinel (W/No. 10212 of 1964) and ex-BR Class 08s Nos 08170 and 08216, along with several other industrial locomotives for repair or parts recovery. The restrictive Kilnhurst works finally closed during 1993, when all stock and work were transferred to RFS's Doncaster works by the August. (Author)

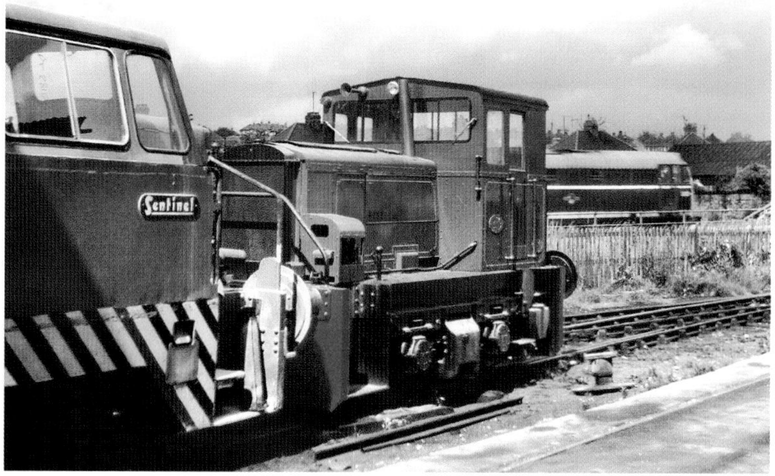

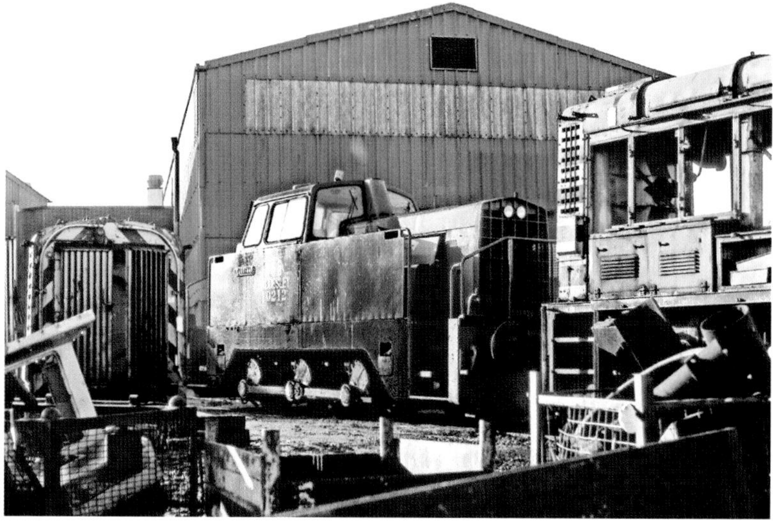

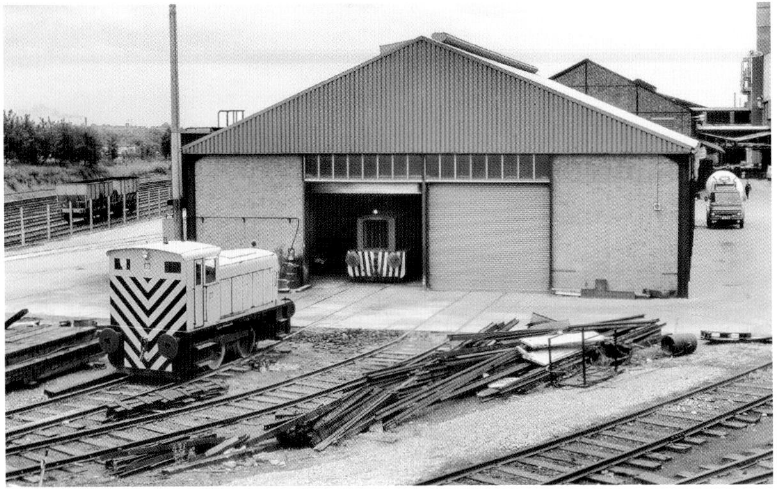

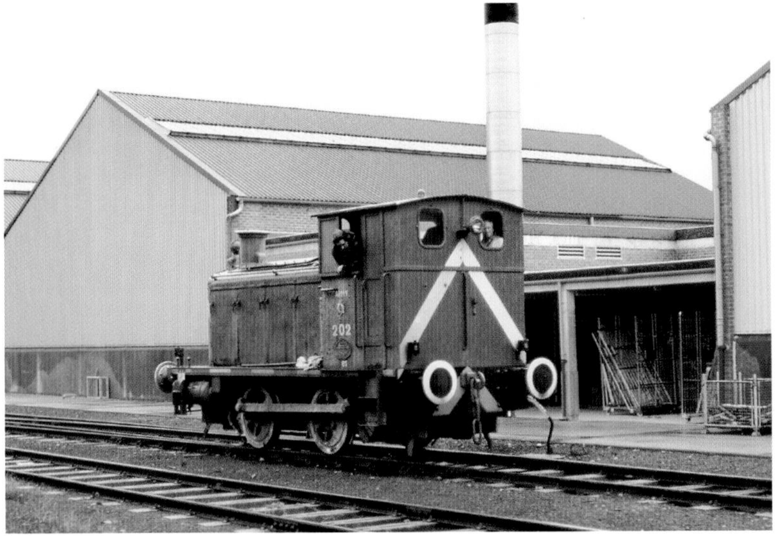

9

INDUSTRIAL MISCELLANY

Left: The British Sugar Corporation's Poppleton factory loco shed in York on 16 August 1982 with the two Ruston & Hornsby shunters; outside was a Class 165DE 0-4-0 diesel-electric (W/No. 395304 of 1956) and inside, transferred from the Selby factory, was a Class 165DS (W/No. 327964 of 1953). In the storage sidings beyond are two LNER-style internal-user hopper wagons, built jointly by Hurst Nelson and Metropolitan Cammell. The Poppleton factory was closed in 2006 and the site has been redeveloped for residential housing. (Roy Burt)

Below left: MoD Army Department Andrew Barclay 193 hp 0-4-0 diesel mechanical No. 202 (W/No. 357 of 1941) at 322 Engineer Park, Hessay, near York, on 16 August 1982. The small storage depot, established during the Second World War, was located on the south side of the York–Knaresborough–Harrogate line and was rail-served until 1991, and for a short time thereafter used as a temporary storage facility for National Railway Museum vehicles. (Roy Burt)

Opposite page: British Oil & Cake Mills (later BOCM Pauls Ltd) Olympia Works at Selby used an internal shunting loco and a rake of internal-user 1930s Charles Roberts-built 20-ton hopper wagons. These were used for transporting raw material at Barlby mill, which produced animal feed and vegetable oil. Some wagons carried LMS registration plates, originating from Bedford Corporation Electricity Department. To the right of the wagons is part of the linseed and rape-seed oil refinery. A wartime John Fowler diesel was replaced by this 1966-built 34 hp 'Trackmobile' road-rail vehicle supplied by Strachan & Henshaw Ltd of Ashton, Bristol, and it is seen at the factory on 4 July 1992. A Mercedes Unimog road-rail vehicle was also acquired in 1982. The mill has since closed and was demolished in July 2012. The site was earmarked for redevelopment for residential housing in 2017. (Author)

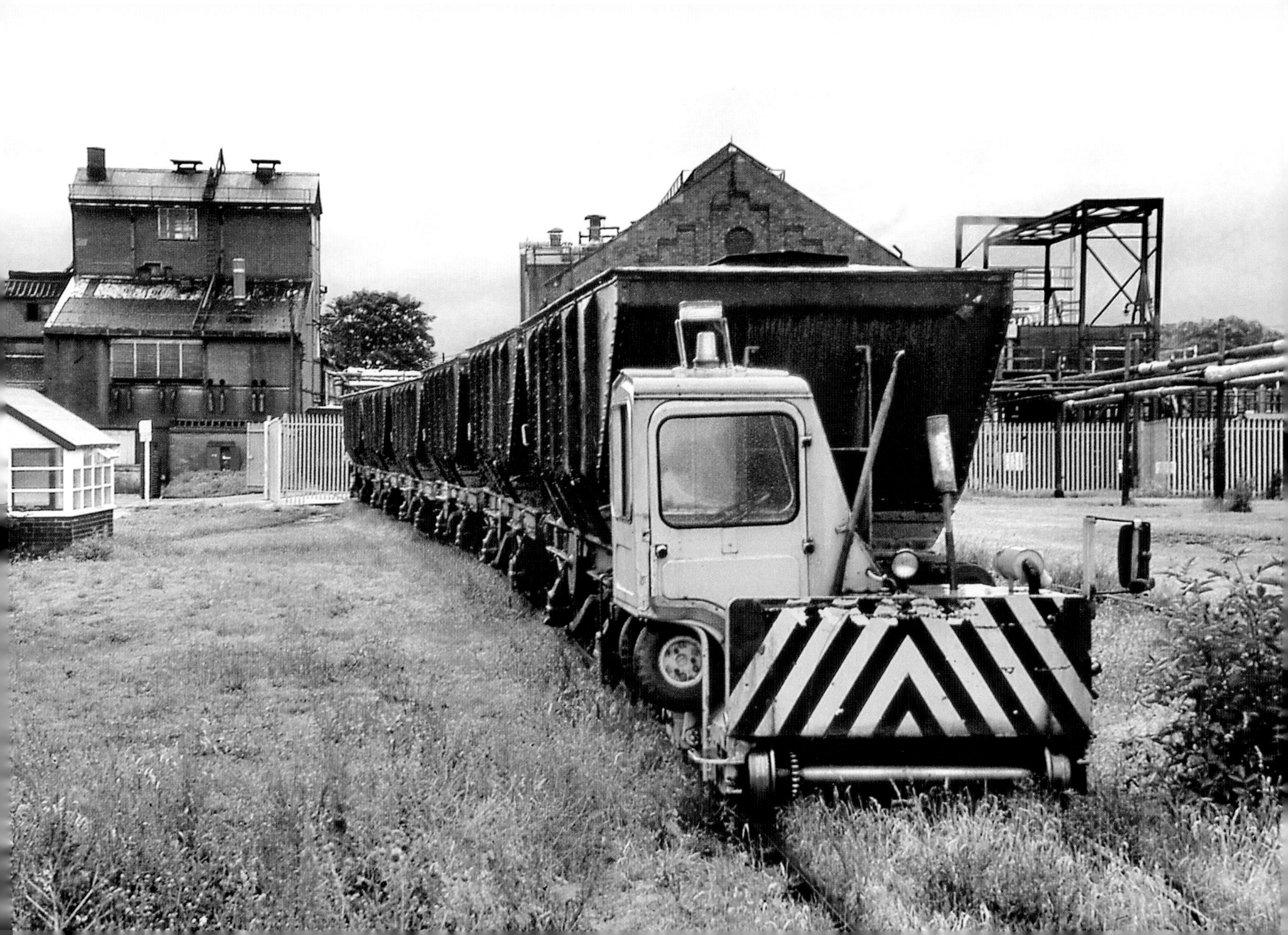

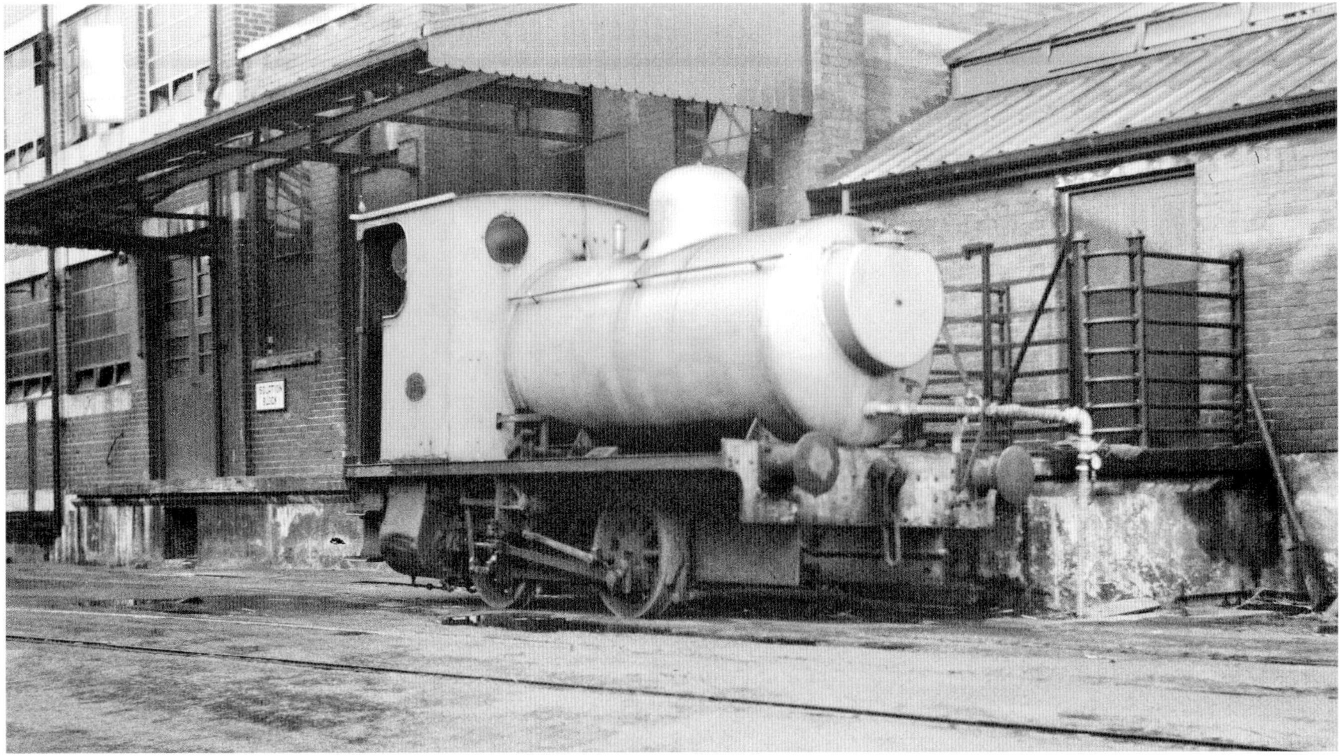

Above: A Hawthorn Leslie 0-4-0 fireless (W/No. 3743 of 1928) at the Sheffield Corporation Abattoir in the 1950s. The Corporation slaughterhouse, alongside the River Don on a site which is now Castlegate, was established in 1929 in a bid to eradicate the many unhygienic and run-down establishments then active in Sheffield. (John Gardner – IRS collection)

Opposite page: British Tissues Ltd used a John Fowler 203 hp 0-4-0 diesel-hydraulic (W/No. 22499 of 1938) for shunting pulp and coal traffic at their Spring Grove paper mills at Oughtibridge near Sheffield, in the sidings connecting with the BR Woodhead Route between Sheffield and Manchester. It had previously worked for Shell at Stanlow as a 150 hp loco with mechanical transmission but was rebuilt by John Fowler before being supplied to British Tissues. The veteran loco was in action on 19 April 1979; however, rail traffic ceased when the Woodhead Route was closed entirely in 1981. The mill was one of the first to use wood pulp to produce paper instead of rags and, as the company name implied, it specialised in tissues, manufacturing the well-known Dixcel brand for many years. All production at the factory ceased by 2015 and there is a plan to redevelop the site for residential housing. (Kevin Lane)

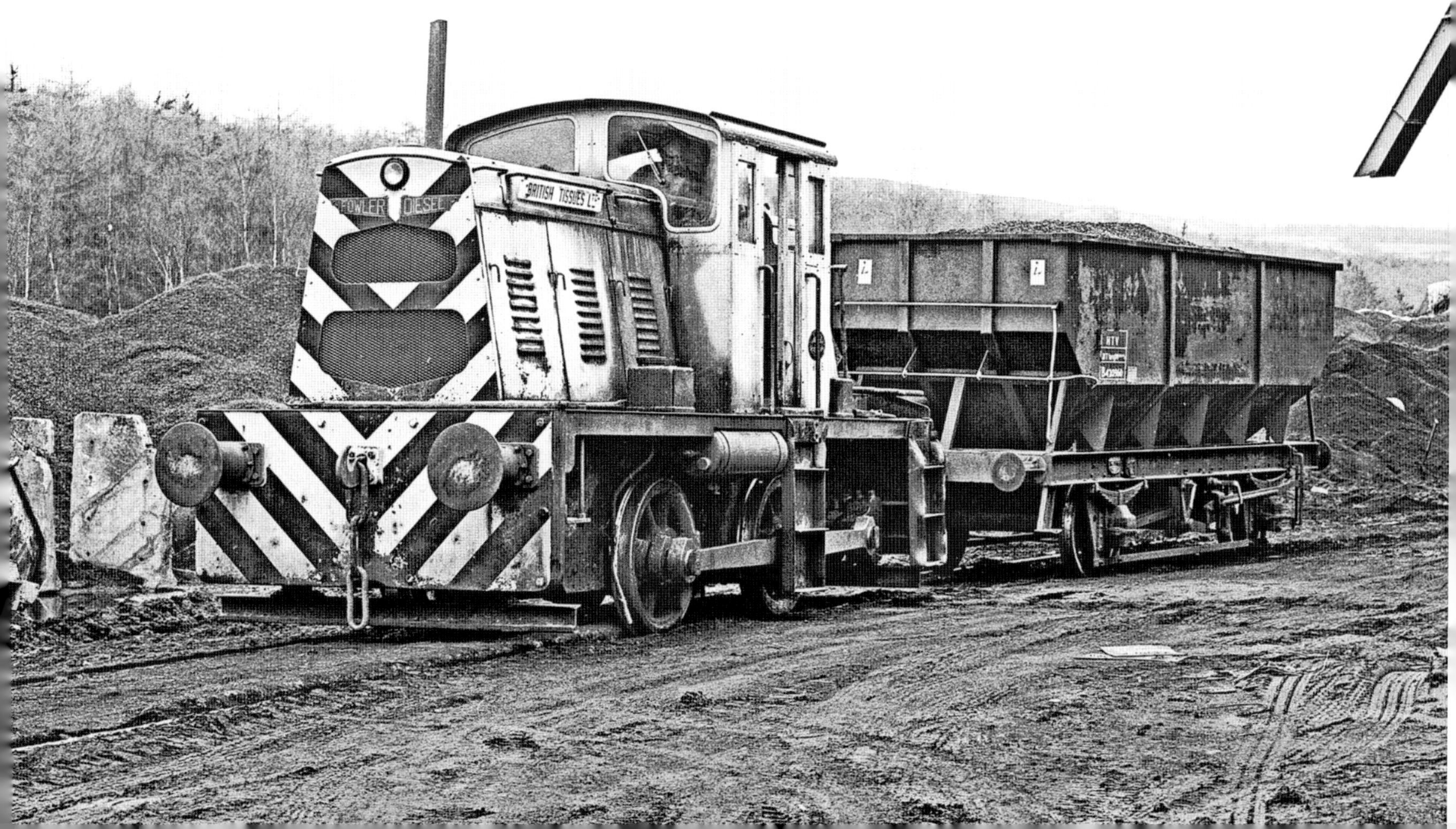
FOWLER DIESEL
BRITISH TISSUES LTD

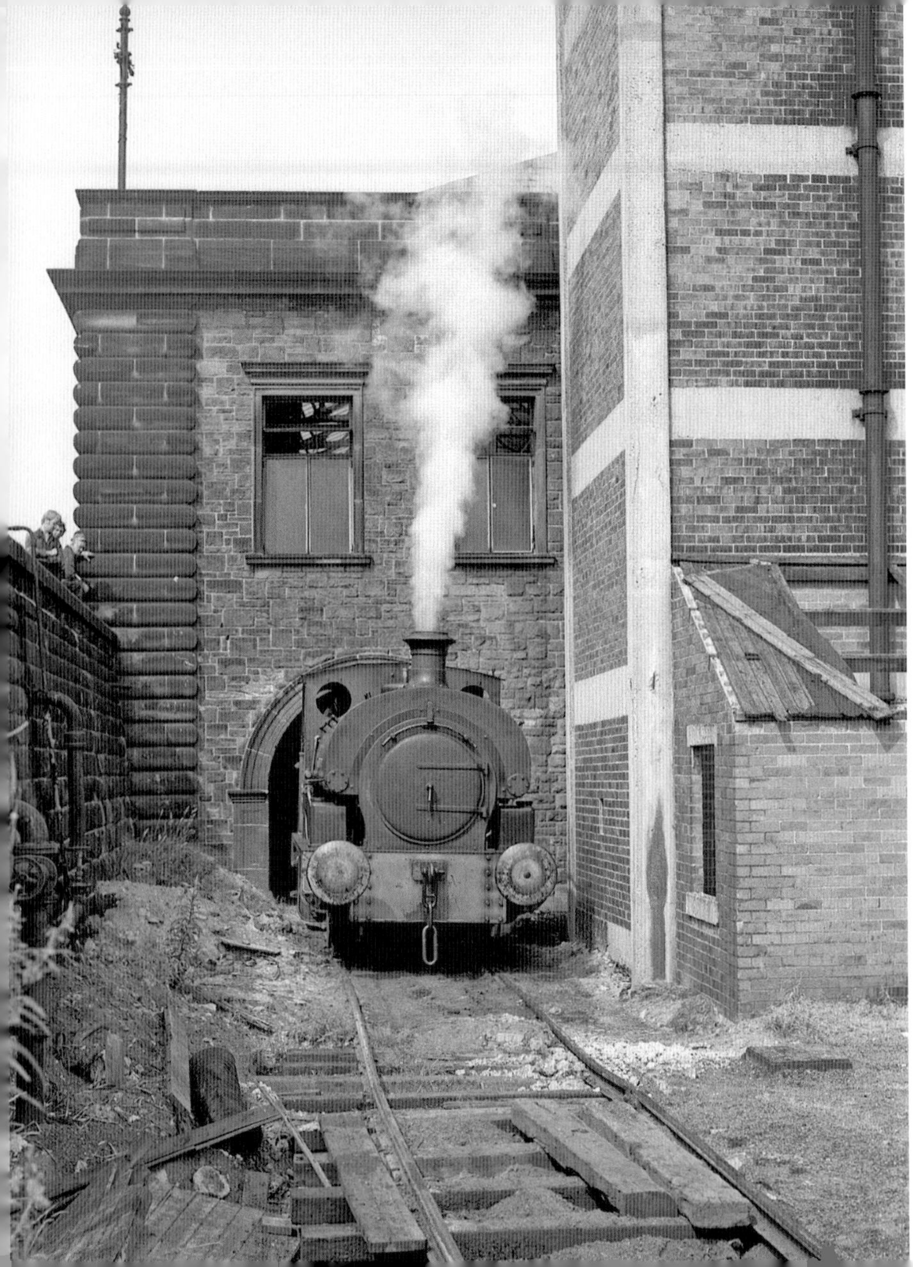

Left: Under the watchful eyes of a group of plant workers, perhaps taking a well-earned tea or lunch break in the fresh air, *Elizabeth* backs a rake of tipper wagons into the Esholt press house on 22 August 1972, to be gravity-loaded with 'cake'. (Richard Stevens)

Opposite page: A 1960s photo of Hudswell Clarke 0-4-0 saddle tank *Nellie* (W/No. 1435 of 1922) setting back towards the Esholt press house with two tipper wagons. (Kevin Lane collection)

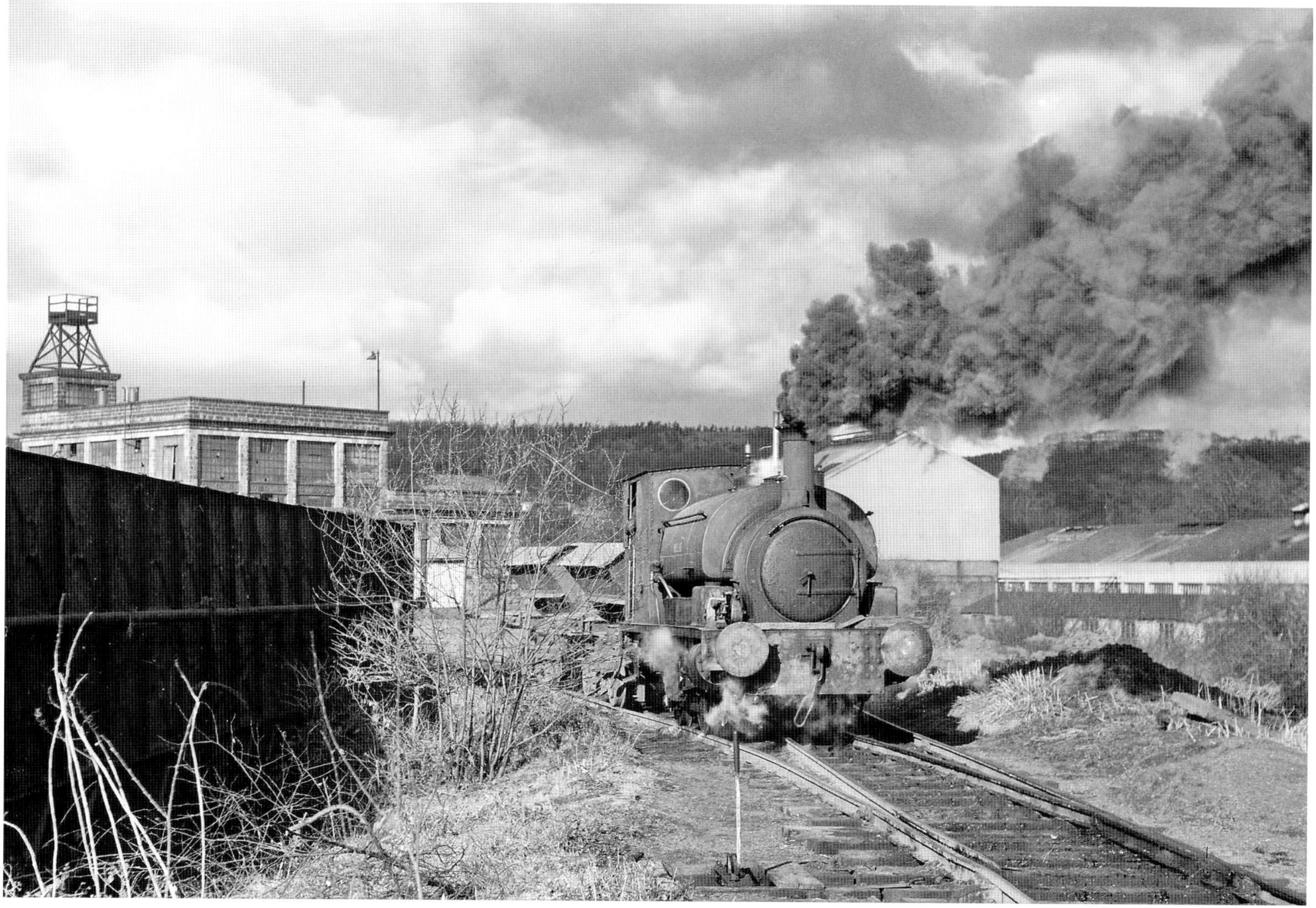

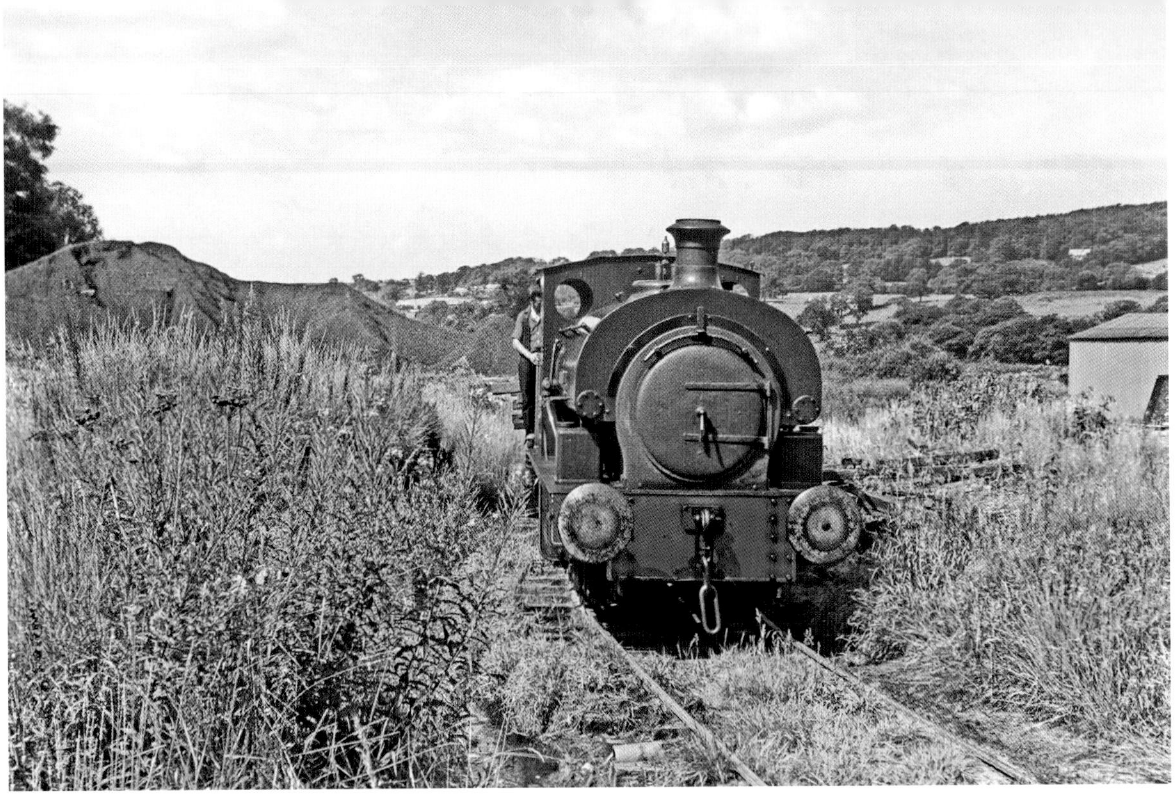

Bradford Corporation's Esholt sewage works was one of the more unusual places to find steam locos at work as late as the 1970s, but at one time, when the works was still under construction in the 1920s, it had eleven of them operating over a track network of some 22 miles, including a main line connection with the Leeds–Keighley line at Apperley Bridge. By the 1960s, however, the railway was reduced to 6½ miles, and used just two locos, both Hudswell Clarke 0-4-0 saddle tanks. The works occupied a huge site of 300 acres and was originally developed to process industrial as well as human waste, recovering lanolin (wool grease) from the waste water discharge of Bradford's woollen industry. Lanolin had multiple applications, including axle grease for railway wagons. At Esholt, it was converted into oil to fire the two Hudswell Clarkes, although in later years gas oil was used. The heart of the works was the press house. This contained 128 steam filter presses which compressed sludge to extract the lanolin. The residue, known as 'cake', a crumbly and odourless material, was loaded into railway tipper wagons and taken to the drying ground on the western edge of the site, where it was left to dry in large piles adjacent to each siding. Some months later it was re-loaded into wagons and taken back to the works to be bagged and sold as fertiliser. The whole operation was a model of environmental good practice, decades before recycling and green issues became fashionable. With a beautiful Aire Valley backdrop, and rosebay willowherb growing by the trackside, the surroundings seemed almost idyllic – but the all-pervasive odour, happily absent from these pages, and the large piles of 'cake' to the left of the picture, give strong clues as to the nature of the operation here. In this scene, on 22 August 1972, *Elizabeth* (W/No. 1888 of 1958) is actually moving track panels on flat wagons rather than 'cake' in tipper wagons. (Richard Stevens)

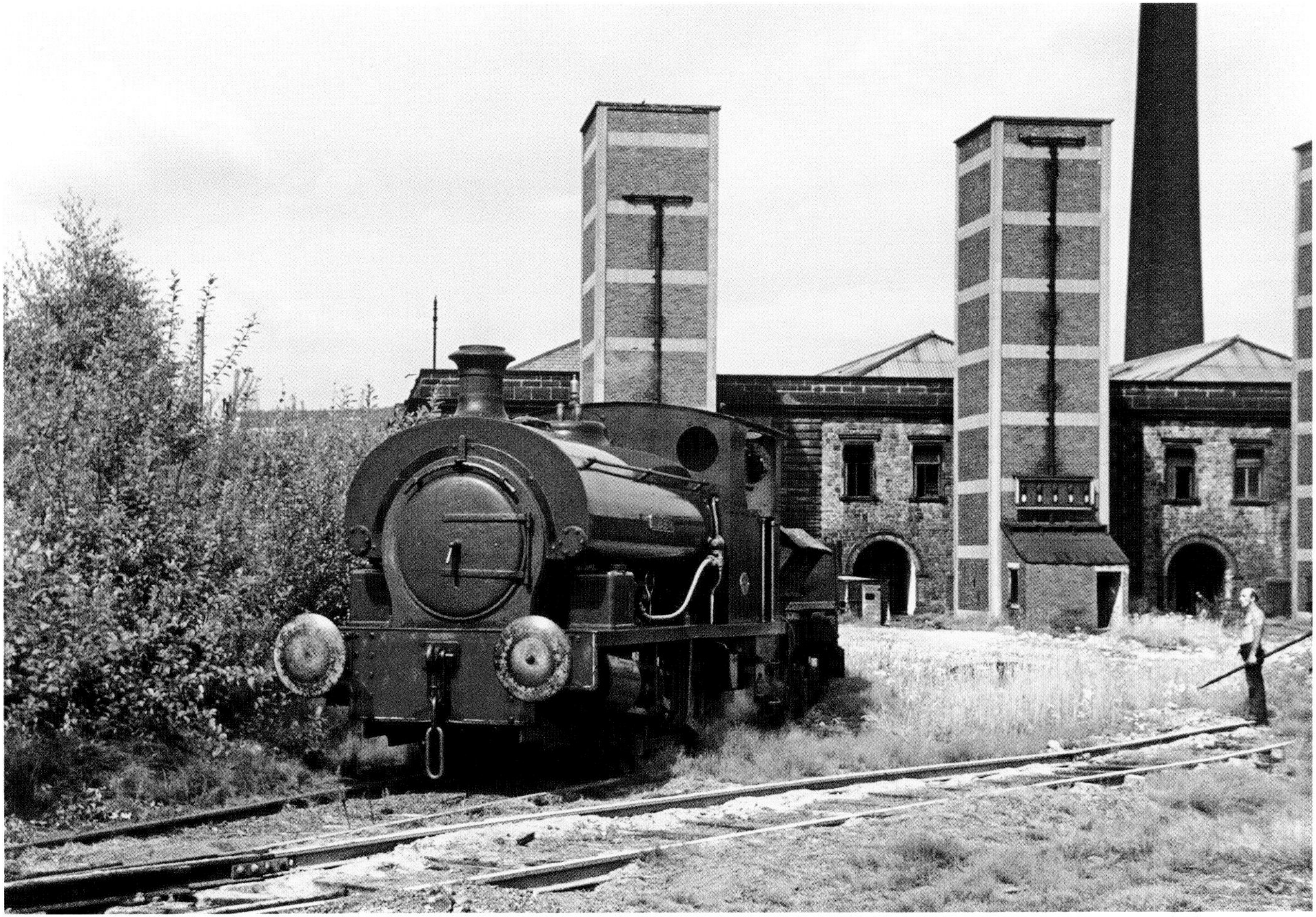

On 22 August 1972, *Elizabeth* is backing empty tipper wagons down one of the six sidings leading into the press house at Esholt. By this time, her older sister, *Nellie*, had been retired to Bradford Industrial Museum and *Elizabeth* was sharing duties with a Hunslet diesel (as seen on page 80). However, she continued in regular use until 1976, with the railway closing completely in 1977, due in large part to the decline of the woollen industry. (Richard Stevens)

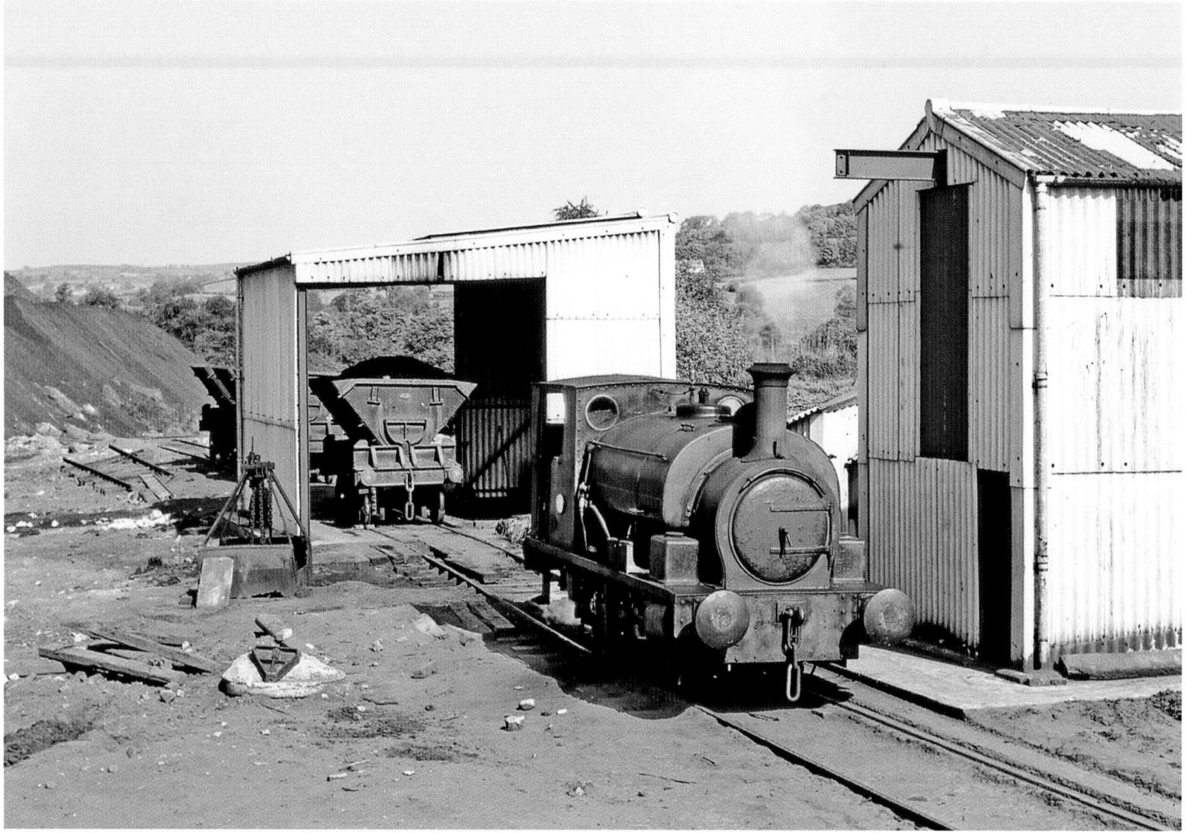

Above: On 9 June 1969, *Nellie* rests between duties outside the 'cake' tipping dock, as the crew take an assumed appropriate refuge for their lunch break. (Author's collection)

Opposite page: A Hunslet 39 hp four-wheel diesel-mechanical (W/No. 7195 of 1974) standing at the lorry loading point at the Yorkshire Water Authority's (YWA) North Bierley water treatment works, Oakenshaw, near Bradford, on 23 January 1990. The 2-foot gauge tramway, first installed in the 1930s, was used five days per week to remove sludge from the filter press house to either a sludge lagoon for tipping, or for immediate discharge into awaiting road vehicles. It was the penultimate water treatment works in the country to use narrow gauge locos, ceasing operations shortly after this visit. (Author)

10

ON THE NARROW GAUGE

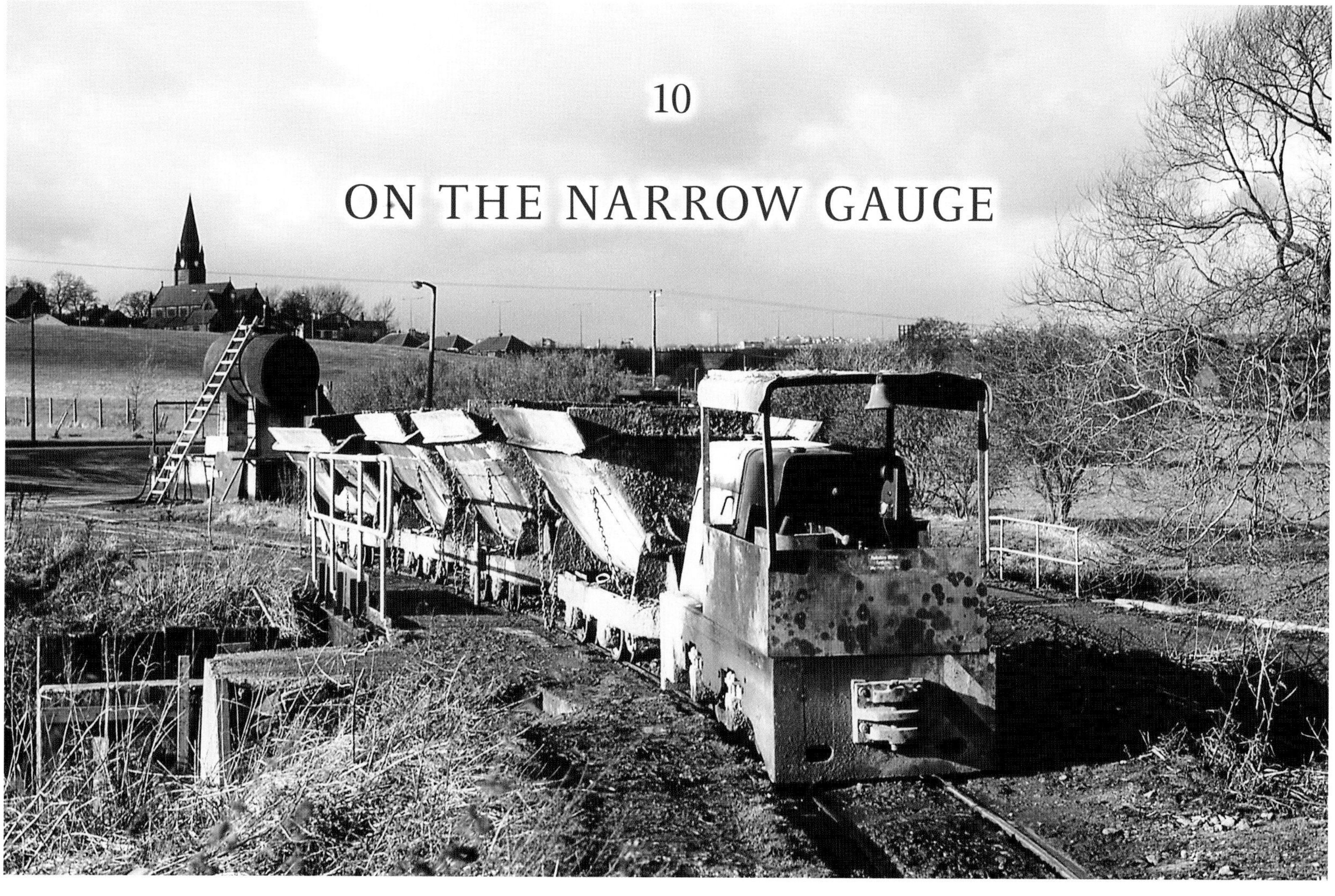

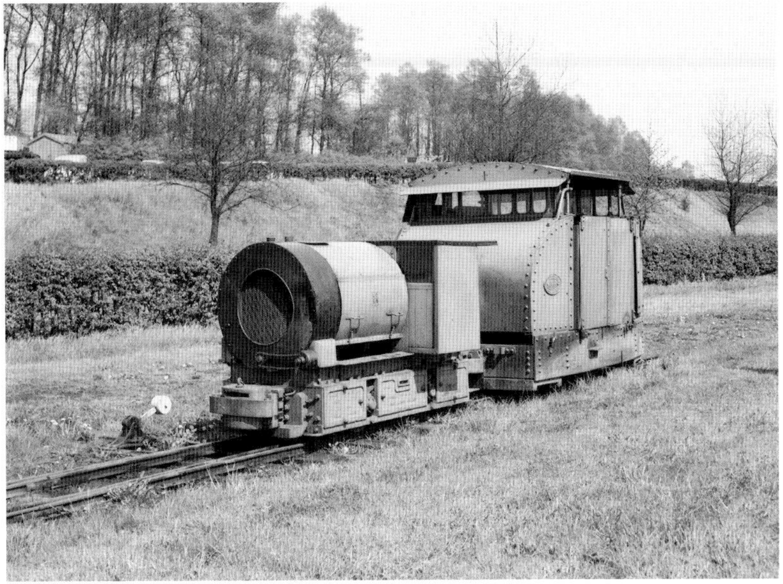

Right: YWA's Knostrop sewage works on 9 May 1962 with a 1-foot 11½-in. gauge four-wheel petrol-mechanical tractor built by textile engineers James C. Kay & Co. Ltd of Bury in 1935, one of only four built, and armoured 40 hp Motor Rail four-wheel petrol-mechanical Simplex tractor No. 1 (W/No. 1369 of 1918), formerly WDLR No. LR3090, one of two acquired from the military. A sewage works was first established at Knowsthorpe Lane, Knostrop, in 1848. Between 1898 and 1906 the site was the focus of research into the processing and disposal of raw sewage. The tramway was installed in 1908, initially worked by two 0-4-0 tank locos, a Hunslet and a Hudswell Clarke, and its purpose was to convey sewage waste in 'V' skips from the detritus and grit tanks plant to the tip. The ex-WDLR Simplex locos replaced steam traction in 1921. The Kay loco was scrapped in 1965, but the Simplexes, along with a Ruston & Hornsby 1960-built LBT Class four-wheel diesel-mechanical, survived until rail traffic ceased during 1979. This Simplex survives, along with numerous other railway exhibits, some in working order, at the Leeds Industrial Museum at Armley Mills. (Brian Webb – IRS collection)

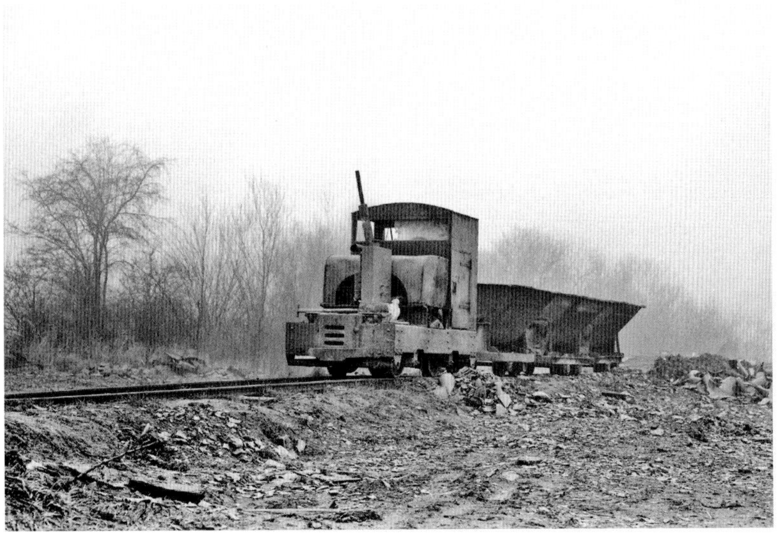

Left: The Alne Brick Company Ltd brickworks, located in the Vale of York near Easingwold and close to the East Coast Main Line, used a 2-foot gauge tramway between the clay pit and kilns. On a misty 23 December 1979, a Motor Rail Simplex four-wheel diesel-mechanical tractor (W/No. 7494 of 1940) stands in the clay pit. (Kevin Lane)

Opposite page: The tipping dock at the Alne Brick Company Ltd on 16 August 1982, with a Motor Rail four-wheel diesel-mechanical Simplex tractor (W/No. 8644 of 1943). Clay tipped from the rake of three 'V' skips generally in use at any given time was then taken to the works by conveyor. (Roy Burt)

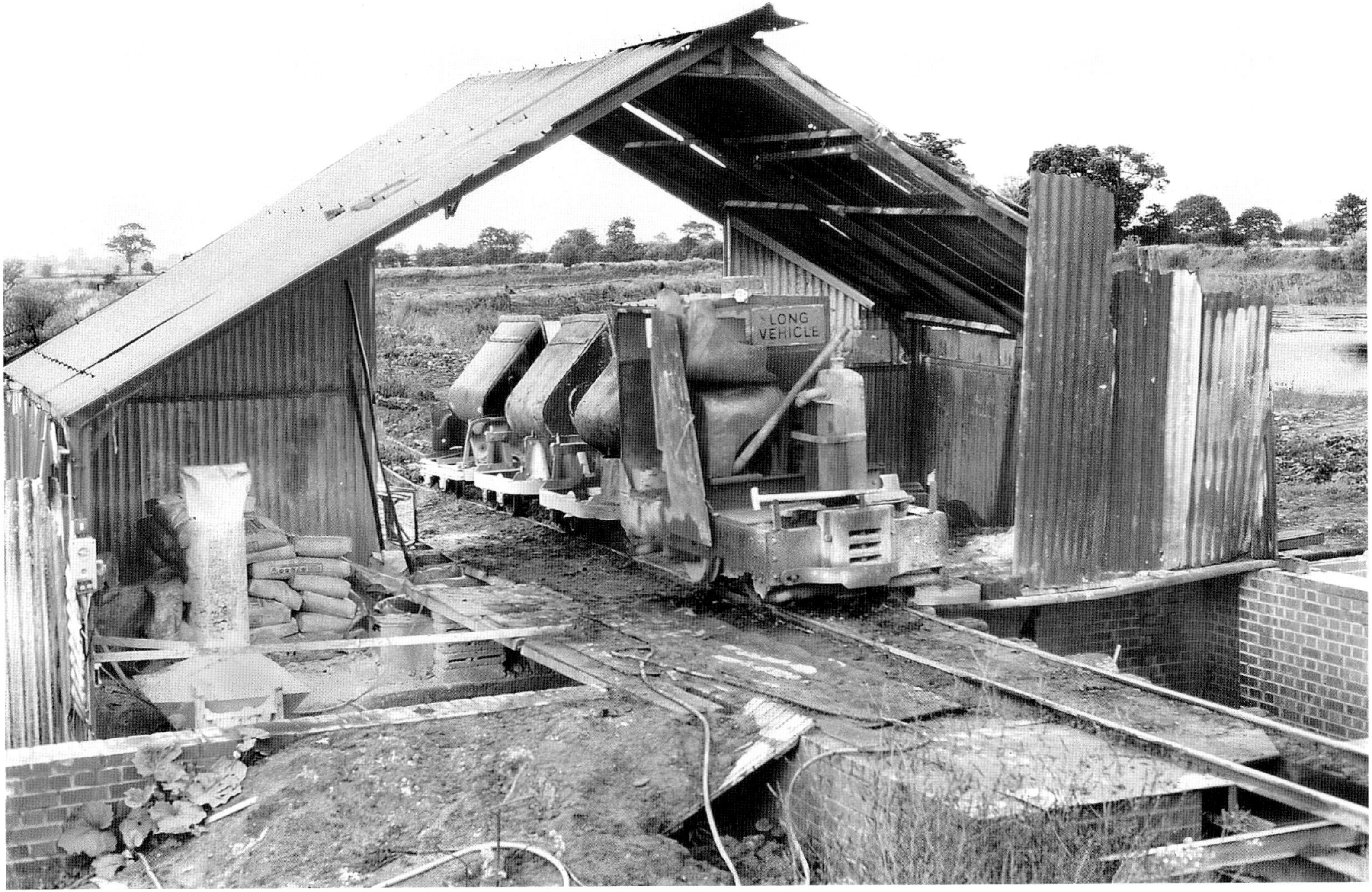
LONG
VEHICLE

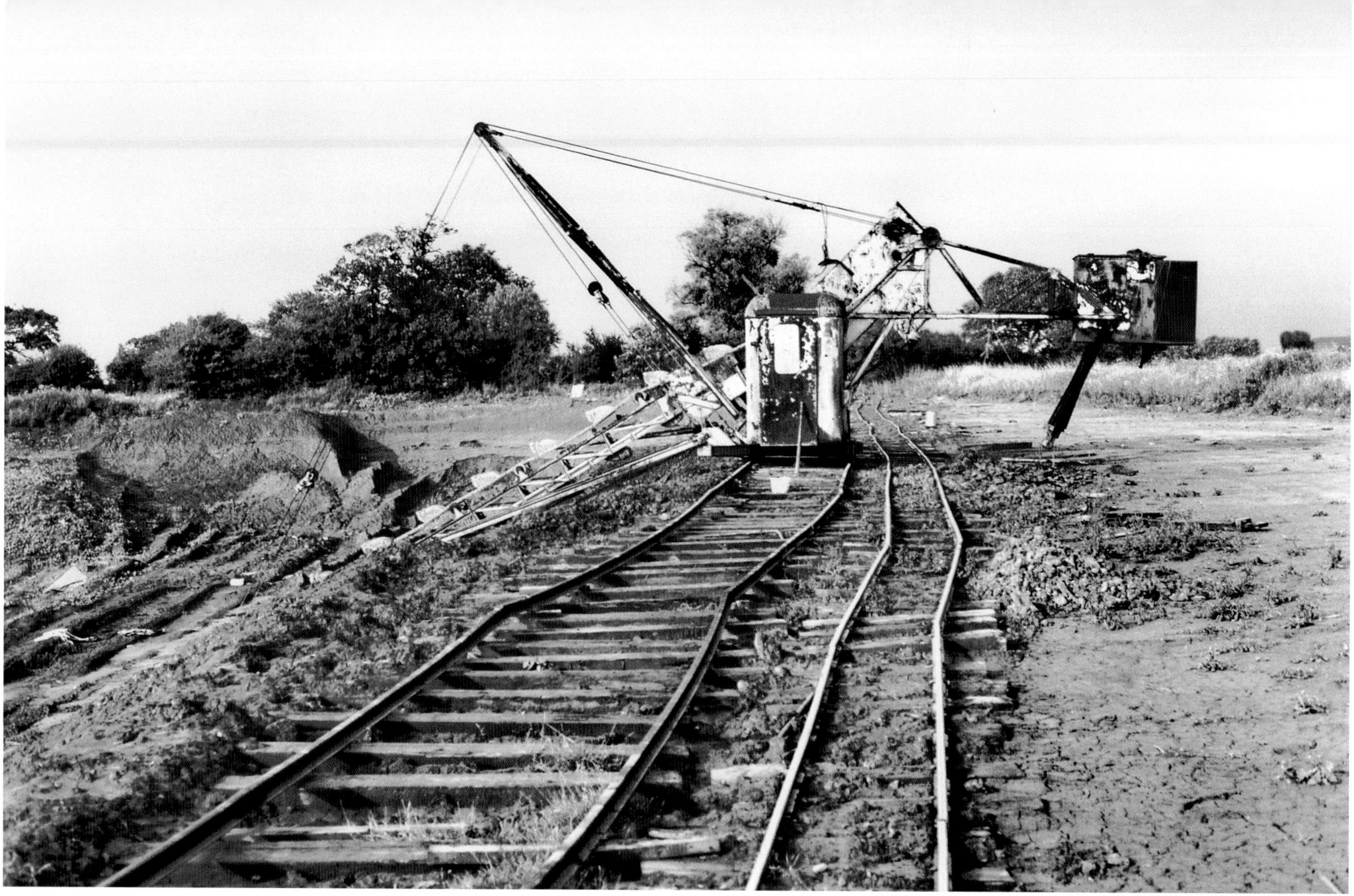

The Alne brickworks also employed a short length of lightly laid standard gauge track installed in the clay pit, along which traversed a German-built counter-balance drag line and bucket excavator, which the operator controlled to place the clay onto the conveyor belt. This was the configuration of the loading point on 23 August 1982. (Roy Burt)

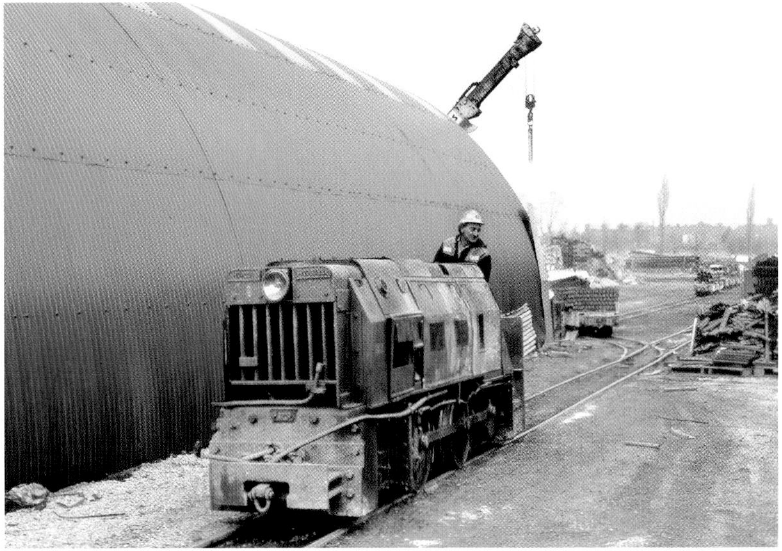

Left: Kiveton Park colliery had a 2-foot gauge system to serve the surface stockyard, which was serviced exclusively by surface-based locos until the late 1980s, although the colliery itself did not close until September 1994. On 16 March 1983, a Hudswell Clarke flameproof 0-4-0 diesel-mechanical (W/No. DM808 of 1953) is seen at the throat of the stockyard sidings. The former mines loco, which was brought to the surface for use in 1978, survived until scrapped around ten years later. It shared surface duties with a sister flameproof Hudswell Clarke and a conventional 1960s-built Motor Rail Simplex. (Roy Burt)

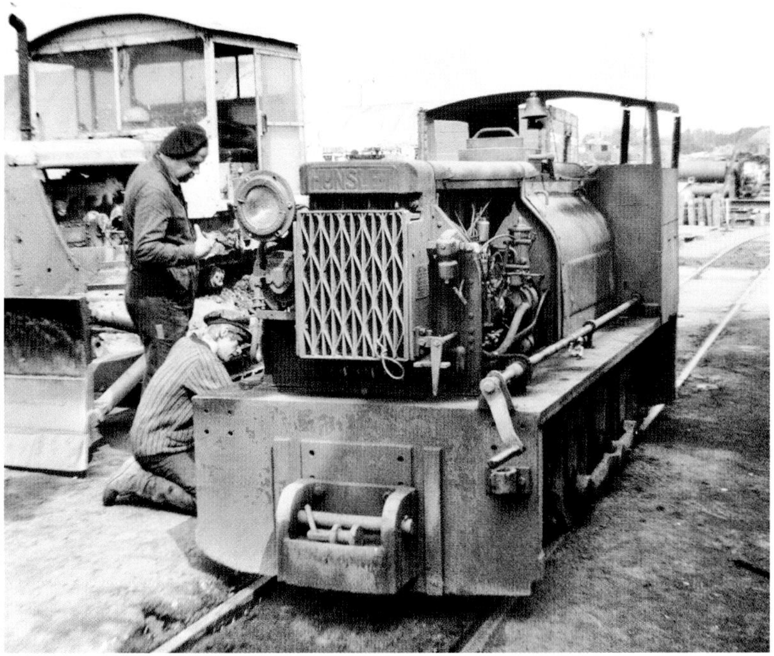

Right: Yorkshire Main colliery at Edlington also used two locos on the surface, exclusively for the 3-foot gauge stockyard system, a standard Hudswell Clarke six-coupled loco, as above, and this flameproof Hunslet 0-4-0 diesel-mechanical mines loco, No. TR7 (W/No. 3427 of 1946). On 14 June 1969, it is seen receiving attention from an apprentice fitter under supervision. The Hunslet, originally supplied new to the colliery for mines use, emerged from the mine for exclusive use on the surface stockyard in August 1953 and it remained on those duties, along with the Hudswell Clarke, until the colliery was closed in October 1985. Both locos were scrapped on site in 1986 by the demolition company, Ogden Demolition Ltd. (Roy Burt)

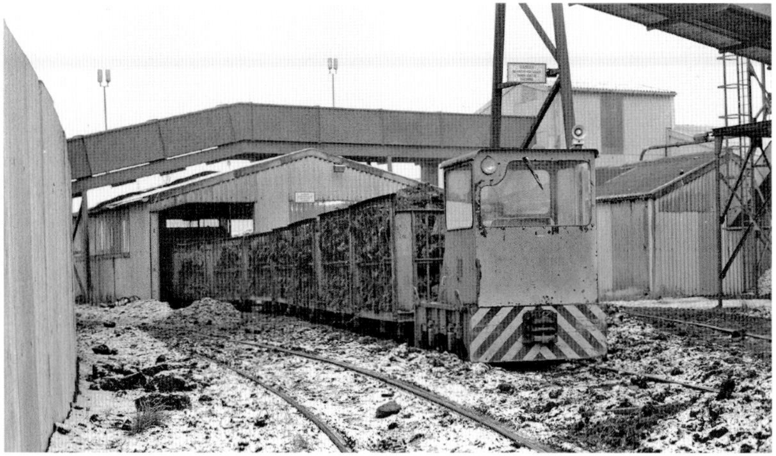

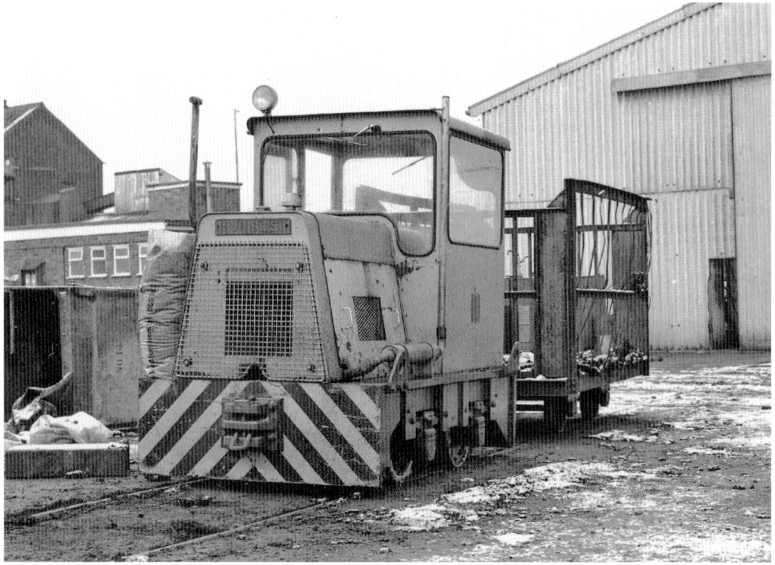

Another volume in this series, which examines Eastern England, covered the 3-foot gauge peat railway on the Crowle and Thorne Moors, namely the operation based around the Levington's peat works at Swinefleet. The company's chief peat extraction works was located at Hatfield Moor, directly on the Yorkshire county boundary. Railway operations at Hatfield, in the later years in the ownership of The Scotts Company (UK) Ltd, comprised around 8 miles of permanent 3-foot gauge track, the peat harvesting on the moor being supported by a fleet of around fifty peat wagons and six 1990-built Schöma 'master and slave' four-wheel diesel-hydraulic locos, supplemented by two older Motor Simplex four-wheel diesel-mechanical locos. The Hatfield mill was also on a much grander scale and far more mechanised than its sister operation at Swinefleet.

Before the introduction of surface milling, turves were loaded on the moor, initially by hand and later by Hymac machine, into the Robert Hudson 1960s-built steel wagons and conveyed to the mill tipping dock. (*Above left*) On 21 December 1978, a decade before the advent of the Schöma 'master and slave' locos, Hunslet four-wheel diesel-mechanical No. 2 (W/No. 7367 of 1974) stands in the snow with a load at the Hatfield mill tipping dock. (Kevin Lane)

On the same date, (*below left*) the second of the pair of 43 hp Hunslet locos (W/No. 7366 of 1974) stands with a peat wagon outside the Hatfield mill workshops, possibly both awaiting attention. (Kevin Lane)

Hand-cutting of peat on the moor, which had in fact taken place for hundreds of years, essentially for home use and small-scale retail trade, ceased by 1970, with the introduction of specialist German cutting machines. By 1986, this style of operation was in turn replaced by the controversial surface milling method, mainly producing horticultural peat. This was a move too far that led to strong opposition and environmental campaigning, resulting in the consequent cessation of all peat harvesting operations on both the Thorne and Hatfield Moors in 2000 and 2006 respectively.

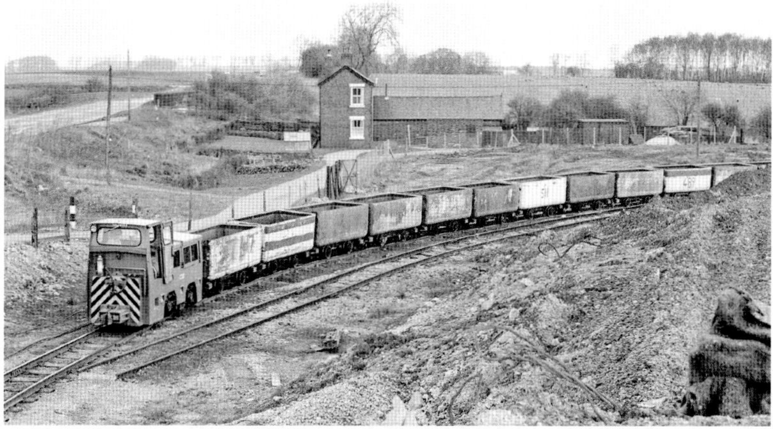

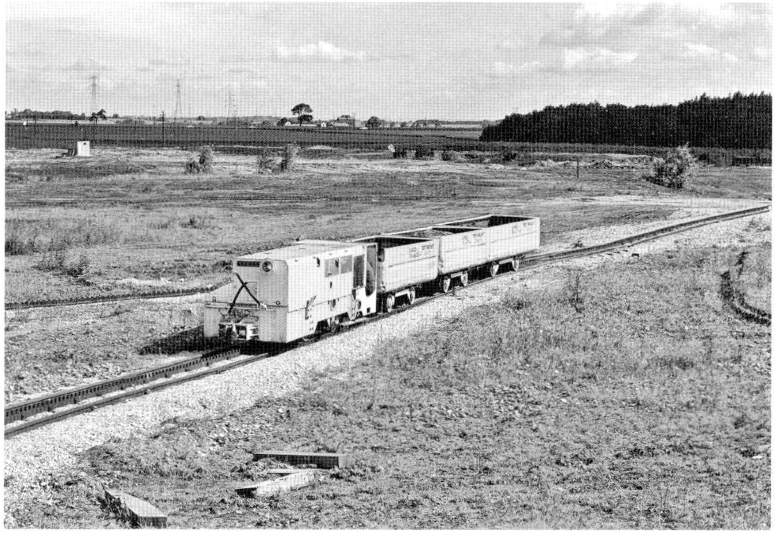

A 2-ft 6-in. gauge surface railway, of a mile and a half in length, ran between Ledston Luck colliery at Kippax and Peckfield washery. The colliery supplied coal for washing by this means between January 1951 and July 1982, when road transport took over, although after this time, until closure of the colliery in October 1986, locos continued to position wagons between a tippler, a conveyor belt feeding the road transport, and a stockpile. Hudswell Clarke had an arrangement with the NCB to use the line for the testing of some of their products. As a joint venture with the NCB, Hunslet also had a purpose-built rack test track, employing gradients of up to 1 in 4, installed at the Ledston Luck colliery spoil tip.

Above right: In April 1980, a Simplex Mechanical Handling four-wheel diesel-hydraulic, possibly No. 18 (W/No. 101T018 of 1979), hauls from Peckfield washery a complete rake of thirty 3½-ton capacity empty side-tipping tubs, a bespoke design for this operation. (Kevin Lane)

Below right: The rack-railway test track, which Hunslet considered as an extension of their Leeds factory activities, was used for driver familiarisation training and trials prior to the loco's delivery to its intended colliery. On 4 July 1978, a flameproof/rack-fitted Hunslet four-wheel diesel-hydraulic (W/No. 7489 of 1977) was in action on the tip line, ten days before its transfer to Kellingley colliery. This line remained in use until 1982, the time when the line to Peckfield ceased the conveyance of coal. (Kevin Lane)

11

PRIVATE RAILWAYS

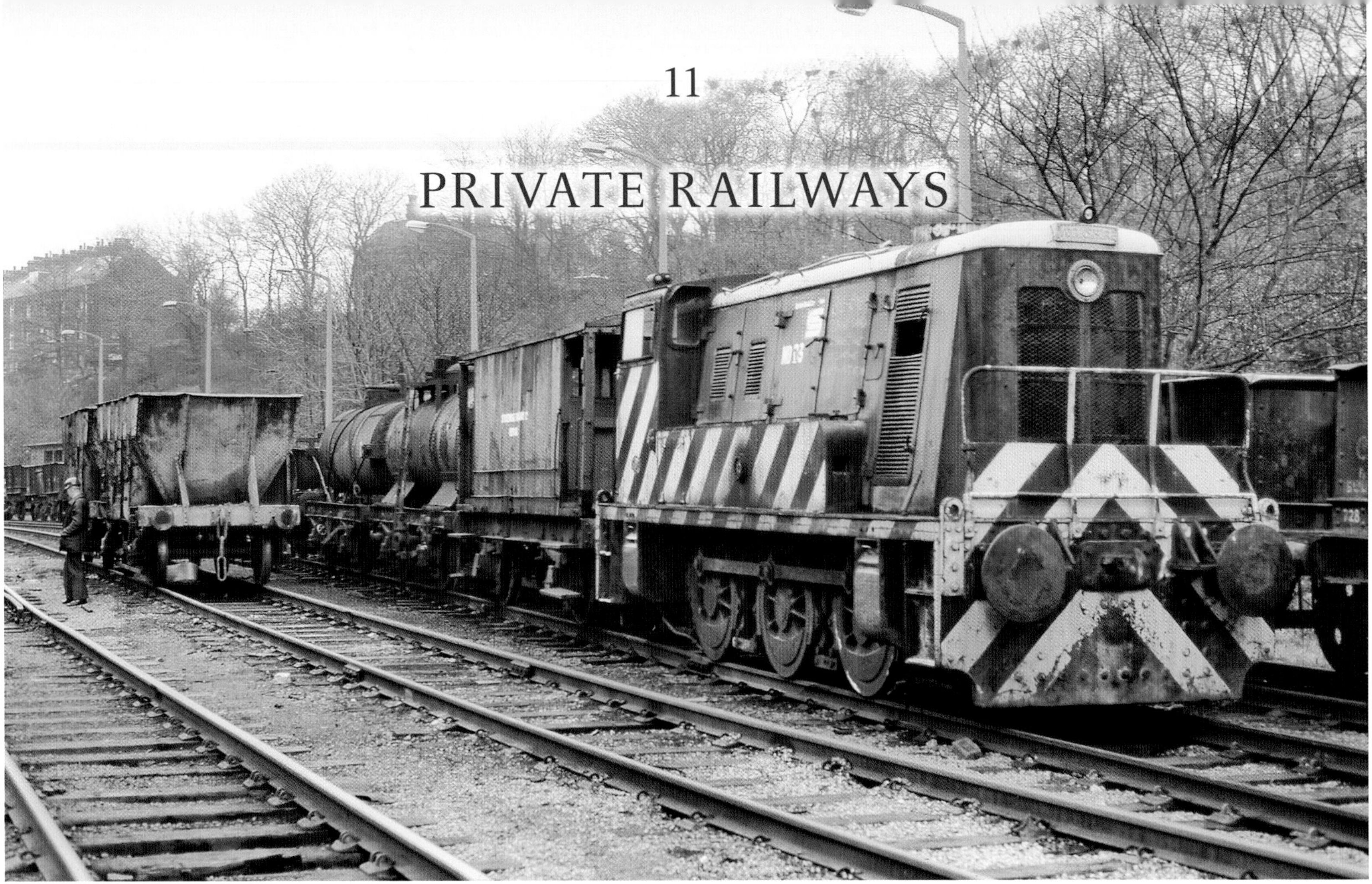

The private Stocksbridge Railway was opened in 1876 and became a subsidiary of the steel company, under various ownerships until 1992, when it ended its separate existence. The line is still in use today, with an exchange point at Ellen Cliffe loop, approximately the mid-way point of the original line from Deepcar to the edge of the Stocksbridge works complex. On 5 May 1983, Yorkshire Engine DE4 Class 440 hp 0-6-0 diesel-electric No. 32 (W/No. 2752 of 1959) stands in the Low Yard of BSC Stocksbridge Works with the Stocksbridge Railway's brake van and a mix of internal freight stock. (Roy Burt)

Private railways specifically associated with industry were relatively widespread until the mid-twentieth century. Three notable survivors beyond the nationalisation period of large industrial and main line railway companies were the Stocksbridge Railway north of Sheffield, the Derwent Valley Light Railway Company (DVLR) near York, and the Middleton Railway at Leeds. The metals of Stocksbridge and Middleton, albeit both now somewhat truncated, survive today, and the DVLR's legacy is celebrated with a demonstration line at the Yorkshire Museum of Farming at Murton, close to the course of the original railway.

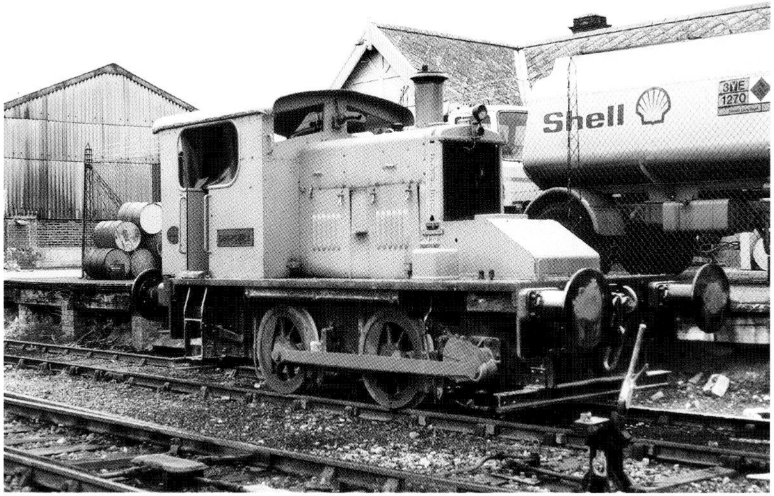

Above right: The DVLR was one of several private railways established around the country following the passing of the 1896 Light Railway Act, opening in July 1913. Passenger services were short-lived, ceasing as early as 1926 due to road competition, but freight traffic prospered on this charming rural line, including agricultural produce to market in York, as well as oil, petroleum, chemicals and coal. During the Second World War the railway carried materials for local airfields and military establishments, but following cessation of hostilities, reduction in traffic volumes saw the line gradually contract; originally running from York (Layerthorpe) to North Duffield, near Selby, by 1972 there was just the stretch between Dunnington and York surviving. The line was completely closed in 1981, much of the track being removed. The Derwent Valley Light Railway Society had already been formed and over time established a centre based at the Yorkshire Museum of Farming at Murton, where a short demonstration line has been laid. Shortly after closure of the DVLR, John Fowler 0-4-0 diesel-mechanical *Churchill* (W/No. 4100005 of 1947) stands in the oil siding at York (Layerthorpe) station on 16 August 1982. From September 1971, this 150 hp loco had worked at the Harvest Mills sidings of Yorkshire Grain Driers Ltd at Dunnington station, originally being supplied new to the Reed Paper Mills at Thatcham in Berkshire. (Roy Burt)

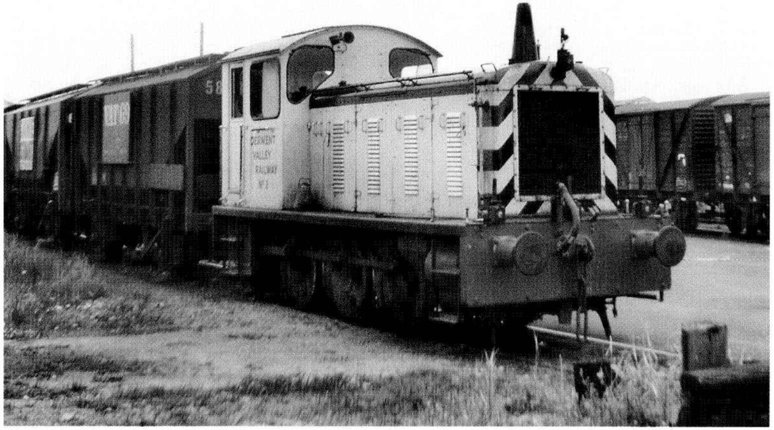

Below right: When the DVLR was still handing an appreciable amount of agricultural traffic, including grain for Harvest Mills at Dunnington, former BR Drewry 1956-built Class 04 No. D2245, Derwent Valley Railway's No. 2, rests with grain wagons in the sidings at Layerthorpe on 27 July 1971. (Roy Burt)

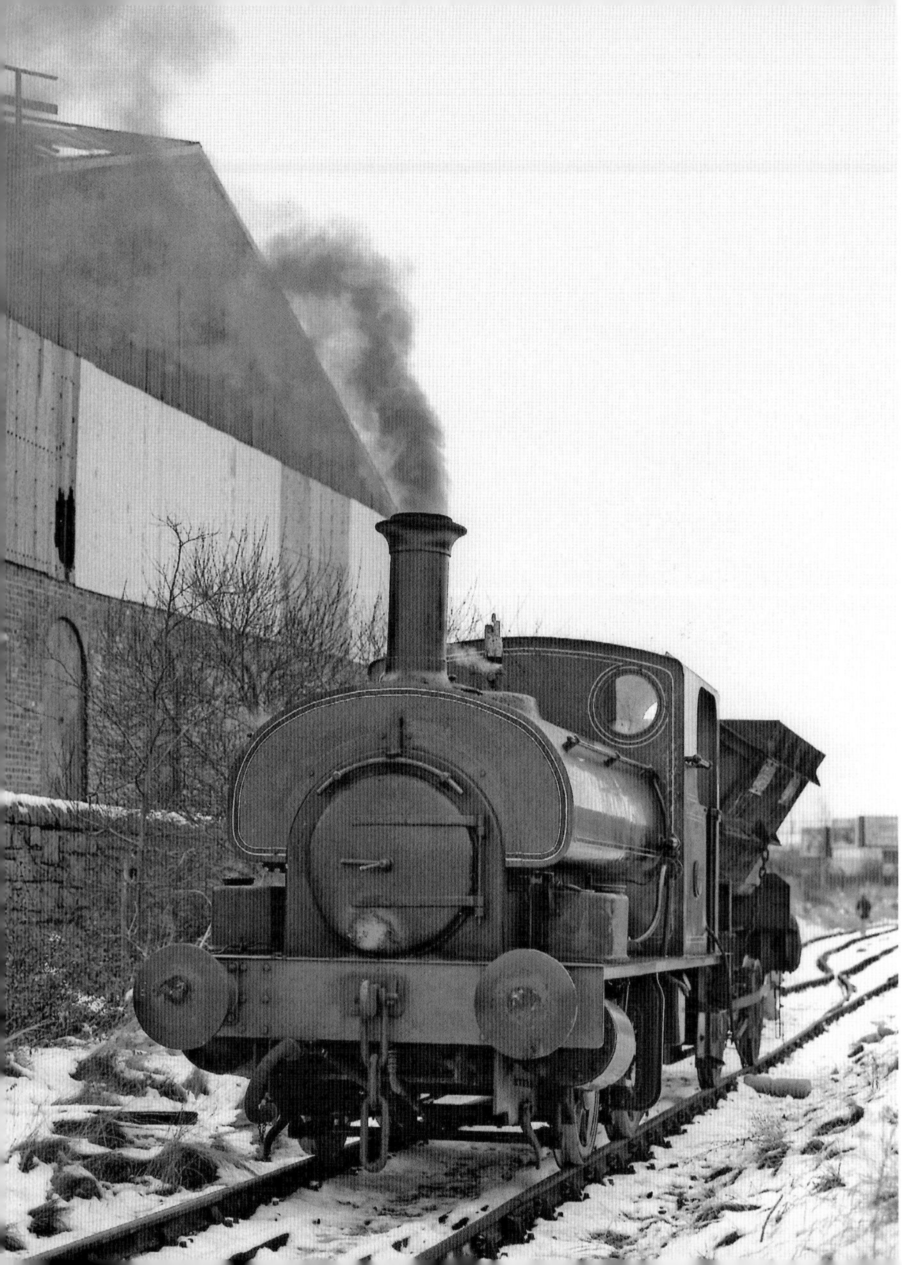

The Middleton Railway, as the world's oldest continuously working public railway, first founded in 1758 by Act of Parliament, most certainly deserves a feature in this book. The waggonway, which enabled coal to be transported cheaply from the Middleton pits, initially to a staith close to the river Aire, enabled Leeds to become a centre for the many developing industries relying on coal as a raw material, including brick and glass manufacture, pottery, metal working and brewing, as well as a source of power for the many mill and factory owners establishing their businesses there. The first commercially successful loco, fitted with the patent Blenkinsop rack and pinion drive, commenced operation on the railway in 1812, the first non-experimental and revenue-earning use of steam traction in the world. The railway was converted from 4 ft 1 in. to standard gauge in 1881, enabling it to enjoy a connection with the Midland Railway at Hunslet Lane, and latterly the GNR at Hunslet East. The Middleton Estate & Colliery Company became part of the NCB on Vesting Day in 1947 and coal traffic was subsequently concentrated principally on the line between Hunslet East and Broom Pit (featured on page 26). From December 1958 the use of NCB locos ceased, and BR worked all colliery traffic, this finally ending in July 1967. The northern part of the Middleton Railway subsequently passed to the Middleton Railway Trust, who continued to work some traffic for the companies whose private sidings had historically connected with the line. After clearance of the Middleton Broom colliery site, following its closure in May 1968, the Trust extended their line to Park Halt. Some fifty years on, the Middleton Railway is a well-established heritage steam railway, most unusually located in a major city.

Left: On 5 January 1997, Hudswell Clarke 0-4-0 saddle tank *Mirvale* (previously featured on page 64) is at work on the Balm Road branch of the heritage Middleton Railway, with a side-tipper wagon formerly used on the Esholt Sewage Works railway. (Author)

Opposite page: Manning Wardle 0-6-0 saddle tank *Sir Berkeley* (W/No. 1210 of 1891) near Tulip Street on the Balm Road branch with a demonstration mixed freight train on 22 September 1996. (Author)

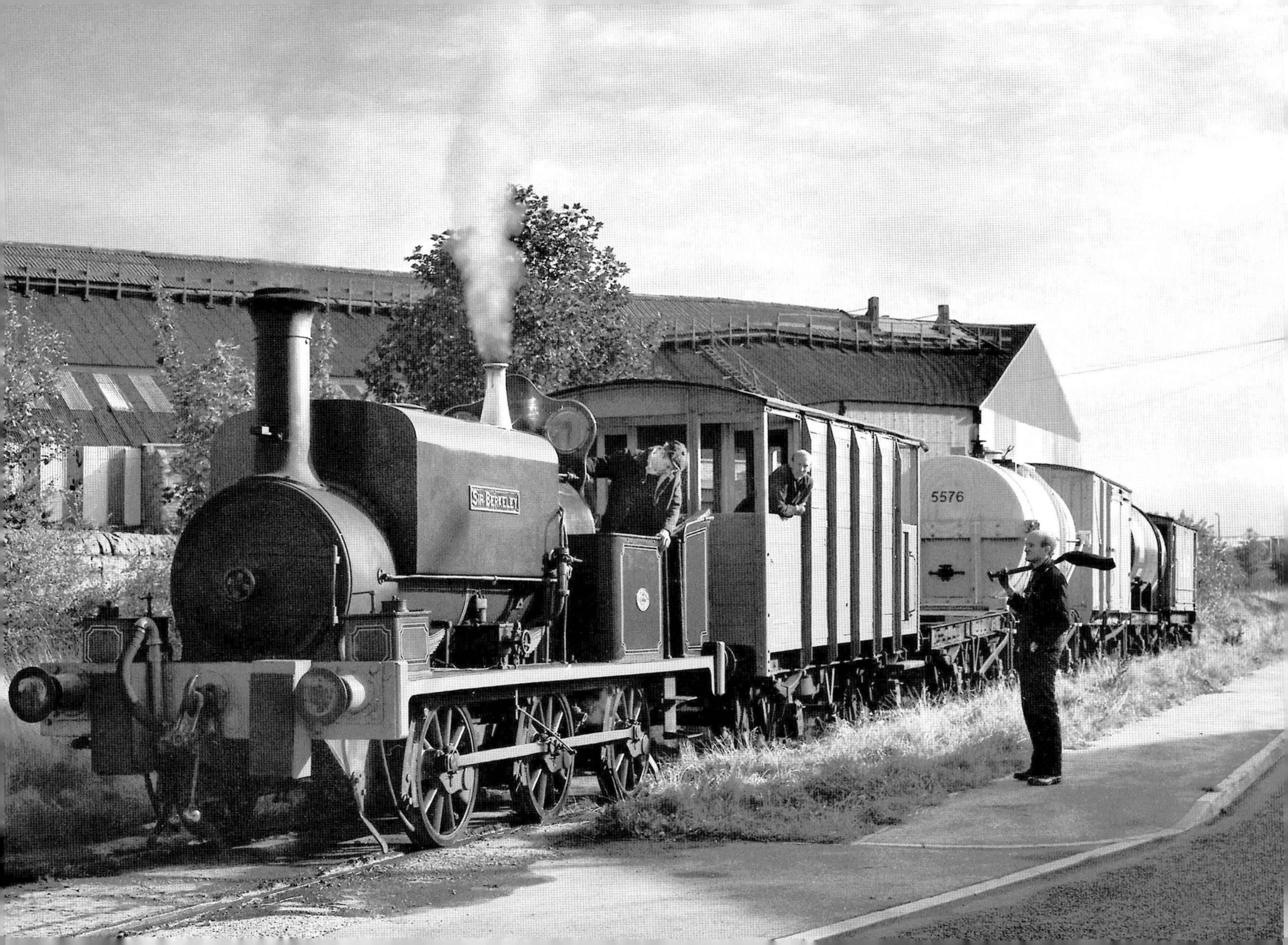
SIR BERKELEY
5576

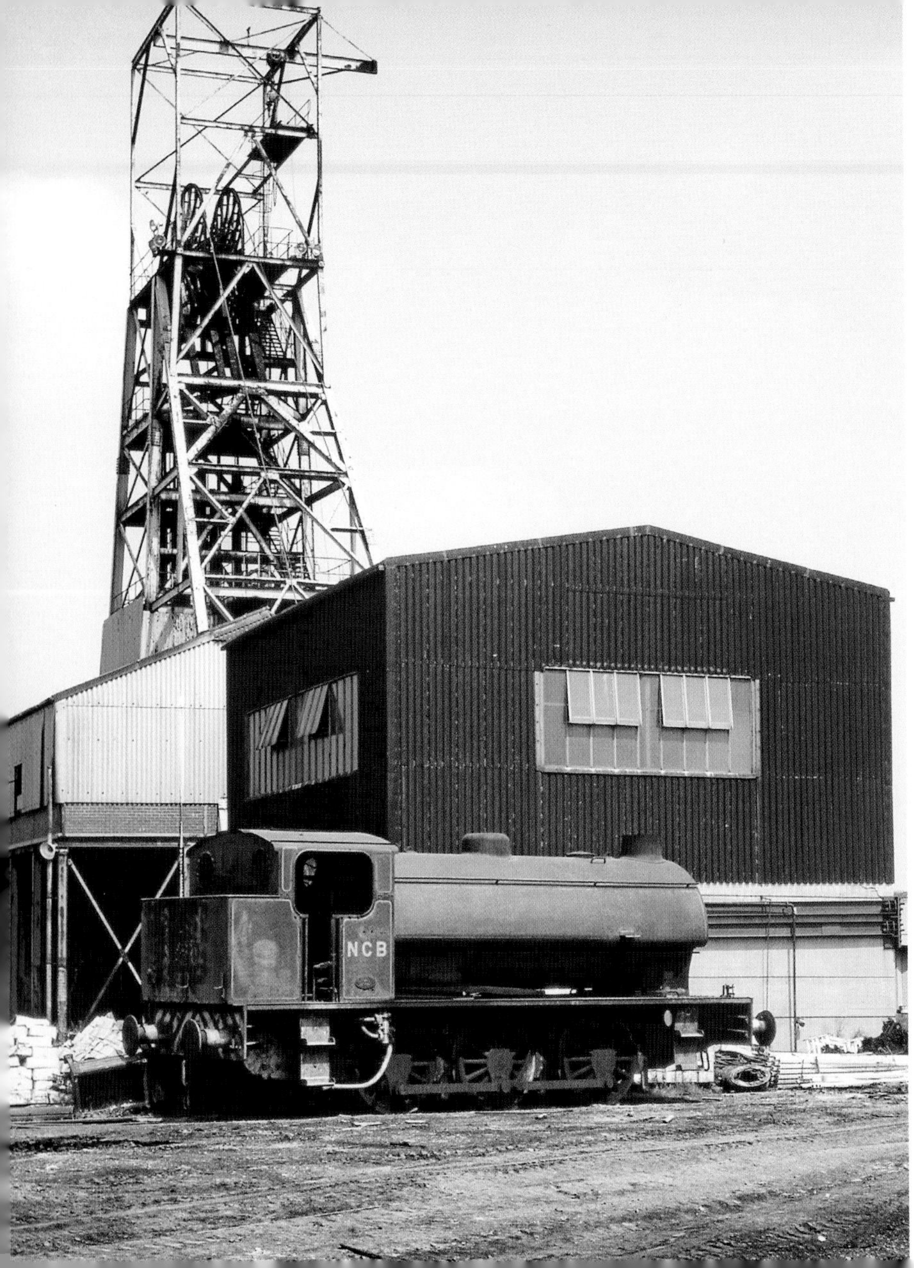

12

THE 'EVENING STARS' OF INDUSTRY

Although the Lancashire collieries of Bickershaw and Bold, and the Derbyshire colliery at Cadley Hill, saw out the last of everyday working NCB steam, some Yorkshire collieries held the distinction of using the last locos built for commercial industrial use in Britain, namely products from the Hunslet Engine Company and Hudswell, Clarke & Co. Ltd. The winter 1981/2 period of steam operation at Wheldale, during which Hunslet's underfeed stoker system was evaluated for various grades of coal, has been documented pictorially in the earlier-published *British Austerity Saddle Tanks* book by this author; but a decade or so before, virtually new steam locos could be seen in action at Peckfield, Skiers Spring, Cadeby, Dodworth, Monk Bretton and Manvers Main collieries.

Left: Hunslet No. 66 (W/No. 3891 of 1965) was a rebuild of Hudswell Clarke-constructed Austerity 0-6-0 saddle tank (W/No. 1763 of 1944) and was photographed at Peckfield colliery on 15 July 1972. Acquired from the Army Department as *WD No. 117* in 1963, it was totally rebuilt by Hunslet and fitted with the underfeed stoker and gas combustion system and sold on to the NCB as a 'new' loco. As the last rebuilt Austerity to be sold into commercial industrial service, it evaded preservationists and was scrapped at Allerton Bywater workshops during December 1973, after less than a decade of service. (John Sloane)

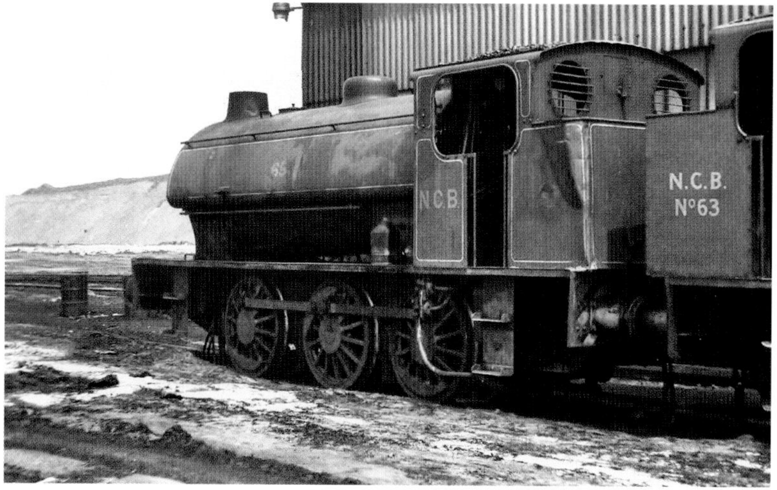

Above right: The last two locos built for British industry, to an order placed in 1963 by the NCB Area No. 3 (Rotherham), were never afforded names; Hunslet Austerity No. 65 (W/No. 3889 of 1964) was the penultimate Austerity steam loco constructed for industry and was delivered to the NCB Manvers colliery and coal preparation plant at Wath-on-Dearne in March 1964. It represented Britain's final development of the steam loco, being fitted by Hunslet with a welded steel firebox, underfeed stoker and gas producer unit, drop grate and improved blast pipe system. With an influx of diesels at Manvers, it saw very little use there after 1971 and was the last steam loco to work at Manvers Main. It was eventually transferred to Cadley Hill colliery in June 1975, where, following a steam test, its boiler was found to need major repairs. Its entire commercial NCB service therefore proved to be remarkably short-lived, a similar story to that of the BR 9F Class of 2-10-0s! (John Sloane)

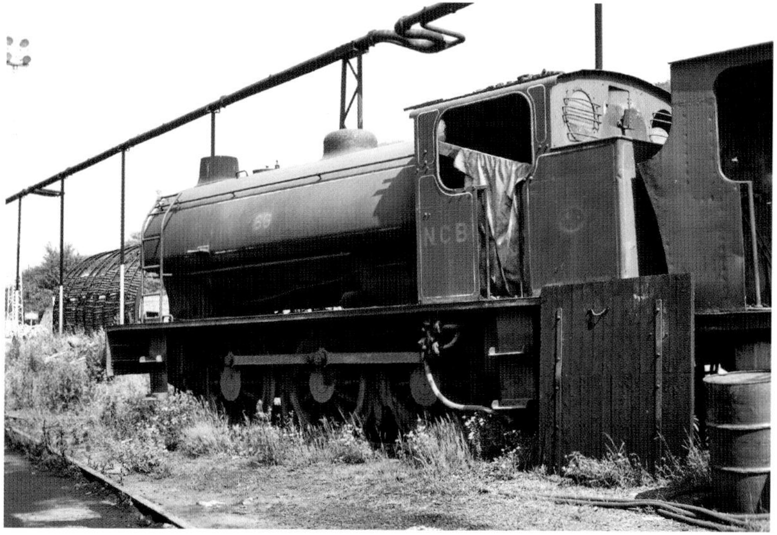

Below right: Hunslet Austerity No. 66 (W/No. 3890 of 1964), the final steam loco to be built for commercial industrial service in Britain, was also delivered to the NCB in March 1964, to Cadeby colliery at Conisbrough. This 'ultimate' loco in steam design for British industry sadly again didn't see too much service, due to the presence of diesel traction at Cadeby. It was last noted in use during the early months of 1970, but its standby role, as when photographed on 15 July 1972 in the latter years of its NCB ownership, assured its survival – it passed into preservation in October 1975, initially with the Quainton Railway Society in Buckinghamshire, but today it is to be found in full working order on the Chasewater Light Railway in Staffordshire and is just as deserving of its place in preservation as BR's *Evening Star*. (John Sloane)

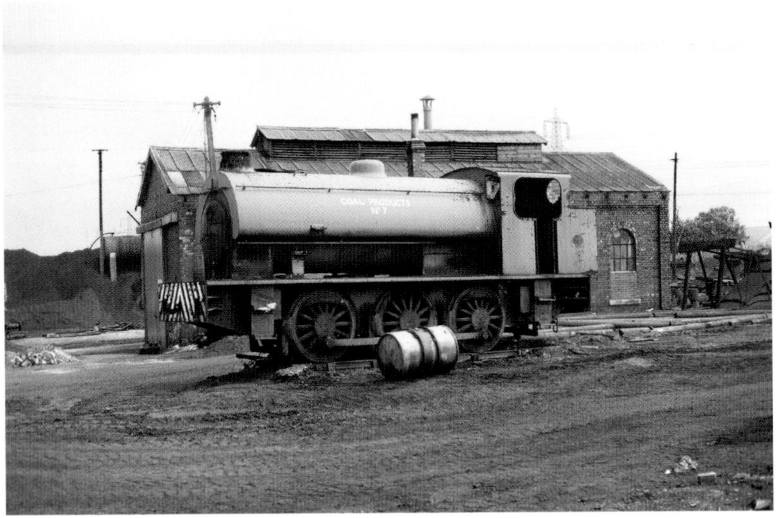

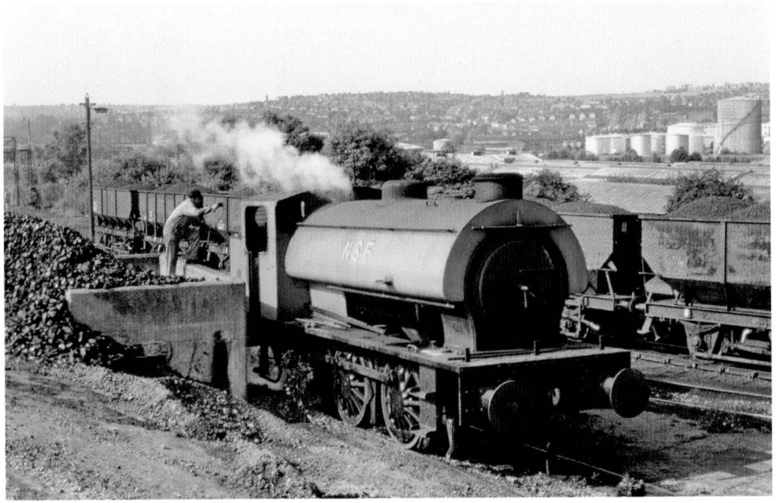

Above left: Hunslet Austerity *Coal Products No. 7* (W/No. 3886 of 1963) was another of Hunslet's later rebuilds, this example acquired from the Army Department in October 1962, originally their *WD No. 123* at Bicester (Hunslet W/No. 2897 of 1943). It was supplied to Glasshoughton coking plant at Castleford in October 1963. By the time of this visit, made on 17 July 1972, it had been relegated to standby status, replaced by two Thomas Hill Vanguard diesel-hydraulic locos. It was scrapped on site by Thos. W. Ward Ltd in November 1974. (John Sloane)

Below left: Another of Hunslet's later conversions from a wartime Austerity, this example was to hold the distinction of being one of the last steam locos to work in industry in Britain on a regular basis. This dubious honour was held by *SWCP No. 2* at the National Smokeless Fuels coking plant at Smithywood, Chapeltown. Originally built for the wartime effort, it was acquired by Hunslet as *WD No. 139* from Chilwell Central Ordnance Depot, Army Department. Along with a sister loco, *WD No. 140*, also acquired from the Army Department at the same time, it was deployed at the Smithywood plant in 1964 following the rebuild work. While *SWCP No. 1* (W/No. 3887 of 1964, rebuilt from Hunslet W/No. 3193 of 1944) gave over a decade of sterling service, passing into preservation in 1978, its sister, *SWCP No. 2* (W/No. 3888 of 1964, rebuilt from Hunslet W/No. 3192 of 1944), soldiered on until at least 25 July 1982, when this photo was taken, predominantly in later years deputising whenever one of the resident diesel locos was unavailable. (Roy Burt)

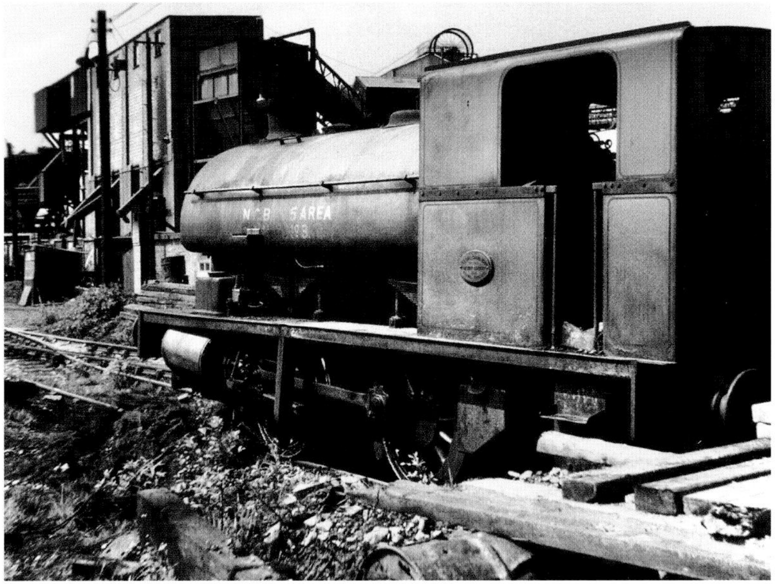

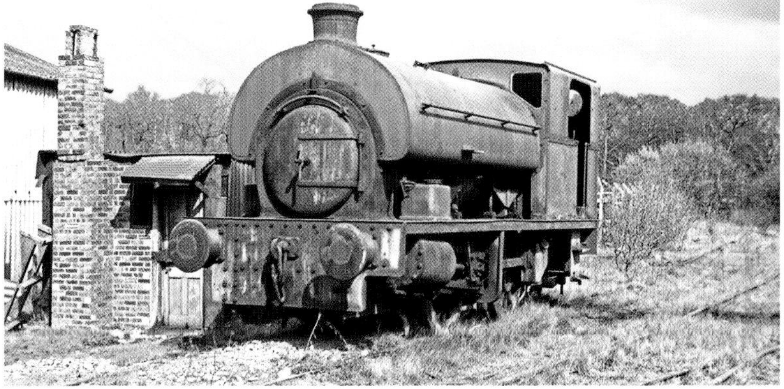

At a time when the final BR Standard Class 9F 2-10-0 locos were being turned out of Swindon works, the NCB South Yorkshire area had already placed an order with Hudswell, Clarke & Co. Ltd for five 0-4-0 saddle tanks for use in their Barnsley and Swinton area collieries. The company had a reputation for building well-designed, yet rugged and reliable products, sold both at home and overseas, and these were to be no exception, being based on a well-established design constructed over a period of three decades at 'The Railway Foundry' in Leeds. To a traditional company design with a full-length saddle tank and the company's signature design of smooth external lines, these locos had 16 x 24-in. outside-cylinders and 3-ft 9-in. driving wheels. Just as British Railways' No. 92220 *Evening Star* emerged from Swindon works in March 1960, following its well-publicised naming, the first two of the NCB order of five saddle tanks were being completed in the erecting shop at the Leeds foundry. These were in fact slightly larger versions of *Elizabeth* (W/No. 1888), which was built to a standard 14 x 22-in. (OC) design and had been supplied new to Bradford Corporation's Esholt Sewage Works two years earlier, in October 1958 (see pages 108–110). Understandably, the more ubiquitous Hunslet Austerity has received much attention over the years, but these 1960s-built steam locos are very much a part of Britain's industrial railway heritage, and yet have received little attention. Bearing the identities *HC No. 1* to *HC No. 5* (works numbers 1889 to 1893), they were delivered to Monk Bretton, Dodworth, Skiers Spring, Barnsley Main and Barrow collieries respectively between September 1960 and September 1961. Sadly, none survived into preservation, all being scrapped between 1975 and 1977, although they at least served the nationalised industry somewhat longer than the 9F Class of locos did for BR! Hudswell Clarke continued to construct diesel locos for a further decade, until 1971, when the company's goodwill and designs passed to Hunslet. (*Above*) By 6 June 1970 *HC No. 3* (W/No. 1891 of 1961) was nearing the end of its active career at Skiers Spring colliery. (John Sloane). (*Below*) On 29 March 1975, *HC No. 4* (W/No. 1892 of 1961) was also out of use at Skiers Spring. (Author's collection)

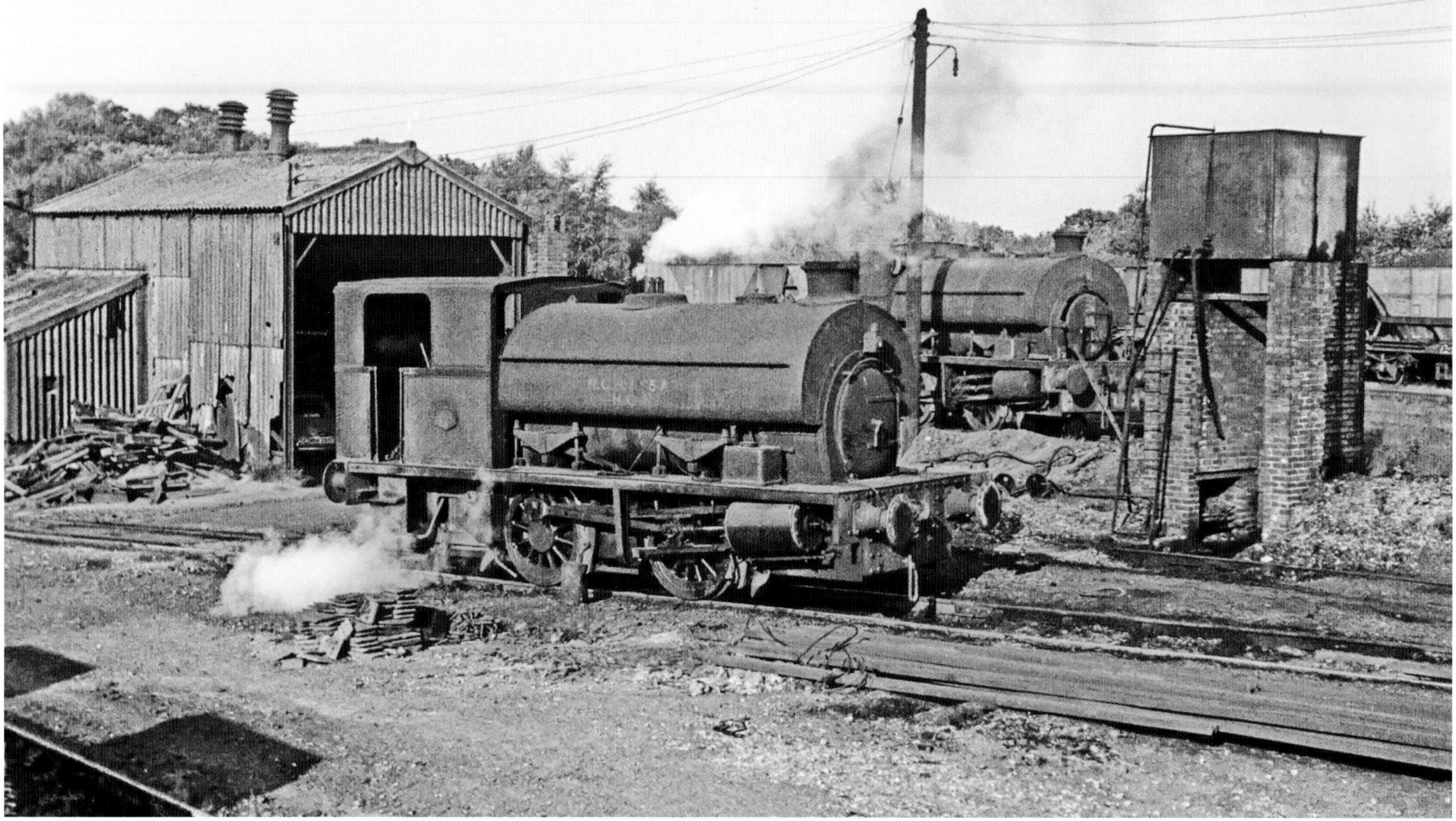

Skiers Spring at Wentworth was a small colliery alongside BR's Sheffield–Barnsley line, near Hoyland. It had two examples of the last batch of steam locos built by Hudswell Clarke and was, until February 1973, the last all-steam colliery in Yorkshire. On 22 August 1972 *HC No. 3* (W/No. 1891 of 1961) was in steam, while *HC No. 4* (W/No. 1892 of 1961) was out of use behind. *HC No. 4* had arrived at Skiers Spring in November 1969 from Wombwell colliery, to join sister locomotive *HC No. 3*, but in fact it did little work there. Most of Rockingham colliery's output was brought to the surface via Skiers Spring drift mine. Both Rockingham and Skiers Spring closed in November 1979. Despite an attempt to save this relatively new locomotive, it was scrapped in January 1977, leaving no surviving examples of this 'eleventh-hour' build of steam locomotive for British industry. (Richard Stevens)